AMERICAN WOMEN
images and realities

AMERICAN WOMEN
Images and Realities

Advisory Editors
ANNETTE K. BAXTER
LEON STEIN

A Note About This Volume

In 1818, Frances Wright D'Arusmont (1795-1852), distant ward of LaFayette and friend of Jefferson, came from England to tour the United States. Her impressions, recorded in personal correspondence, were published in 1821 and immediately acclaimed. But a return trip in 1824 led to a journey on the Mississippi River which modified her initial enthusiasms about the New World and focused her interest on the evils of slavery. She founded a black Utopian settlement in Nashoba, near Memphis. It failed, among rumors that it had encouraged free love. In lectures, pamphlets and in the *Free Enquirer,* which she edited with Robert Dale Owen, she advocated liberation of blacks, equality for women, liberalized divorce laws, birth control, political action, workingmen's parties, and revolution—earning from the self-righteous the title of "great red harlot of infidelity."

LIFE, LETTERS AND LECTURES

1834/1844

Frances Wright D'Arusmont

ARNO PRESS

A New York Times Company
New York • 1972

Reprint Edition 1972 by Arno Press Inc.

Course of Popular Lectures and Supplement
Course of Lectures were reprinted from copies
in The Princeton University Library.

American Women: Images and Realities
ISBN for complete set: 0-405-04445-3
See last pages of this volume for titles.

Manufactured in the United States of America

Publisher's Note: This selection has been
reprinted from the best available copy.

- - - - - - - - - - - - -

Library of Congress Cataloging in Publication Data

D'Arusmont, Frances Wright, 1795-1852.
    Life, letters, and lectures, 1834-1844.

    (American women: images and realities)
    CONTENTS: Course of popular lectures; with three
addresses, on various public occasions, and a reply to
the charges against the French reformers of 1789. [etc]
    I. Title. II. Series.
HQ1615.D37A3   301.24'2'0924 [B]   72-2598
ISBN 0-405-04454-2

CONTENTS

COURSE

OF

POPULAR LECTURES;

WITH

THREE ADDRESSES,

ON

VARIOUS PUBLIC OCCASIONS,

AND

A REPLY TO THE CHARGES AGAINST THE FRENCH
REFORMERS OF 1789.

DELIVERED

BY FRANCES WRIGHT,

In New-York, Philadelphia, Boston, &c.

London :

JAMES WATSON, 18, COMMERCIAL PLACE,

CITY ROAD, FINSBURY.

(Adjoining the New Mechanics' Hall of Science.)

CONTENTS.

PREFACE.

THE substance of the three first lectures which appear in the present volume, was first delivered in Cincinnati, during the course of the last summer.

The motives that actuated me to step forward in a manner ill suited to my taste and habits, which are rather those of a quiet observer and reflecting writer, than of a popular reformer or public speaker, will appear sufficiently in the discourses themselves. I may observe, however, that from the age of seventeen, when I first accidently opened the page of America's national history, as pourtrayed by the Italian Bocca, the only work on a subject so politically heterodox which had found a place in the aristocratical libraries which surrounded my youth—from that moment my attention became rivetted on this country, as on the theatre where man might first awake to the full knowledge and the full exercise of his powers. I immediately collected every work which promised to throw any light on the institutions, character, and condition of the American people: and as, at this period, little satisfactory information on these subjects could be gleaned in Europe, I visited this country in person. The " Views" then rapidly formed I published on my return to England, with the single object of awakening the attention of European reformers to the great principles laid down in American government. Those principles had indeed so warmed my own feelings, as to have influenced my perceptions. During my first visit to America, I seemed to hear and see her declaration of independence every

A

where. I studied her institutions, and mistook for the energy of enlightened liberty what was, perhaps, rather the restlessness of commercial enterprise. I saw her population active
and thriving, and conceived that to be the effect of wise social
regulations, which had, perhaps, rather its source in the temporary state of an artificial market. I saw neither princes nor
bayonets, nor a church married to the state, and conceived, in
very truth, that liberty had here quickened the human mind
until it was prepared to act under the influence of reason
instead of fear. It was true that I saw this country at a favourable moment, when peace had opened to her the ports of the
world, and set a second seal on her republican liberties and
national independence. Still, however favourable the time
might be, my own enthusiasm doubtless conspired to throw a
Claud-Lorraine tint over a country which bore the name of Republic. It required a second visit, and more minute inspection, to enable me to see things under the sober light of truth,
and to estimate both the excellences that are, and those that
are yet wanting.

This second visit, while it has exposed to my view evils and
abuses differing in degree rather than in nature from those of
Europe, has rivetted me in mind and feeling yet more strongly
to a country where are enshrined all the liberties and all the
hopes of the human race. From a visitor, therefore, I have
become a resident and a citizen.

While yet imperfectly acquainted with the state of things in
my adopted country—with the breadth of distance between
American principles and American practice—between the theory of American government and its actual application—my
attention had been attracted towards the political anomaly and
moral injustice presented by the condition of the coloured
population in the slave-holding states, as well as by the feelings exhibited, and practices legally countenanced, towards
that race, generally throughout the union. Four years of extensive and minute observation, with deeper reflection, and
more varied, as well as more reasoned experience, have convinced me that American negro slavery is but one form of the
same evils which pervade the whole frame of human society

And as, in common with all human errors, it has its source in ignorance, so must one common panecea supply its and their remedy. The spread and increase of knowledge alone can enable man to distinguish that the true interests of each point to the equal liberties, equal duties, and equal enjoyments of all ; and that then only, will the principles set forth in the first national instrument of American government, the declaration of independence, be practically exhibited—when the law of force shall give place to the law of reason, when wealth shall be the reward of industry, and all things shall be estimated in a ratio calculated in the order of their utility.

Satisfied that the melioration of the human condition can be reached only by the just informing of the human mind, I have applied such powers as I possess to the furtherance of this pleasing, though laborious task. In the citadel of human error, as exhibited in this country, it is easy to distinguish two main strong holds, which, if once carried, the fastness would probably surrender at the first summons. These are : First, the neglected state of the female mind, and the consequent dependence of the female condition. This, by placing the most influential half of the nation at the mercy of that worst species of quackery, practised under the name of religion, virtually lays the reins of government, national as well as domestic, in the hands of a priesthood, whose very subsistence depends, of necessity, upon the mental and moral degradation of their fellow creatures.

Second, the inaptness and corruption of the public press, ridden by ascendant influences, until it is abandoned alike by the honest and the wise, and left in the hands of individuals too ignorant to distinguish truth, or too timid to venture its utterance. The former of these evils, as somewhat unusually exhibited last summer in the towns and cities of the western country, first led me to challenge the attention of the American people.

The city of Cincinnati had stood for some time conspicuous for the enterprise and liberal spirit of her citizens, when, last summer, by the sudden combination of the clergy of three orthodox sects, a *revival*, as such scenes of distraction are wont

to be styled, was opened in houses, churches, and even on the
Ohio river.   The victims of this odious experiment on human
credulity and nervous weakness, were invariably women.
Helpless age was made a public spectacle, innocent youth
driven to raving insanity, mothers and daughters carried lifeless from the presence of the ghostly expounders of damnation;
all ranks shared the contagion, until the despair of Calvin's
hell itself seemed to have fallen upon every heart, and discord
to have taken possession of every mansion.

A circumstantial account of the distress and disturbance on
the public mind in the Ohio metropolis led me to visit the
afflicted city; and since all were dumb, to take up the cause of
insulted reason and outraged humanity.

The consequences of the course of lectures I then first delivered, on three successive Sundays, in the Cincinnati court-
house, and re-delivered in the theatre, were similar to those
which have been witnessed elsewhere;—a kindling of wrath
among the clergy, a reaction in favour of common sense on the
part of their followers, an explosion of the public sentiment in
favour of liberty, liberality, and instructional reform, and a
complete exposure of the nothingness of the press, which, at a
time when the popular mind was engrossed by questions of the
first magnitude, sullenly evaded their discussion, betraying
alike ignorance the most gross, and servility the most shame-
less.   All that I then observed, conspired to fix me in the determination of devoting my time and labour to the investigation and exposure of existing evils and abuses, and to the
gradual development of the first principles of all moral and
physical truth, every where so perplexed and confounded by the
sophistry of false learning, the craft of designing knavery, and
the blunders of conceited ignorance.

The two means which presented themselves, were those of
popular discourses, and a periodical publication, which should
follow up the same objects, consistently and fearlessly, and, by
instituting inquiry on matters of real interest, aid in drawing
off the public attention from the squabbles of party, the ver-
biage of theory, the gossippings of idleness, and the ravings of
zeal without knowledge.

The present volume contains the first, or introductory course, closing at the seventh lecture ; in which I have attempted to sketch an outline of the field of truth, and, at the same time, to expose such existing errors as must tend to blind the intellectual sight to its perception.

The second course, which will be found sketched at the close of the fifth lecture, on Morals, will attempt the development and practical application of those simple principles by which the conduct of human beings, one towards the other, may be justly regulated, and the face of human society be harmonized into beauty.

In the seventh discourse, on " Existing Evils and their Remedy," I was induced by circumstances, and the impatience of the public mind, somewhat to anticipate a subject whose more complete development will form an important item in the second course, as laid out of the close of the fifth lecture, already referred to, and to which I shall apply myself so soon as some duties of a more private nature may permit.

In attempting reform by means of instructional improvement at the present day, the labourer is perplexed by the alternate dullness and vivacity, inertness and restlessness of the human mind. At first, curiosity is slow to awaken ; then it runs too fast ; anon it slumbers, as if all truth were seized, and its every feature distinguished, when perhaps not a single impression received is in accurate accordance with fact and with reason.

The effects of a pernicious education are in nothing more conspicuous, than in the universal activity of the imagination and the inertness of the judgment. To treat any subject with perspicuity, a certain order and arrangement are indispensable. Let this order be disturbed, and arrangement interrupted, and things the most simple appear confused, and truths the most evident, difficult or doubtful. But to proceed step by step—to trace the outline and consider the details—to substantiate first principles, and then trace them out in their various applications, demands attention too patient, and reflection too dispassionate, for minds habitually unsettled by the day-dreams of fancy, and accustomed to adopt conclusions without examining premises. The first effort of the reformer is to awaken, but soon he finds it yet more necessary to compose. The spur is hardly applied when the rein is wanting, and the impatience of curiosity is soon a greater hindrance to progress than the apathy of ignorance.

All this, however, a little perseverance, sustained be zeal and tempered by prudence, might speedily vanquish, were it not, most unhappily, the momentary interest of a large and increasing body of men to feed the worst passions of the hour, and to counteract the labours of truth's advocates by every means possible for art to devise or violence to dare. Still, in this country, the progress of the human mind, if impeded, cannot be arrested. And truly, if regard be had to the conflicting interests and sinister influences which now pervade society, we may rather marvel at the success obtained than at the difficulties encountered.

The views which I have felt it my duty to present to the American people—the only people free to choose between truth and error, good and evil—are as yet but faintly sketched. The outline only is presented, and those first principles laid down in whose general and minute application I shall hereafter seek the law of nations and the law of men. While attempting the development of these first principles, I have been often challenged to their premature application to existing laws and usages ; not seeing that with these the enquirer after truth has little to do, and that it must be rather for our laws and usage to bend to principles, than for these to shape themselves to our laws and usages. As a lecturer, therefore, I have rather applied myself to develope what is true than to expose what is false ; reserving my comments on the passing opinions and practices of the age for the pages of the periodical of which I am a joint editor.

The Free Enquirer, formerly the New Harmony Gazette, was the first periodical established in the United States for the purpose of fearless and unbiassed enquiry on all subjects. It was conducted in Indiana, with more or less consistency and ability, for the space of three years, when I assumed its joint proprietorship, and removed it to New-York, under a name more expressive of its character. Since that period, it has been conducted, I am sure, with honesty, and, I hope, not without utility. Its editors have had singly in view the discovery of truth and the well being of man. If their zeal has been warm, their spirit has, I trust, been gentle. If they have spared no error on account of its popularity, they have neither sought the exposure of the erring, nor resented the hostility of the violent. They have kept true to the pledge given in their prospectus—they have sought truth "alone, and for itself;" "they have devoted their pages without fear, without reserves, without pledge to men, parties, sects, or systems, to free, unbiassed and universal enquiry ;" and, while taking for their premises the principles developed in the following discourses, they have tested, as they will continue to test, the laws, opinions, and practices of men, by that only standard of truth, supplied by nature herself, and by the powers of the human mind.

FRANCES WRIGHT.

New-York, 4th October, 1829.

INTRODUCTORY ADDRESS,

TO THE SECOND COURSE.

[As delivered for the second time in New York.]

THE circumstances under which I now meet this assemblage of the people of New York, are, I believe, unparalleled in the history of the world. All nations have had their revolutions— all cities, in the hitherto unfortunate annals of the human race, their disturbances, and their disturbers; but truly, the sight and the sound is alike novel, of privilege and pretension arraying all the forces of a *would-be* hierarchy and a *would-be* aristocracy, to assassinate the liberties of a free state in the person of a single individual, and to outrage public order and public decency, by ribald slanders and incendiary threats, against the reputation and person of a woman. Truly the signs are novel which mark this hour, and truly the place assigned to myself by the clamour and artifice of a body of men, trembling for privileges and profits, and eager to drown with noisy words that which they cannot confute by argument might cower the strength of one less confident in her cause or less ardent for its success. But, so surely as I know the strength of the ground which I have assumed, and the weakness of that which *they* have to defend, will I stand fast, and stand firm. And did I need, in this hour, ought beyond or without my own bosom to sustain me, I should find it in my conviction of the destined triumph of the cause I serve, and in the pure decision of wiser and happier generations to come, who (be what it may, the momentary issue of this hour, and its momentary consequences, to me,) shall write my name and preserve my memory among those of the champions of human liberty and heralds of human improvement.

I know of none, from the modest Socrates and gentle Jesus, down to the least or the greatest reformers of our own time, who have remembered the poor, the ignorant, or the oppressed, raised their voice in favour of more equal distributions of knowledge and liberty, or dared to investigate the causes of vice and wretchedness, with a view to their remedy; I know of none, I say, who have not been the mark of persecution, drank the poison of calumny, or borne the cross of martyrdom.

B

What better and wiser have endured, I shall not lack courage to meet. Having put my hand to the plough, I will not draw back, nor, having met the challenge so long cast at human nature and human reason, alike by privilege and superstition, will I refuse to meet all hazards in their cause.

I have already pledged myself to show evidence for all my opinions ; I pledge myself farther, to *show all my opinions*, for, so truly as I have taken man for my study, and his happiness for my object, do I believe that all my opinions can bring facts to their support, and will, sooner or later, find an echo in every thinking mind and feeling heart.

It hath been asked again and again, amid all the confusion of reports and assertions, threats and declamations, conjured up to fright the timidity of woman, and alarm the protecting tenderness of man, why I do not reply to the slander of enemies, and supply arguments to friends ?

If among the present assemblage there be any who have followed all or some of my previous discourses, I would put it to their memory and their reason, if I, on those occasions, presented arguments and evidence for the opinions advanced : and if any one of those arguments has been by a single individual refuted, or that evidence, in whole or in part, by one single individual impugned. And I will here call upon you to observe, that my opponents have had the command of the whole press and all the pulpits of this city. To what account have these been turned ? To heap on my name and person, outrage and abuse. To libel my audience, intimidate women, attack the interests of men, invoke the interference of the magistracy of the city, and threaten the lessees of this house with "riot, fire, and bloodshed."

My friends, I appeal to your reason, if, by resorting to such measures, my opponents have not substantiated their own weakness, and supplied an acknowledgment, that so far as I have spoken they cannot gainsay me ?

And now, then, I will ask, and that rather for the sake of good order and common sense, than for any personal interest of mine, if on the topics I *have* spoken, I have neither outraged your reason nor your feelings, and remain unanswered by my enemies—if it be not at the least probable that on the topics I have *not* spoken, I may be rational also. I have nothing in my head or my heart to hold back from such of my fellow creatures, as may desire to read either, with a view to the eliciting of truth. I have already sketched out to you the subject matter of many future investigations, embracing all our weightiest duties and responsibilities, as reasoning and sentient beings.

But, as I have opened our discussions in order, so *in order* must I pursue them, if pursued at all. We cannot speak to all things at once, nor demonstrate the last problem in Euclid, ere we have substantiated the first.

In compliance with the wishes of a mass of the citizens, as conveyed to me by individuals, and attested by my own observations of the many disappointed of entrance in our former places of meeting, I have consented to redeliver my elementary course on the nature of all knowledge, physical and moral.

Without a thorough understanding of the primary truths which it has been my attempt, in this elementary course, familiarly to elucidate, the public mind must be unfit for any discussion ; therefore it is, that I commence with these primary truths ; and therefore it is, that I shall decline the discussion of all other topics, until our first premises being laid, we are supplied with a standard by which to test all existing opinions and existing practice.

Whenever hereafter I may be called, in peace and with seriousness, to deliver my views on any subject of general interest to my fellow beings, I will meet their wishes. My opinions, whatever they may be, I am not accustomed to *defend*, but I will willingly *explain ;* and explain with that simplicity, which befits inquiry after truth, and that tenderness to the feelings of others, which I think I am not apt to forget.

Before we open our discussions of the evening, I would suggest to the audience, the propriety of bearing in mind the circumstances under which we meet, the former futile attempts to disturb our meetings in the Masonic Hall, and the possible presence of some mistaken and misguided individuals, ready to excite false alarm, and to take advantage of any the least disturbance, with a view to the injury of the cause of human improvement, which we are met to promote, and to the injury of the lessees of the building which we now occupy.

In case of any attempt to disturb our meeting, by cries of alarm, I beg the audience to bear in mind, that the house is under vigilant and double police.

I shall now, then, present you with the opening discourse, formerly delivered in the Masonic Hall. And, as it will be in matter and words the same, you will judge of the accuracy of the reports presented in your daily papers.

LECTURE I.

On the Nature of Knowledge.

WHO among us, that hath cast even an occasional and slightly observant glance on the face of society, but must have remarked the differing opinions, which distract the human mind; the opposing creeds and systems, each asserting its claim to infallibility, and rallying around its standard pertinacious disciples, enthusiastic proselytes, ardent apologists, fiery combatants, obsequious worshippers, conscientious followers, and devoted martyrs? If we extend our observation over the surface of our globe, and consider its diversified population, however varied in hue and feature, we find it yet more varied in opinions, in one opinion only invariably agreed, viz. that of its infallibility. The worshipper of sculptured idols bows before the image of his hand, and shrinks with unfeigned terror, if a sacrilegious intruder profane the sanctuary of his superstition. The adorer of the bright luminary which marks our days and seasons, sees in the resplendent orb, not a link in the vast chain of material existence, but the source of all existence; and so from the most unpretending savage, to the most lettered nation of a lettered age, we find *all* shaping their superstitions, according to the measure of their ignorance or their knowledge, and each devoutly believing his faith and practice to be the true and the just. Or let us confine our observation within the limits of the country we inhabit—how varying the creeds arising out of one system of faith! How contradictory the assertions and expectations of sects, all equally positive, and equally, we may presume, conscientious! How conflicting the opinions and feelings of men upon all subjects, trivial or important! until we are tempted to exclaim, " Where, then, is right or wrong but in human imagination, and what is truth more than blind opinion?" Few of us prone to study or observation, yet educated after existing methods, but must have asked these questions, and halted for a reply.

Should the problem here started be, I say not impossible, but even difficult of solution, lamentable must be the human

condition to the end of time ! Had truth no test—no standard
—no positive, no tangible existence, behold us, then, sold to
error, and, while to error, to misery, through all the generations of our race! But, fortuuately, the answer is simple ;
only too simple, it would appear, for mystery-loving, mystery-
seeking man, to perceive and acknowledge.

Let not the present audience imagine, that I am about to
add one more to the already uncountable, unnameable systems, which distract the understandings of men, or to draw
yet new doctrines and precepts from the fertile alembic of the
human brain. I request you to behold in me an inquirer, not
a teacher ; one who conceives of truth as a jewel to be found,
not to be coined ; a treasure to be discovered by observation,
and accumulated by careful, persevering industry, not invented
and manufactured by learned art or aspiring quackery, like
the once fashionable elixer of immortality and philosopher's
stone. My object will be simply to take with you a survey of
the field of human inquiry ; to ascertain its nature, its extent,
its boundaries, its limits ; to discover, in the first place, what
there is for us to know ; secondly, the means we possess for
acquiring such knowledge as is of possible attainment, and,
thirdly, having satisfied ourselves as to what can be known,
and as to what we know, to seek in our knowledge the test of
our opinions.

It must be admitted, that, as all our opinions must rest
upon some evidence, real or imagined, so upon the truth or
falsehood of the evidence admitted, must rest the truth or
falsehood of the opinions based thereupon. It is evident,
therefore, that before we can apply any safe or certain test to
our opinions, we must well understand the nature of true
evidence; before we can reflect, we must have something to
reflect upon ; before we can think accurately respecting any
thing, we must know accurately all relating to it ; and wheresoever our knowledge be complete, will our opinion be just.

Seeing, then, that just opinions are the result of just knowledge, and perceiving, as we must all perceive, how much confusion arises to society out of the conflicting opinions, which
divide alike nations and families into sects and parties, it is
equally our interest and our duty, to aim at the acquisition of
just knowledge, with a view to the formation of just opinions.
And, as we shall hereafter have occasion to observe, just practice being the result of past opinions, and human happiness
being the certain result of just practice, it is equally our

interest and our duty to aim at the formation of just opinions, with a view to the attainment of happiness.

We shall, therefore, open our investigations by an inquiry into the nature and object of just knowledge ; and if we succeed in ascertaining these, we will farther examine the causes which at present impede our progress, and the means best calculated at once to remove such impediments, and to advance us in the course which it is our interest to pursue.

If we consider man in comparison with other animals, we find him distinguished by one principle. This principle, which is shared by no other existence within the range of our observation, gives him all his pre-eminence. It constitutes, indeed, all his existence. By its neglect or cultivation he remains ignorant and degraded, or becomes intelligent and happy ; and, as he owes to it all that has elevated him above the brute in past time or at the present, so in it may he find rich hope and promise for the future.

Much does it behove us, then, earnestly to consider this distinguishing principle of our nature. Much does it behove us to understand the fulness of its importance and its power, and to know that, as without it we should be as the beasts of the field, so with it we may rise in the scale of being, until every vice which now degrades, every fear which unnerves, and every prejudice which enchains us, shall disappear beneath its influence.

I advert to the simple but all-important principle of improvement. Weak as we are, compared to the healthy strength we are conscious would be desirable ; ignorant as we are, compared to the height, and breadth, and depth of knowledge which extends around us far as the universal range of matter itself ; miserable as we are, compared to the happiness of which we feel ourselves capable, yet in this living principle we see nothing beyond or above us, nothing to which we or our descendants may not attain, of great, of beautiful, of excellent. But to *feel* the power of this mighty principle, to urge it forward in its course, and accelerate the change in our condition which it promises, we must awaken to its observation.

Are we yet awake to this? Do we know what we are, or have we ever asked ourselves what we might be? Are we even desirous of becoming wiser, and better, and happier ? and, if desirous, are we earnestly applied to effect the change?

It is probable that some vague desire of advancing in

knowledge pervades every bosom. We find every where some deference paid to the great principle of our nature in the growing demand for schools and colleges. We seem to have discovered that the faculties of man demand care for their developement; and that, like the marble of the quarry, he must be shaped and polished ere he will present the line of beauty.

But, alas! here is the difficulty. If agreed that something must be done, we see but darkly what that something is. While eager to be doing, we are still in doubt both as to the end to be attained and the means to be employed. While anxious to learn, we are but too often ignorant of the very nature of knowledge. We are unacquainted with her haunts and her habitation, and seek her where she is not to be found. It may be useful, then, before we engage in the labyrinth of learning, that we examine carefully what knowledge is.

If we ask this in our schools, we shall be told, that knowledge is an acquaintance with the structure of our own language; a familiarity with foreign, especially with dead languages. We shall, moreover, hear of history, geography, astronomy, &c. Do we ask the same in our colleges, we shall hear farther of law, medicine, surgery, theology, mathematics, chemistry, and philosophy, natural and mental: and we shall be farther told, that when a youth has mastered all these sounding names, and puzzled through all the learning, useful or useless, attached to them—he is well taught and thoroughly educated. It may be so. And yet may he be also very ignorant of what it most imports him to know. Nay, more! in despite of an intimate acquaintance with all the most esteemed branches of knowledge, he may be utterly unacquainted with the object and nature of knowledge itself. Let us, then, enquire again, *what knowledge is.*

It is not, in the first place, acquaintance with ourselves? and secondly, with all things to which we stand in relation?

How are we to obtain this acquaintance? By observation and patient inquiry.

What are the means we possess from this observation and inquiry? Our senses; and our faculties, as awakened and improved in and by the exercise of our senses.

Let us now examine what are the objects really submitted to the investigation of our senses.

These may be all embraced under the generic term matter, implying the whole of existence within the range of our inspection.

Were we to proceed minutely in our analysis, we should observe that matter, as existing around us, appears under three forms, the gaseous, the liquid, and the solid; and that under one or other of these forms may be accurately classed all that is submitted to our observation—all, in short, that we can see, hear, feel, taste, or smell. But to enter at present into such details would be foreign to our purpose.

I shall, therefore, pass on to observe that the accurate and patient investigation of matter, in all its subdivisions, together with all its qualities and changes, constitutes a just education. And that in proportion as we ascertain, in the course of investigation, the real qualities and actual changes of matter, together with the judicious application of all things to the use of man, and influence of all occurrences on the happiness of man, so do we acquire knowledge. In other words, knowledge is an accumulation of facts, and signifies *things known*. In proportion, therefore, as the sphere of our observation is large, and our investigationof all within that sphere careful, in proportion is our knowledge.

The view of knowledge we have here taken is simple; and it may be observed, that not in this case only, but in all others, accuracy and simplicity go hand in hand. All truth is simple, for truth is only fact. The means of attaining truth are equally simple. We have but to seek and we shall find; to open our eyes and our ears; without prejudice to observe; without fear to listen, and dispassionately to examine, compare, and draw conclusions.

The field of knowledge is around, and about, and within us. Let us not be alarmed by sounding words, and let us not be *deceived* by them. Let us look to things. It is things which we have to consider. Words are, or, more correctly, should be, only the signs of things. I say they *should be ;* for it is a most lamentable truth, that they are now very generally conceived to constitute the very substance of knowledge Words, indeed, should seem at present contrived rather for the purpose of confusing our ideas, than administering to their distinctness and arrangement. Instead of viewing them as the shadows, we mistake them for the substance; and conceive that in proportion as we enlarge our vocabulary, we multiply our acquirements.

Vain, then, will be the attempt to increase our knowledge, until we understand where we are to look for it, and in what it consists. Here is the first stepping stone. Let our foot but firmly strike it, and our after progress is easy.

And in what lies the importance of this first step in human knowledge? In the accuracy which it brings to all our ideas. It places us at once on firm ground, introduces us into the field of real inquiry, and lays the reign of the imagination in the hand of the judgment. Difficult were it to exaggerate the importance of the step which involves such consequences. Until we bring accuracy to our thoughts, and, we may add, accuracy to the words employed for their expression—we can make no progress. We may wander, indeed, and most certainly shall wander, in various paths; but they will be paths of error. The straight broad road of improvement it will not be ours to tread, until we take heed unto our feet, and know always whither we are going.

Imagine—and how easy is it to imagine, when we have but to look around us or within ourselves—imagine the confusion of hopes, desires, ambitions, and expectations, with which the scholar enters, and but too often leaves the halls of science. On entering them, he conceives that some mysterious veil, like the screen of the holy of holies, is about to be withdrawn, and that he is to look at things far removed from real life, and raised far above the vulgar apprehension. On leaving them, he has his memory surcharged with a confusion of ideas, and a yet more confusion of words. He knows, perhaps, the properties of ciphers and of angels; the names and classification of birds, fishes, quadrupeds, insects, and minerals; the chemical affinities of bodies; can measure star from star; analyze invisible substances; detail in chronological order the rise and fall of nations, with their arts, sciences, and sects of philosophy. He can do all this, and more; and yet, perhaps, is there neither arrangement in his knowledge, distinctness in his ideas, nor accuracy in his language. And, while possessed of many valuable facts, there is blended with all and with each, a thousand illusions. Thus it is with so many wordy pedants, and hair-brained or shallow disputants, are sent forth from the schools of all countries, while those who do honour to their species, by rendering service in their generation, are, most generally, what is called self-taught. And the reason of this is evident. Our existing modes of education, being equally false and deficient, and the instruction of our schools full of fallacies, theories, and hypotheses, the more regularly a youth is trained in fashionable learning, the more confused is usually his perception of things, and the more prostrated his reason by the dogmatism of teachers, the sophism of words, and the false principles engrafted by means of pretended science, ostentatiously inculcated or real science, erroneously imparted. While, on the other hand, a vigorous intellect, if stimulated by fortunate circumstances to inquiry, and left to accumulate information by the efforts of its own industry, though its early progress may be slow, and its aberrations numerous, yet in the free exercise of its powers, is more likely to collect accurate knowledge, than those who are methodically fed with learned error and learnedly disguised truth.

I shall have occasion, in a more advanced stage of our inquiries, to examine minutely the errors in the existing mode of instruction, and which are of a nature to perplex the human mind from infancy to age, and to make even learning an additional stumbling-block in the way of knowledge. For the present, I would confine myself to the establishing the simple position, that *all real knowledge is derived from positive sensations.*

In proportion to the number of senses we bring to bear upon an object, is the degree of our acquaintance with that object. Whatever we see, and feel, and attentively examine with *all* our senses, we *know ;* and respecting the things thus investigated, we can afterwards form a correct opinion. Wherever, respecting such things, our opinions are erroneous, it is where our investigation of them has been insufficient, or our recollection of them imperfect ; and the only certain way of rectifying the error, is to refer again to the object itself.

Things which we have not ourselves examined, and occurrences which we have not ourselves witnessed, but which we receive on the attested sensations of others, we may *believe,* but we do not *know.* Now, as these two modes of intellectual assent are generally, if not universally, confounded ; and, as their accurate distinction is, in its consequences, of immense importance, I shall risk the straining of your attention for a few minutes, while I attempt its elucidation.

To select a familiar, and at the moment a pertinent example. The present audience *know* that an individual is now addressing them, because they see her person, and hear her voice. They may *believe* that some other speaker occupies the pulpit of a church in this town, if assured to that effect by a person of ordinary veracity ; but, let the testimony of that person be as well substantiated in their opinion as possible, the fact received through his reported sensations, they would *believe ;*

the fact of my presence, admitted upon their own sensations, they will *know*.

My hearers will understand that my object in presenting these definitions, is not to draw a mere verbal distinction, but a distinction between different states of the human mind ; the distinction in words only being important, in that it is necessary to a clear understanding of the mental phenomena it is desirable to illustrate.

Did the limits of our present discourse permit such a developement, or did I not apprehend to weary the attention, it would not be difficult to draw the line between knowledge and belief, and again between the different grades of belief, through all the varieties of intellectual assent from the matter-of-fact certainty supplied by knowledge, down to the lowest stage of probability, supplied by belief. But having suggested the distinction, I must leave you to draw it for yourselves ; requesting you only to observe—that, as your own positive sensations can alone give you knowledge of a thing, so is your belief of any thing stronger, in proportion as you can more accurately establish, or approach nearer to, the sensations of those whose testimony you receive.

Thus : if a friend, or, more particularly, if several friends of tried veracity and approved judgment, relate to us a circumstance of which they declare themselves to have been attentive spectators—our belief is of the highest kind. If they relate a circumstance which they shall have received from another, or from other individuals, for whose veracity and judgment they also vouch, our belief, though in a measure accorded, is very considerably weakened ; and so on, until, after a few more removes from the original sensations of the reported spectators, our belief is reduced to zero.

But farther, it is here of importance to observe that belief— that is, the belief of a well trained mind—can never be accorded to the attested sensations of others, should those attested sensations be contradicted by our own well established experience, or by the unvarying and agreeing experience of mankind. Thus : should one, or twenty, or a thousand individuals, swear to the fact of having seen a man, by effort of his unaided volition ; raise himself through the air to the top of the steeple in this city, we should believe—what ? Not the eccentric occurrence, however attested, but one of two very common occurrences—either that the individuals were seeking to impose upon us, or that their own ignorant credulity had been deceived by false appearances.

But now let us suppose a case, very likely to be presented in form of an objection, although in reality capable of furnishing a forcible elucidation of the simple truth we are now attempting to illustrate. Let us suppose that some of our organs should become diseased—those of sight, for instance; and that we should, in consequence, imagine the appearance of an object not perceptible to more healthy individuals. If the phantasy presented nothing uncommon in any of its parts, or inconsistent with the course of previous sensations, we should at first, undoubtedly, yield credence to our eyes; until, in consequence, perhaps, of some incongruity, we should be led to appeal to our other senses, when, if they did not concur with the testimony of our vision, we should distinguish the appearance, immediately, for the effect of disease, and apply ourselves, on the instant, to its investigation and remedy.

But again, let us suppose (a case by no means uncommon in the history of the human pathology) that two of our senses should be diseased—our sight and our hearing; and that we should in consequence see the spectral illusion of a human being; and, farther, imagine such illusion to discourse with us. Our belief would be now strongly accorded to this twofold evidence; but we should still have a resource in our sense of touch. Should this last not confirm the evidence supplied by our vision and our hearing, we should suspect as in the former case, the health of our organs, and consult on the subject with an able physician.

But let us now suppose that *all* the organs of sense, in some individual, should become suddenly diseased, and sight, hearing, feeling, taste, and smell, should *combine* to cheat him into the belief of existences not perceptible to the more healthy sensations of his fellow creatures. I do not conceive that such an individual, however, naturally strong or highly cultivated his judgment, and even supposing his judgment to retain its activity in the midst of the general disorder, could for any length of time struggle with the delusion, but must gradually yield intellectual assent to his diseased sensations, however incongruous these might be, or however at variance with past experience. I conceive that an individual thus diseased in all his organs of sense, must rapidly lose all control over his reasoning faculties, and present, consequently, to his fellow creatures, the afflicting spectacle of one labouring under mental insanity.

If we look to the unfortunate maniac, or to the sufferer tossing in fever delirium, we shall perceive how implicit the credence given to his diseased sensations. The phantoms which he hears, and feels, and sees, are all realities to him, and, as realities, govern his thoughts and decide his actions. How, in such cases, does the enlightened physician proceed? He does not argue with the incongruous ideas of his patient; he examines his disordered frame, and as he can restore healthy action to all its parts, so does he hope to restore healthy sensations to the body, and accurate ideas to the mind. Here, then, we see, in sickness as in health, our sensations supplying us with all intellectual food. In fever, they supply us with dreams; in health, if accurately studied, with knowledge.

The object of these observations is to show, that as we can only *know* a thing by its immediate contact with our senses, so is *all knowledge compounded of the accurately observed, accumulated, and agreeing sensations of mankind.*

The field of knowledge, then, we have observed to be the field of nature, or of material existence around and within us. The number of objects comprised within the circle of human observation, is so multiplied, and the properties or qualities of these objects so diversified, that with a view to convenient and suitable divisions in the great work of inspecting the whole, and also with a view to the applying more order and method in the arrangement of the facts collated in the wide field of nature, they have been classed under different heads, each of which we may call *a branch of knowledge*, or, more succinctly, *a science.*

Thus: do we consider the various living tribes which people the elements? We class our observations under the head of natural history. Do we direct our attention to the structure and mechanism of their bodies? We designate the results of our inspection under the heads anatomy and physiology. Do we trace the order of occurrences and appearances in the wide field of nature? We note them under natural philosophy. Do we analyze substances and search out their simple elements? chemistry. Do we apply ourselves to the measurement of bodies, or calculate the heights and distances of objects? geometry. And so on, through all the range of human observation, extending from the relative position of the heavenly bodies, and accurate calculation of their courses, to the uses, habits, structure, and physiology of the delicate plant which carpets our earth.

Now, all the sciences, properly so called, being compounded of facts, ascertained or ascertainable by the sensations of each individual, so all that is not so ascertainable is not knowledge, only belief, and can never constitute for us matter-of-fact certainty, only greater or less probability. In elucidation, we might remark that the facts we glean, in the study of chemistry, supply us with knowledge; those received upon testimony, as in the study of history, supply us with probabilities, or with improbabilities, as it may be, and constitute belief.

Now, again—as our knowledge is supplied by our own individual sensations, and our belief by the attested sensations of others, it is possible, while pretending to communicate knowledge, only to communtcate belief. This we know to be the system pursued in all our schools and colleges, where the truths of the most demonstrable sciences are presented under the disguise of oral or written lessons, instead of being exposed, in practical illustrations, to the eye, and the ear, and the touch, in the simple, incontrovertible fact. This method, while it tends to hide and perpetuate the errors of teachers, so does it also inculcate credulity and blind belief in the scholar, and finally establishes the conclusion in the mind, that knowledge is compounded of words, and signs, and intellectual abstractions, instead of facts and human sensations.

Greatly, very greatly to be desired, is a just mode of instruction. It would not only shorten the road of knowledge, it would carpet it with flowers. We should then tread it in childhood with smiles of cheerfulness; and, as we followed its pleasant course, horizon after horizon would open upon us, delighting and improving our minds and feelings, through life, unto our latest hour. But if it is of the first importance to be launched aright in infancy, the moment we distinctly perceive what knowledge is, we may, at any age, start boldly for its attainment.

I have said, we may start *boldly*—ay! and there lies the surety of our success. If we bring not the good courage of minds covetous of truth, and truth only, prepared to hear all things, examine all things, and decide upon all things, according to evidence, we should do more wisely to sit down contented in ignorance, than to bestir ourselves only to reap disappointment. But let us once look around upon this fair material world, as upon the book which it behoves us to read; let us understand, that in this book there are no puzzling mysteries, but a simple train of occurrences, which it imports us to observe, with an endless variety of substances and existences, which it imports us to study—what is there, then, to frighten us? what is there not rather, to encourage our advance?

Yet how far are we from this simple perception of simple things! how far from that mental composure which can alone fit us for inquiry! How prone are we to come to the consideration of every question with heads and hearts preoccupied! how prone to shrink from any opinion, however reasonable, if it be opposed to any, however unreasonable, of our own! How disposed are we to judge, in auger, those who call upon us to think, and encourage us to inquire! To question our prejudices, seems nothing less than sacrilege; to break the chains of our ignorance nothing short of impiety!

Perhaps at this moment, she who speaks is outraging a prejudice—(shall I be forgiven the word?) Perhaps among those who hear me, there are who deem it both a presumption and an impropriety for a woman to reason with her fellow creatures.

Did I know, of a surety, this prejudice to prevail among my hearers, I should, indeed, be disposed to reason with *them.* I should be tempted to ask, whether truth had any sex; and I should venture farther to ask, whether they count for nothing, for something, or for every thing, the influence of women over the destinies of our race.

Shall I be forgiven for adverting, most unwillingly, to myself? Having assumed an unusual place, I feel, that to my audience some explanation is due.

Stimulated in my early youth, by I know not what of pitying sympathy with human suffering, and by I know not what persuasion, that our race was not of necessity born to ignorance, and its companion, vice, but that it possessed faculties and qualities which pointed to virtue and enjoyment; stimulated, at once, by this pity for the actual condition of man, and this hope of a possible melioration, I applied myself to the discovery of the causes of the one, and of the means for effecting the other.

I have as little the inclination to obtrude on you the process of investigation and course of observation I followed through the period of an eventful youth, as you would probably have to listen to them. Suffice it, that I have been led to consider the growth of knowledge, and the equal distribution of knowledge, as the best—may I say, the only means for reforming the condition of mankind. Shall I be accused of presumption for imagining that I could be instrumental in promoting this, as it appears to me, good work ? Shall I appear additionally presumptuous for believing that my sex and my situation tend rather to qualify than to incapacitate me for the undertaking.

So long as the mental and moral instruction of man is left solely in the hands of hired servants of the public—let them be teachers of religion, professors of colleges, authors of books, or editors of journals or periodical publications, dependent upon their literary labours for their daily bread, so long shall we hear but half the truth; and well if we hear so much. Our teachers, political, scientific, moral, or religious ; our writers, grave or gay, are *compelled* to administer to our prejudices, and to perpetuate our ignorance. They dare not speak that which, by endangering their popularity, would endanger their fortunes. They have to discover not what is true, but what is palatable : not what will search into the hearts and minds of their hearers, but what will open their purse strings. They have to weigh every sentiment before they hazard it, every word before they pronounce it, lest they wound some cherished vanity, or aim at some favourite vice. A familiar instance will bring this home to an American audience.

I have been led to inspect, far and wide, the extensive and beautiful section of this country which is afflicted with slavery. I have heard in the cities, villages, and forests of this afflicted region, religious shepherds of all persuasions haranguing their flocks; and I have never heard *one* bold enough to comment on the evil which saps the industry, vitiates the morals, and threatens the tranquility of the country. The reason of this forbearance is evident. The master of the slave is he who pays the preacher, and the preacher must not irritate his paymaster. I would not here be understood to express the opinion, that the preaching of religious teachers against slavery would be desirable. I am convinced of the contrary—convinced that it would be of

direful mischief to both parties, the oppressor and the oppressed.
To judge from the tone but too generally employed by
religious writers in the northern states, where (as denunciation
against the vice of the south risks no patronage and wins
cheap credit for humanity) negro philanthropy is not so scarce
—to judge, I say, from the tone employed by northern religionists, when speaking of their southern neighbours, and
their national crime and affliction, one must suppose them as
little capable of counselling foreign as home offenders—as
little capable of advising in wisdom as of judging in mercy,
or speaking with gentleness. The harshest physician with
which I am acquainted is the religious physician. Instead
of soothing, he irritates; instead of convincing, he disgusts;
instead of weighing circumstances, tracing causes, allowing
for the bias of early example, the constraining force of
implanted prejudice, the absence of every judicious stimulus,
and the presence of every bad one; he arraigns, tries,
convicts, condemns—himself accuser, jury, judge, and execu-
tioner; nobly immolating interests which are not his,
generously commanding sacrifices which he has not to share,
indignantly anathematizing crimes which he cannot commit,
and virtuously kindling the fires of hell to consume sinners, to
whose sins, as he is without temptation, so *for* whose sins he is
without sympathy. I would not be understood, therefore, as
regretting in this matter the supineness of the southern clergy;
I would only point it out to you, desirous that you should
observe how well the tribe of Levi know when and where to
smite, and when and where to spare.

And though I have quoted an instance more peculiarly
familiar to Americans, every country teems with similar examples. The master vice, wherever or whatever it be, is never
touched. In licentious aristocracies, or to look no farther than
the towns and cities of these states, the rich and pampered few
are ever spared, or so gently dealt with, as rather agreeably to
tickle the ear, than to probe the conscience, while the crimes
of the greatly-tempted, greatly-suffering poor, are visited with
unrelenting vigour.

Is any discovery made in science, tending to open to us
farther the book of knowledge, and to purge our minds of
superstitious beliefs in occult causes and unsubstantiated
creeds—where has it ever found opposers—or, might we not
say, persecutors? Even among our hired preachers and
licensed teachers of old doctrines and old ways. Is any

C

inquiry instituted into the truth of received opinions and the advantage of existing practice—who are the last to encourage it? nay, the foremost to cry out " heresy!" and stop the mouth of knowledge? Who but those who live by the ignorance of the age, and the intolerance of the hour? Is any improvement suggested in our social arrangements, calculated to equalize property, labour, instruction, and enjoyment; to destroy crime by removing provocation; vice, by removing ignorance; and to build up virtue in the human breast by exchanging the spirit of self abasement for that of self respect—who are the foremost to treat the suggestions as visionary, the reform as impossible? Even they who live by the fears and the vices of their fellow creatures; and who obtain their subsistence on earth by opening and shutting the door of heaven.

Nor, as we have seen, are our licensed and pensioned teachers the only individuals interested in disguising the truth. All who write for the public market, all who plead in our courts of law, all who harangue in our halls of legislature, all who are, or who aspire to be, popular servants or popular teachers of the people, all are *compelled* to the support of existing opinions, whether right or wrong—all, more or less, do, and more or less must, pander to the weaknesses, vices, and prejudices of the public, who pays them with money or applause.

I have said not only that they do, but that they *must;* and most assuredly they must conciliate the popular feeling, or forego the popular favour. Here is intended no satire upon any individuals, professions, nor employments. The object is merely to expose a fact, but a fact highly important to be known; that as, to be popular, men must not speak truths, so, when we would hear truths, we must seek them from other mouths and other pens than those which are dependent upon popular patronage, or which are ambitious of popular admiration.

And here, then, is the cause why I have presumed to reason with my fellow creatures; why, in my earliest years, I devoted myself to the study of their condition, past and present; why I searched into their powers and their capabilities, examined their practice, and weighed their opinions; and why, when I found these both wanting, I volunteered to declare it. I believe that I see some truths important for my fellow beings to know; I feel that I have the courage and the indepen-

dence to speak that which I believe; and where is the friend
to his species that will not say, " *Happy, most happy shall it
be for human kind, when all independent individuals, male
or female, citizens or foreigners, shall feel the debt of kindness they owe to their fellow beings, and fearlessly step forth
to reveal unbought truths and hazard unpopular opinions.*"

Until this be done, and done ably, fearlessly, and frequently,
the reign of human error must continue; and, with human
error, human vice, and human suffering. The advocates of
just knowledge must be armed with courage to dare all
things, and to bear all things, for the truths they revere ; and
to seek, as they may only find, the reward of their exertions
in the impression, great or little, slow or rapid, as it may
be, which their exertions may produce on public opinion, and
through the public opinion, on the public practice.

We have now sufficiently considered, so far as I have found
possible in a single discourse on so wide a topic, the main
subject of our introductory inquiries: viz. the nature and
object of just knowledge. We have examined, also, some of
the errors vulgarly entertained on the subject, and many of
the impediments which now obstruct our advances in the
road of improvement. We have seen that just knowledge is
easy of acquirement, but that few are interested in revealing
its simple principles ; while many are driven by circumstances
to interpret or dissemble them. We have remarked that,
to accelerate the progress of our race, two means present
themselves ; a just system of education, and a fearless spirit
of inquiry ; and that while the former would remove all
difficulties from the path of future generations, the latter
would place far in advance even the present. We have also
observed on the advantage which would accrue to mankind,
if all independent individuals would volunteer the task, for
which appointed teachers and professional men are now but
too frequently unfit, by devoting themselves to the promul-
gation of truth, without regard to fashionable prejudice. I
have been led, also, incidentally to advert to the influence
exerted over the fortunes of our race by those who are too
often overlooked in our social arrangements and in our civil
rights—I allude to women.

Leaving to a future opportunity the more complete development of the important subject, we have this evening
approached—the nature of all knowledge—as well as the
equally important subject of youthful education, I shall, at

our next meeting, consider the other two enumerated means of improvement, viz. by free inquiry. And as this is for us of the present generation the *only* means, so shall I endeavour to show how much it is our interest, and how imperiously it is our duty to improve it to the uttermost.

It is with delight that I have distinguished, at each successive meeting, the increasing ranks of my own sex. Were the vital principle of human equality universally acknowledged, it would be to my fellow beings without regard to nation, class, sect, or sex, that I should delight to address myself. But until equality prevail in condition, opportunity, and instruction, it is every where to the least favoured in these advantages, that I most especially and anxiously incline.

Nor is the ignorance of our sex matter of surprise, when efforts, as violent as unrelaxed, are every where made for its continuance.

It is not as of vore. Eve puts not forth her hand to gather the fair fruit of knowledge. The wily serpent now hath better learned his lesson ; and, to secure his reign in the garden, beguileth her *not* to eat. Promises, entreaties, threats, tales of wonder, and, alas! tales of horror, are all poured in her tender ears. Above, her agitated fancy hears the voice of a god in thunders; below, she sees the yawning pit ; and, before, behind, around, a thousand phantoms, conjured from the prolific brain of insatiate priestcraft, confound, alarm, and overwhelm her reason !

Oh! were that worst evil withdrawn which now weighs upon our race, how rapid were its progress in knowledge ! Oh! were men—and, yet more, women, absolved from fear, how easily, and speedily, and gloriously would they hold on their course in improvement ! The difficulty is not to convince, it is to *win attention.* Could truth only be heard, the conversion of the ignorant were easy. And well do the hired supporters of error understand this fact. Well do they *know*, that if the daughters of the present, and mothers of the future generation, were to drink of the living waters of knowledge, their reign would be ended—"their occupation gone." So well do they know it, that, far from obeying to the letter the command of their spiritual leader, " Be ye fishers of men," we find them every where *fishers of women.* Their own sex, old and young, they see with indifference swim by their nets ; but closely and warily are their meshes laid, to entangle the female of every age.

Fathers and husbands! Do ye not also understand this fact? Do ye not see how, in the mental bondage of your wives and fair companions, ye yourselves are bound? Will ye fondly sport yourselves in your imagined liberty, and say, "it matters not if our women be mental slaves?" Will ye pleasure yourselves in the varied paths of knowledge, and imagine that women, hoodwinked and unawakened, will make the better servants and the easier playthings? They are greatly in error who so strike the account; as many a bankrupt merchant and sinking mechanic, not to say drowning capitalist, could bear witness. But setting aside dollars and cents, which men, in their present uncomfortable state of existence, are but too prone exclusively to regard, how many nobler interests of the mind and the heart cry "treason!" to this false calculation?

At our next meeting, we shall consider these interests, which will naturally present themselves during our investigations on the subject of free inquiry. In what just knowledge consists we have cursorily examined; to put ourselves in the way of attaining that knowledge, be our next object.

LECTURE II.

Of Free Inquiry, considered as a means for obtaining just Knowledge.

THE subject we have to examine this evening, is that of free inquiry, considered as a means for the attainment of just knowledge.

At our last meeting, we endeavoured to investigate the nature and object of just knowledge, together with the means proper for its attainment. We discovered these means to be two: a judicious education, and a free spirit of inquiry.

From the first and best means, a judicious education, we of the present generation are unfortunately excluded. Whereever our lot may have been cast, or whatever may be our attainments, we must all be conscious that we are what we are in spite of many disadvantages; and that, however wise or good our vanity may pronounce us to be, we should have been much wiser, and, consequently, better and happier, had a judicious education more carefully developed our tender faculties, and brought order and accuracy to all our nascent ideas. But the forest is grown; and, straight or crooked, the trees have to stand pretty much as early circumstances have inclined them. Still, something may be done; nay! if we bring fearless and determined spirits to the work, *much* may be done—much for ourselves, and every thing for our descendants. It rests with us to command, for the rising generation, that education, whose want we, in our own case, deplore. It rests with us to open, with a golden key, the gates of just knowledge for our children ; and to marshal them in those smooth, broad, pleasant paths, which we ourselves have never trod. Equally true it is, that we cannot for ourselves, command that first, best means for attaining the first, best good. Our opinions have, unfortunately, to be changed, not simply formed ; our advance in knowledge must involve forgetting as well as acquiring. We have not, in our own minds, to till a virgin soil, but one surcharged with weeds, rank, entangled, and poisonous. Still it is ours to redeem the soil. We may set the edge of our ploughshares, apply them with a steady and nervous hand, and scatter the good seed in good time to reap a harvest.

The second means for the attainment of knowledge is ours, if we choose to exercise it ; that is, if we feel the importance of the object, and have courage to employ the means. The importance of the object we *must* feel, if we feel at all for ourselves or for our race ; if we are not wholly indifferent to the rank we hold in the scale of being: not wholly indifferent to our moral excellence, to our mental elevation ; to our own utility ; to the liberty and happiness of our species through all the ages of time to come. And, if such be the mighty consequences depending on the object, shall we lack the courage to employ the means? And what means? to open our eyes and our ears ; to throw wide the gates of our understanding; to dare the exercise of our intellectual faculties, and to encourage in others, as in ourselves, a habit of accurate and dispassionate investigation.

We have seen, also, that it is not our own improvement merely that it must be advanced or impeded according to our courage or timidity, but that of future generations, whose destiny it is ours to influence. Strongly, then, are we pledged to lay aside indolence and fear; and to engage honestly in the task of weeding out our prejudices and establishing our opinions.

There is a common error that I feel myself called upon to
notice ; nor know I the country in which it is more prevalent
than in this.   Whatever indifference may generally prevail
among men, still there are many eager for the acquisition of
knowledge ; willing to inquire, and anxious to base their
opinions upon correct principles.   In the curiosity which
motives their exertions, however, the vital principle is but
too often wanting.   They come selfishly, and not generously,
to the tree of knowledge.   They eat, but care not to impart
of the fruit to others.   Nay, there are who, having leaped the
briar fence of prejudice themselves, will heap new thorns in
the way of those who would venture the same.

And have Americans yet to learn that the interests of all
are compounded of the interests of each? and that he who, in
pursuing his own advantage, immolates one interest of his
fellow beings, fails in justice as a man, commits treason as a
citizen?   And oh! what interest so dear as that of mental
improvement?   Who is without that interest? or of whom is
not that interest sacred?   Man, woman, child—who has not
a claim to the exercise of his reason? or what injustice may
compare with that which says to one, " thought is good for
thee," and to another " knowledge is to thee forbidden ?"

But will this imputation startle my hearers? Will they
say, America is the home of liberty, and Americans brethren
in equality. It is so? and may we not ask here as elsewhere,
how many are there, not anxious to monopolize, but to univer-
salize knowledge? how many, that consider their own improvement in relation always with that of their fellow beings, and
who feel the imparting of truth to be not a work of supererero-
gation, but a duty ; the withholding it, not a venial omission,
but a treachery to the race.   Which of us have not seen
fathers of families pursuing investigations themselves, which
they hide from their sons, and, more especially, from their
wives and daughters?   As if truth could be of less importance
to the young than to the old ; or as if the sex which in all
ages has ruled the destinies of the world, could be less worth
enlightening than that which only follows its lead!

The observation I have hazarded may require some explanation. Those who arrogate power usually think themselves
superior *de facto* and *de jure*. Yet justly might it be made
a question whether those who ostensibly govern are not always
unconsciously led. Should we examine closely into the state
of things, we might find that, in all countries, the governed

decide the destinies of the governors, more than the governors those of the governed ; even as the labouring classes influence more directly the fortunes of a nation than does the civil officer, the aspiring statesman, the rich capitalist or the speculative philosopher.

However novel it may appear, I shall venture the assertion, that, until women assume the place in society which good sense and good feeling alike assign to them, human improvement must advance but feebly. It is in vain that we would circumscribe the power of one half of our race, and that half by far the most important and influential. If they exert it not for good, they will for evil; if they advance not knowledge, they will perpetuate ignorance. Let women stand where they may in the scale of improvement, their position decides that of the race. Are they cultivated?—so is society polished and enlightened. Are they ignorant?—so is it gross and insipid. Are they wise?—so is the human condition prosperous. Are they foolish?—so is it unstable and unpromising. Are they free?—so is the human character elevated. Are they enslaved? —so is the whole race degraded. Oh! that we could learn the advantage of just practice and consistent principles! that we could understand, that every departure from principle, how speciously soever it may appear to administer to our selfish interests, invariably saps their very foundation! that we could learn that what is ruinous to some is injurious to all! and that whenever we establish our own pretensions upon the sacrificed rights of others, we do in fact impeach our own liberties, and lower ourselves in the scale of being!

But to return. It is my object to show, that before we can engage successfully in the work of inquiry, we must engage in a body ; we must engage collectively; as human beings desirous of attaining the highest excellence of which our nature is capable ; as children of one family, anxious to discover the true and the useful, for the common advantage of all. It is my farther object to show that no co-operation in this matter can be effective which does not embrace the two sexes on a footing of equality ; and, again, that no co-operation in this matter can be effective which does not embrace human beings on a footing of equality. Is this a republic—a country whose affairs are governed by the public voice—while the public mind is unequally enlightened? Is this a republic, where the interest of the many keep in check those of the few —while the few hold possession of the courts of knowledge and the many stand as suitors at the door? Is this a republic, where the rights of all are equally respected, the interests of all equally secured, the ambitions of all equally regulated, the services of all equally rendered? Is this such a republic—while we see endowed colleges for the rich, and barely *common schools* for the poor; while but one drop of coloured blood shall stamp a fellow creature for a slave, or, at the least, degrade him below sympathy; and while one half of the whole population is left in civil bondage, and, as it were sentenced to mental imbecility.

Let us pause to inquire if this be consistent with the being of a republic. Without knowledge, could your fathers have conquered liberty? and without knowledge, can you retain it? Equality! where is it, if not in education? Equal rights! they cannot exist without equality of instruction. "All men are born free and equal!" they are *born*, but do they so *live?* Are they educated as equals? and, if not, can they *be* equal? and, if not equal, can they be free? Do not the rich command instruction, and they who have instruction must they not possess the power? and when they have the power, will they not exert it in their own favour? I will ask more; I will ask, *do* they not exert it in their own favour? I will ask if two professions do not now rule the land and its inhabitants? I will ask, whether your legislatures are not governed by lawyers and your households by priests? And I will farther ask, whether the deficient instruction of the mass of your population does not give to lawyers their political ascendancy; and whether the ignorance of women be not the cause that your domestic hearths are invaded by priests? Are not these matters of popular interest? matters for popular inquiry? We shall examine tomorrow whether you have not now in your hands all the means necessary for equalizing instruction, not merely among your children but yourselves; so far, at least, as to place your liberties beyond risk of attainder.

This examination will involve all your interests, national and social. Your political institutions have taken equality for their basis; your declaration of rights, upon which your institutions rest, sets forth this principle as vital and inviolate. Equality is the soul of liberty; there is, in fact, no liberty without it—none that cannot be overthrown by the violence of ignorant anarchy, or sapped by the subtilty of professional craft. That this is the case your reasons will admit; that this is the case your feelings *do* admit—even those which are the least amiable and the least praiseworthy. The jealousy betrayed by the uncultivated against those of more polished address and manners, has its source in the beneficial principle to which we advert, however, (in this, as in many other cases,) misconceived and perverted. Cultivation of mind will ever lighten the countenance and polish the exterior. This external superiority which is but a faint emanation of the superiority within, vulgar eyes can see and ignorant jealously will resent. This, in a republic, leads to brutality; and, in aristocracies, where this jealousy is restrained by fear, to servility. Here it will lead the waggoner to dispute the road with a carriage; and, in Europe, will make the foot passenger doff his hat to the lordly equipage which spatters him with mud, while there he mutters curses only in his heart. The unreasoning observer, will refer the conduct of the first to the *republican institutions*—the reflecting observer, to the *anti-republican education.* The instruction befitting free men is that which gives the sun of knowledge to shine on all; and at once secures the liberties of each individual, and disposes each individual to make a proper use of them.

Equality, then we have shown to have its seat in the mind. A proper cultivation of the faculties would ensure a sufficiency of that equality for all the ends of republican government, and for all the modes of social enjoyment. The diversity in the natural powers of different minds, as decided by physical organization, would be then only a source of interest and agreeable variety. All would be capable of appreciating the peculiar powers of each; and each would perceive that his interests, well understood, were in unison with the interests of all. Let us now examine whether liberty, properly interpreted, does not involve, among your unalienable rights as citizens and human beings, the right of equal means of instruction.

Have ye given a pledge, sealed with the blood of your fathers, for equal rights of all human kind sheltered within your confines? What means the pledge? or what understand ye by human rights? But understand them as ye will, define them as you will, how are men to be secured in *any* rights without instruction; how to be secured in the *equal exercise* of those rights without *equality of instruction?* By instruction understand me to mean knowledge—*just knowledge*; not talent, not genius, not inventive mental powers. These will vary in every human being ; but knowledge is the same for every mind, and every mind may and *ought to be* trained to receive it. If, then, ye have pledged, at each anniversary of your political independence, your lives, properties, and honour, to the securing your common liberties, ye have pledged your lives, properties, and honour, to the securing of your *common instruction*. Or will you secure the end without securing the means ? ye shall do it, when ye reap the harvest without planting the seed.

Oh ! were the principle of human liberty understood, how clear would be the principle of human conduct! It would light us unerringly to our duties as citizens. It would light us unerringly to our duties as men. It would lead us aright in every action of our lives ; regulate justly every feeling and affection of our hearts, and be to us a rule more unerring than laws, more binding than oaths. more enforcing than penalties. Then would passion yield to reason, selfishness to justice, and equal rights of others supply the sole, but the sure, immutable limits of our own.

As we have somewhat swerved from our leading subject to consider the nature of equality, let us again pause to consider that of liberty. We have seen that they are twin sisters ; and so were they viewed by the effulgent mind of Jefferson, when from his fearless pen dropped the golden words. " All men are born free and equal." Those words his fellow citizens and descendants will have interpreted, when they shall have shed on the minds of the rising generation, and as far as possible on their own, the equal effulgence of just knowledge ; before which every error in opinion and every vice in practice will fly as the noxious dews of night before the sun.

Let us, then, pause to consider these immortal words, graven by an immortal pen on the gates of time, " All men are born free and equal."

All men are born free and equal! That is : *our moral feelings acknowledge it to be just and proper, that we respect those liberties in others, which we lay claim to for ourselves ; and that we permit the free agency of every individual, to any extent which violates not the free agency of his fellow creatures.*

There is but one honest limit to the rights of a sentient being ; it is where they touch the rights of another sentient being. Do we exert our own liberties without injury to others—we exert them justly ; do we exert them at the expense of others—unjustly. And, in thus doing, we step

from the sure platform of liberty upon the uncertain threshold
of tyranny. Small is the step; to the unreflecting so imper-
ceptibly small, that they take it every hour of their lives as
thoughtlessly as they do it unfeelingly. Whenever we slight,
in word or deed, the feelings of a fellow creature ; whenever,
in pursuit our own individual interests, we sacrifice the interest
of others ; whenever, through our vanity or our selfishness,
we interpret our interests unfairly, sink the rights of others
in our own, arrogate authority, presume upon advantages of
wealth, strength, situation, talent, or instruction ; whenever
we indulge idle curiosity respecting the private affairs, opinions, and actions of our neighbours ; whenever, in short, we
forget what in justice is due to others, and, equally, what in
justice is due to ourselves, we sin against liberty—we pass
from the rank of freemen to that of tyrants or slaves. Easy
it were to enumerate the many laws by which, as citizens, we
violate our common liberties ; the many regulations, habits,
practices, and opinions, by which, as human beings, we
violate the same. Easy it were ? Alas ! and say I so ?
when to enumerate all these our sins against liberty, would
be well nigh to enumerate all that we do, and feel, and
think, and say ! But let us confine ourselves within a familiar
though most important example.

Who among us but has had occasion to remark the ill-
judged, however well-intentioned government of children by
their teachers ; and, yet more especially, by their parents?
In what does this mismanagement originate ? In a misconception of the relative position of the parent or guardian, and
of the child : in a departure, by the parent, from the principle
of liberty, in his assumption of rights destructive of those of
the child ; in his exercise of authority, as by right divine,
over the judgment, actions, and person of the child ; in his
forgetfulness of the character of the child, as a human being,
born "free and equal" among his compeers ; that is, having
equal claims to the exercise and development of all his
senses, faculties, and powers, with those who brought him into
existence, and with all sentient beings who tread the earth.
Were a child thus viewed by his parent, we should not see
him, by turns, made a plaything and a slave ; we should not
see him commanded to believe, but encouraged to reason ; we
should not see him trembling under the rod, nor shrinking from
a frown, but reading the wishes of others in the eye, gathering
knowledge wherever he threw his glance, rejoicing in the pre-

sent hour, and treasuring up sources of enjoyment for future years. We should not then see the youth launching into life without compass or quadrant. We should not see him doubting at each emergency how to act, shifting his course with the shifting wind, and, at last, making shipwreck of mind and body on the sunken rocks of hazard and dishonest speculation, nor on the foul quicksands of debasing licentiousness.

What, then, has the parent to do, if he would conscientiously discharge that most sacred of all duties, that, weightiest of all responsibilities, which ever did or ever will devolve on a human being? What is he to do, who, having brought a creature into existence, endowed with varied faculties, with tender susceptibilities, capable of untold wretchedness or equally of unconceived enjoyment; what is he to do, that he may secure the happiness of that creature, and make the life he has given blessing and blessed, instead of cursing and cursed? What is he to do?—he is to encourage in his child a spirit of inquiry and equally to encourage it in himself. He is never to advance an opinion without showing the facts upon which it is grounded; he is never to assert a fact, without proving it to be a fact. He is not to teach a code of morals, any more than a creed of doctrines; but he is to direct his young charge to observe the consequences of actions on himself and on others; and to judge of the propriety of those actions by their ascertained consequences. He is not to command his feelings any more than his opinions or his actions; but he is to assist him in the analysis of his feelings, in the examination of their nature, their tendencies, their effects. Let him do this, and have no anxiety for the result. In the free exercise of his senses, in the fair development of his faculties, in a course of simple and unrestrained inquiry, he will discover truth, for he will ascertain facts; he will seize upon virtue, for he will have distinguished beneficial from injurious actions; he will cultivate kind, generous, just, and honourable feelings, for he will have proved them to contribute to his own happiness and to shed happiness around him.

Who, then, shall say, inquiry is good for him and not good for his children? Who shall cast error from himself, and allow it to be grafted on the minds he has called into being? Who shall break the chains of his own ignorance, and fix them, through his descendants, on his race? But, there are some, who, as parents, make one step in duty, and halt at the second. We see men who will aid the instruction of their

sons, and condemn only their daughters to ignorance. "Our
sons," they say, "will have to exercise political rights, may
aspire to public offices, may fill some learned profession, may
struggle for wealth and acquire it.   It is well that we give
them a helping hand; that we assist them to such knowledge
as is going, and make them as sharp witted as their neighbours. But for our daughters," they say—if indeed respecting
them they say any thing—" for our daughters, little trouble
or expense is necessary. They can never *be any thing*; in
fact, they *are nothing*. We had best give them up to their
mothers, who may take them to Sunday's preaching; and
with the aid of a little music, a little dancing, and a few fine
gowns, and fit them out for the market of marriage."
   Am I severe? It is not my intention. I know that I am
honest, and I fear that I am correct. Should I offend, however, I may regret, I shall not repent it; satisfied to incur
displeasure, so that I render service.
   But to such parents I would observe, that with regard to
their sons, as to their daughters, they are about equally
mistaken. If it be their duty, as we have seen, to respect in
their children the same natural liberties which they cherish
for themselves—if it be their duty to aid as guides, not to
dictate as teachers—to lend assistance to the reason, not to
command its prostration,—then have they nothing to do with
the blanks or the prizes in store for them, in the wheel of
worldly fortune. Let possibilities be what they may in
favour of their sons, they have no calculations to make on
them. It is not for them to ordain their sons magistrates nor
statesmen ; nor yet even lawyers, physicians, or merchants.
They have only to improve the one character which they
receive at the birth. They have only to consider them as
human beings, and to ensure them the fair and thorough
development of all the faculties, physical, mental, and moral,
which distinguish their nature. In like manner, as respects
their daughters, they have nothing to do with the injustice of
laws, nor the absurdities of society. Their duty is plain,
evident, decided. In a daughter they have in charge a
human being; in a son, the same. Let them train up these
human beings, under the expanded wings of liberty. Let
them seek *for* them and *with* them, just knowledge; encouraging, from the cradle upwards, that useful curiosity
which will lead them unbidden in the paths of free inquiry;
and place them, safe and superior to the storms of life, in the

security of well-regulated, self-possessed minds, well-grounded, well-reasoned, conscientious opinions, and self-approved, consistent practice.

I have as yet, in this important matter. addressed myself only to the reason and moral feelings of my audience; I could speak also to their interests. Easy were it to show, that in proportion as your children are enlightened, will they prove blessings to society and ornaments to their race. But if this be true of all, it is more especially true of the now more neglected half of the species. Were it only in our power to enlighten part of the rising generation, and should the interests of the whole decide our choice of the portion, it were the females, and not the males, we should select.

When, now a twelvemonth since, the friends of liberty and science pointed out to me, in London, the walls of their rising university, I observed, with a smile, that they were beginning at the wrong end: "Raise such an edifice for your young women, and ye have enlightened the nation." It has already been observed, that women, wherever placed, however high or low in the scale of cultivation, hold the destinies of human-kind. Men will ever rise or fall to the level of the other sex; and from some causes in their conformation, we find them, however armed with power or enlightened with knowledge, still held in leading strings even by the least cultivated female. Surely, then, if they knew their interests, they would desire the improvement of those who, if they do not advantage, will injure them; who, if they elevate not their minds and meliorate not their hearts, will debase the one and harden the other; and who, if they endear not existence, most assuredly will dash it with poison. How many, how omnipotent are the interests which engage men to break the mental chains of women! How many, how dear are the interests which engage them to exalt rather than lower their condition, to multiply their solid acquirements, to respect their liberties, to make them their equals, to wish them even their superiors! Let them inquire into these things. Let them examine the relation in which the two sexes stand, and ever must stand, to each other. Let them perceive, that, mutually dependent, they must ever be giving and receiving, or they must be losing:—receiving or losing in knowledge, in virtue, in enjoyment. Let them perceive how immense the loss, or how immense the gain. Let them not imagine that they know aught of the delights which intercourse with the

other sex can give, until they have felt the sympathy of mind
with mind, and heart with heart; until they bring into that
intercourse every affection, every talent, every confidence,
every refinement, every respect. Until power is annihilated
on one side, fear and obedience on the other, and both restored
to their birthright—equality. Let none think that affection
can reign without it ; or friendship, or esteem. Jealousies,
envyings, suspicions, reserves, deceptions—these are the
fruits of inequality. Go, then! and remove the evil first
from the minds of women, then from their condition, and then
from your laws. Think it no longer indifferent whether the
mothers of the rising generation are wise or foolish. Think
it not indifferent whether your own companions are ignorant
or enlightened. Think it not indifferent whether those who
are to form the opinions, sway the habits, decide the destinies,
of the species—and that not through their children only, but
through their lovers and husbands—are enlightened friends or
capricious mistresses, efficient coadjutors or careless servants,
raasoning beings or blind followers of superstition.

There is a vulgar persuasion, that the ignorance of women,
by favouring their subordination, ensures their utility. 'Tis
the same argument employed by the ruling few against the
subject many in aristocracies; by the rich against the poor in
democracies; by the learned professions against the people in
all countries. And let us observe, that if good in one case, it
should be good in all; and that, unless you are prepared to
admit that you are yourselves less industrious in proportion to
your intelligence, you must abandon the position with respect
to others. But, in fact, who is it among men that best
struggle with dfficulties?—the strong-minded or the weak?
Who meet with serenity adverse fortune?—the wise or the
foolish? Who accommodate themselves to irremediable
circumstances? or, when remediable, who control and mould
them at will?—the intelligent or the ignorant? Let your
answer in your own case, be your answer in that of women.

If the important inquiry which engaged our attention last
evening was satisfactorily answered, is there one who can
doubt the beneficial effects of knowledge upon every mind,
upon every heart? Surely it must have been a misconception
of the nature of knowledge which could alone bring it into
suspicion. What is the danger of truth? Where is the
danger of fact? Error and ignorance, indeed, are full of
danger. They fill our imagination with terrors. They place

us at the mercy of every external circumstance. They incapacitate us for our duties as members of the human family,
for happiness as sentient beings, for improvement as reasoning
beings. Let us awake from this illusion. Let us understand
what knowledge is. Let us clearly perceive that accurate
knowledge regards all equally; that truth, or fact, is the same
thing for all humankind; that there are not truths for the
rich and truths for the poor, truths for men and truths for
women; there are simply *truths*, that is, *facts*, which all
who open their eyes, and their ears, and their understandings
can perceive. There is no mystery in these facts. There is
no witchcraft in knowledge. Science is not a trick; not a
puzzle. The philosopher is not a conjuror. The observer of
nature who envelopes his discoveries in mystery, either knows
less than he pretends, or feels interested in *withholding* his
knowledge. The teacher whose lessons are difficult of comprehension, is either clumsy or he is dishonest.

We observed, at our last meeting, that it was the evident
interest of our appointed teachers to disguise the truth. We
discovered this to be a matter of necessity, arising out of their
dependence upon the public favour. We may observe yet
another cause, now operating far and wide—universally,
omnipotently—a cause prevading the whole mass of society,
and springing out of the existing motive principle of human
action—competition. Let us examine, and we shall discover
it to be the object of each individual to obscure the first
elements of the knowledge he professes—be that knowledge
mechanical and operative, or intellectual and passive. It is
thus that we see the simple manufacture of a pair of shoes
magnified into an art, demanding a seven years' apprenticeship,
when all its intricacies might be mastered in as many months.
It is thus that cutting out a coat after just proportions is
made to involve more science, and to demand more study,
than the anatomy of the body it is to cover. And it is thus,
in like manner, that all the branches of knowledge, involved
in what is called scholastic learning, are wrapped in the fogs
of pompous pedantry; and that every truth, instead of being
presented in naked innocence, is obscured under a weight of
elaborate words, and lost and buried in a medley of irrelevant ideas, useless amplifications, and erroneous arguments,
Would we unravel this confusion—would we distinguish the
true from the false, the real from the unreal, the useful from
the useless—would we break our mental leading strings—

D

would we know the uses of all our faculties—would we be virtuous, happy, and intelligent beings—would we be useful in our generation—would we possess our own minds in peace, be secure in our opinions, be just in our feelings, be consistent in our practice—would we command the respect of others, and—far better—would we secure our own—let us inquire.

Let us inquire! What mighty consequences, are involved in these little words! Whither have they not led? To what are they not yet destined to lead? Before them thrones have given way. Hierarchies have fallen, dungeons have disclosed their secrets. Iron bars, and iron laws, and more iron prejudices, have given way; the prison house of the mind hath burst its fetters; science disclosed her treasures; truth her moral beauties: and civil liberty, sheathing her conquering sword, hath prepared her to sit down in peace at the feet of knowledge.

Let us inquire! oh, words fraught with good to man and terror to his oppressors! Oh words bearing glad tidings to the many and alarm only to the few! The monarch hears them, and trembles on his throne! The priest hears them, and trembles in the sanctuary; the unjust judge—and trembles on the judgment seat. The nations pronounce them and arise in their strength. Let us inquire; and behold, ignorance becomes wise, vice forsakes its errors, wretchedness conceives of comfort, and despair is visited by hope. Let us inquire!—when all shall whisper these little words, and echo them in their hearts, truly the rough places shall be made smooth, and the crooked paths straight. Let us inquire; and behold, no evil but shall find its remedy, no error but shall be detected, and no truth but shall stand revealed! Let us inquire! These little words, which presume in nothing, but which promise all things, what ear shall they offend? what imagination shall they affright? Not yours, sons of America! Not yours. What hold ye of good or great? what boast ye of rights, of privileges, of liberty, beyond the rest of the nations, that by inquiry hath not been won, by inquiry improved and protected? Let us inquire, said your ancestors, when kingly and priestly tyranny smote them on the banks of the Thames or the Seine. Let us inquire, said your fathers, when imperious princes and arrogant parliaments questioned their charters and trampled on their rights. Let us inquire, said Henry, said Jefferson, said Franklin, said the people and congress of '76. Let us inquire; and behold, the inquiry gained to them and their descendants a country—lost to kings and their empires a world!

And shall the sons fear to pronounce, in peace, under the shadow of the olive and the laurel planted by their fathers— shall they, I say, fear to pronounce those little words which, by their ancestors, were uttered under ban and forfeiture, outlawry, and excommunication, in prison, and under scaffolds, before the bayonets of tyranny and the threatening thunders of leagued armies?

Or, is the race of human improvement ended, and the work of reform completed? Have we attained all truth, rectified all error, so that, sitting down in wisdom and perfection, we may say, " our duty is achieved, or destiny fulfilled?" Alas for our nature, alas for our condition, alas for reason and common sense, if such should be the answer of our presumption, such the decision of our ignorance! Where is the mind so vast, the imagination so sublime, that hath conceived the farthest limits of human improvement, or the utmost height to which human virtue may attain? Or, say! where is the heart so insensible, the mind so debased, that, looking abroad on the face of society, as now disfigured with vice, rapine, and wretchedness, can seriously think and feel farther inquiry superfluous, farther reformation impossible?

Did the knowledge of each individual embrace all the discoveries made by science, all the truths extracted by philosophy from the combined experience of ages, still would inquiry be in its infancy, improvement in its dawn. Perfection for man is in no time, in no place. The law of his being, like that of the earth he inhabits, is *to move always, to stop never*. From the earliest annals of tradition, his movement has been in advance. The tide of his progress hath had ebbs and flows, but hath left a thousand marks by which to note its silent but tremendous influx.

The first observations of Indian and Egyptian astronomers; the first application of man to civil industry; the first associations of tribes and nations, for the purpose of mutual protection; the invention of an alphabet, the use of each ornamental, and, far better, of each useful art,—stand as so many tide-marks in the flood of recorded time, until, applying a lever to his own genius, man invented the printing press, and opened a first highway to inquiry. From that hour, his progress has been accelerating and accelerated. His strides have been those of a giant, and are those of a giant growing

D 2

n his strength. Mighty was the step he made, when, in Germany, he impeached the infallibility of Rome; mightier yet when, in England, he attacked the supremacy of kings; mightier by far, when appealing to his own natural rights, he planted in this new world the more new standard of equal liberty; and mightier still shall be his impulse in the onward career of endless improvement, when, rightly reading and justly executing his own decree, he shall extend to every son and daughter within the confines of these free states, liberty's first and only security—virtue's surest and only guide— national, rational, and equal education.

Something towards this has been done, and in no division of this promising republic more than in New-England and the commonwealth of New-York. But, as it may hereafter be my attempt to show, in the efforts yet made and making, the masterspring hath not been touched, the republican principle hath not been hit, and, therefore, is the reform imperfect.

If this be so—and who that looks abroad shall gainsay the assertion?—if this be so—and who that looks to your jails, to your penitentiaries, to your houses of refuge, to your hospitals, to your asylums, to your hovels of wretchedness, to your haunts of intemperance, to your victims lost in vice and hardened in profligacy, to childhood without protection, to youth without guidance, to the widow without sustenance, to the female destitute and female outcast, sentenced to shame and sold to degradation—who that looks to these shall say, that inquiry hath not a world to explore, and improvement yet a world to reform!

Let us inquire. Who, then, shall challenge the words? They are challenged. And by whom? By those who call themselves the guardians of morality, and who *are* the constituted guardians of religion. Inquiry, it seems, suits not them. They have drawn the line, beyond which human reason shall not pass—above which human virtue shall not aspire! All that is without their faith, or above their rule, is immorality, is atheism, is—I know not what.

My friends, I will ask you, as I would ask them would they meet the question, what means we possess for settling the point now at issue between the servants of faith and the advocates of knowledge, but what are supplied by inquiry?

Are we miserable creatures, innately and of necessity; placed on this earth by a being who should have made us for misery here and damnation hereafter ; or are we born ductile as the gold and speckless as the mirror, capable of all inflection and impression which wise or unwise instruction may impart, or to which good or evil circumstance may incline ? Are we helpless sinners, with nought but the anchor of faith to lean upon ? Or are we creatures of noblest energies and sublimest capabilities, fitted for every deed of excellence. feeling of charity, and mode of enjoyment ? How may we settle this problem but by inquiry ? How shall we know who hath the right and who hath the wrong but by inquiry ? Surely the matter is not small, nor the stake at issue trifling. Every interest dearest to the heart, every prospect most exhilirating to the mind, is involved in the question and trembles on the decision.

Oh ! then, let us gird up our minds in courage, and compose them in peace. Let us cast aside fear and suspicion, suspend our jealousies and disputes, acknowledge the rights of others and assert our own. And oh ! let us understand that the first and noblest of these rights is, the cultivation of our reason. We have seen what just knowledge is ; we have ascertained its importance to our worldly prosperity, to our happiness, to our dignity. We have seen, that it regards us, not only individually, but relatively and collectively. We have seen that to obtain it, we have but to seek it, patiently and fearlessly, in the road of inquiry ; and that to tread that road pleasantly, securely, profitably, we must throw it open to both sexes—to all ages—to the whole family of human-kind.

It now remains for us to distinguish what are the most important subjects of human inquiry. The field of knowledge is wide and the term of our existence short. With many of us life is considerably spent and much charged with worldly and domestic occupation. Still have we leisure sufficient, if we be willing to employ it, for the acquisition of such truths as are most immediately associated with our interests and influential over our happiness.

At our next meeting we shall inquire what these truths of primary importance are, together with the means now in your hands for their general distribution and popular acquisition.

LECTURE III.

Of the more Important Divisions and Essential Parts of Knowledge.

In our preceding discourses we have investigated, first, the nature and object of just knowledge ; secondly, the means for attaining that knowledge. It remains for us to distinguish those parts or divisions of knowledge, with which it most concerns us to be familiar.

We ascertained at our first meeting just knowledge to consist in, first, acquaintance with ourselves ; and secondly, with all things to which we stand in relation.

Now we stand in relation, more near or more remote, to all substances and all existences within the range of our observation ; that is to the whole of matter, of which whole we ourselves form a part.

We shall understand this relation more accurately if we bear in mind, that the simple elements of all things are eternal in duration and ever changing in position. We may analyze or discompose all substances, from the rocks of the mountain to the flesh of our own bodies ; we may destroy sentient existences—the ox in the market. or the insect beneath our foot ; we may watch the progress of rapid or more gradual decomposition by age or disease in our own bodies ; but let us not imagine that here is destruction, here is only change. We may evaporate water into steam, or convert it into air; we may transform the blazing diamond into the elements of dull carbon ; we may stop the current juices in the plant or the tree, and leave it fading and withering until we find only an earthy heap on the soil ; we may arrest the action of organic life, and stretch the warm and sentient being a cold. dull clod of corruption at our feet— yet have we neither taken from, nor added to, the elements before us. We have changed one substance into other substances. ended one existence to start others into being. The same matter is there : its appearance only is changed, and its qualities diversified. These facts being so, as observation and experience attest, it follows, not merely that we form at this moment a part of one great whole, but that we ever have and ever shall form a part of the same. Under various forms, with varying qualities, the elements which now compose our bodies have ever held, and will ever hold a place, in the vast infinitly of matter : and consequently, ever mingling and mingled with the elements of all things, we stand, in our very nature, allied and associated with the air we breathe, the dust, the stone, the flower we tread; the worm that crawls, the insect that hums around us its tiny song, the bird that wheels its flight through the blue ether, and all the varied multitude of animal existences, from the playful squirrel to the lordly elephant.

Thus related, as we are to all things, and all things to us, how interesting a theatre that in which we stand! How calculated to awaken our intellectual faculties, and excite our moral feelings ! Our sympathy is attracted to every creature, our attention to every thing. We see ourselves in the midst of a family endlessly diversified in powers, in faculties, in wants, in desires; in the midst of a world whose existence is one with our own, and in whose history each mode of being is an episode,

Were this simple view of things opened to us with our opening reason, royal indeed were our road in improvement. Easily, as pleasantly, should we tread all the paths of knowledge: and advancing, without check or backsliding, become familiar with every object within the circle of each opening horizon, until the whole map of material existence, with all its occurrences and changes, lay revealed to our sight and apprehension. Then would our education be simply a voyage of discovery. We should have only to look within us and to look without us, to store up facts and to register them for future generations. Far other is our occupation now. Instead of establishing facts, we have to overthrow errors ; instead of ascertaining what *is*, we have to chase from our imaginations what *is not.* Before we can open our eyes, we have to ask leave of our superstition ; before we can exercise our faculties, we have to ask leave of each other. When I think how easy and delightful the task would be to present you with a simple table of just knowledge—to arrange under the single head of MATTER AND ITS PHENOMENA all the *real* objects of human investigation and real subjects of human inquiry; and when I picture to myself all the imaginary objects which now engage your attention, and all the fanciful subjects on which your imaginations run riot—I know not where to begin, and am fain to ask pardon of you and pardon of myself for the unmeaning words I must employ, the unreal subjects we must consider. But, waving these for a moment, let us inquire what, under these two divisions of knowledge—acquaintance with ourselves and acquaintance with the world without us—are the subjects of primary interest ; and in what degree we are at present engaged in their consideration.

First, acquaintance with ourselves. We must allow this to be important. If any thing concerns us, it should be our own bodies and minds. What do we understand of their structure? what of their faculties and powers ? If we understand not these, how may we preserve the health of either ? How may we avoid injurious habits, understand our sensations, profit by experience, and establish ourselves in bodily temperance and mental sobriety?

Without pausing to develope all the importance of these studies, we will take its admission for granted ; and place therefore, at the head of our list, anatomy, physiology, and the natural history of man.

In passing to the world without us, we come to a subject of equal importance; one, indeed, which accurately considered, comprises the knowledge of ourselves in common with that of all existences—physics, or a knowledge of the material world.

Under this head we may remark many distinct subjects of inquiry. The motion of the heavenly bodies, and that of our earth considered as one of them. The form and structure of the earth, with all the appearances and substances it exhibits ; the physiology of animals, their habits, instincts, and moral character ! with those of all the swarms of existences which diversify matter with endless variety. But, leaving these with other subdivisions, we may confine ourselves to the remark, that without some general acquaintance with the three great branches of physics, commonly called chemistry, natural philosophy, and natural history, more especially that of man, we can know nothing ; nothing of ourselves, nothing of the world about us, nothing of the relation we bear to things, nor of theirs to us, nor of theirs to each other. The best road to correct reasoning is by physical science ; the way to trace effects to causes is through physical science; the only corrective, therefore, of superstition is physical science.

Nor let us imagine this difficult of attainment. Of all human accomplishments, it is the easiest. For why ? it con-

sists exclusively of facts. It is not that even here human
ingenuity has never devised confusion. But, thanks to the
persevering labours of some enlightened individuals, many of
them persecuted in their generation, and not a few persecuted in our own, we now understand that if we would
investigate nature, in whole or in part, we must use our eyes,
ears, and understandings, simply treasure up facts, judge
from facts, and reason from the premises of facts.

Admitting, as we must, the importance of this mode of
judging and reasoning, we shall perceive the peculiar advantage and necessity of commencing our researches in the
world of fact and science of things.

Before we can proceed to examine our opinions, we must
ascertain facts drawn from the attentive observation of matter.
We must know the anatomy of the matter composing our own
bodies, and that of the matter composing all other bodies.
We must familiarize our senses and our understandings with
the multiform and yet unvarying phenomena of nature. We
must know what does happen and what does *not* happen.
We must trace in the physical world, cause to cause; or,
more properly, occurrence to occurrence; and whenever we
do not perceive the clenching link between two occurrences,
we must not *imagine* it; we must say *we do not know it*,
and we must go, with our five senses open, in search of it.
Had human beings, in all ages of the world, done this, where
should we not now be in just knowledge? It is time that
we seek out the right road. We have groped long enough in
error; lived long enough in fairy land; dreamed more than
enough of things unseen and causes unknown. We have,
indeed, dreamed so much and observed so little, that our
imaginations have grown larger than the world we live in,
and our judgments have dwindled down to a point.

Having obtained a general view of the philosophy of
matter, we may then carry our investigations into the other
branches of knowledge, according to our leisure, taste, and
opportunity. We may apply ourselves to the past history of
man, as handed down to us by tradition, oral or in writing;
and comparing these traditions with what we know of the
nature of man and the nature of things, of matter and its
phenomena, we may judge of their credibility. If we are not
prepared thus to judge by accurate analogy, we may receive
every fable for matter of fact, swallow every fairy tale for true
history, suppose every mythology sound philosophy, and mis-

take equally the tricks of conjurors and the phenomena of nature for miracles.

We may then peruse with equal interest and advantage the narratives of travellers, and engage in general reading with little risk of taking facts for granted without evidence, or receiving the visions of weak understandings for the lessons of wisdom. We may then, too, examine our opinions with some hope of discriminating between the erroneous and the correct; we may then change or form our opinions with good security for basing them on a solid foundation; we may then exercise our reason, for we shall have facts to exercise it upon; we may then compare popular creeds, and investigate unpopular doubts; we may then weigh all things in the balance of reason, seat our judgment on her throne, and listen to her decisions.

But, it may be asked, how are the generality of men, and more especially, of women, to find time and opportunity for such preparatory investigations as we acknowledge to be absolutely indispensible? Should we discover that they now spend more time and more opportunity in useless investigations, than they need devote to the most useful; that they now waste more anxious thought, more precious time, and more hard-earned money in fruitless inquiry—inquiry which never can be answered, and whose answer, if possible, could profit them nothing—than would suffice to gratify every laudable curiosity, and store their minds with knowledge, whose utility should be felt at every moment of their lives—should we discover this, would there be no effort made to turn time and opportunity to better account, and to divert thought and money into the more useful channel?

We spake of inquiry. Behold! my friends, a subject for it! Ask yourselves how ye employ your leisure hours—how ye employ your leisure *day*, the first of the week! Ask, for what have ye raised spacious buildings through your cities and villages, and for what ye pay a host of teachers, interested, as we have seen—as we have *proved*—in deceiving you!

I must pause a moment to conciliate the feelings of my audience: I know the influence exercised by religious teachers, and I know the sway yielded to them ; I know the hostility I must excite by exposing the circumstances which render worse than nugatory the lessons of the pulpit, and which interest the press in confirming the errors which the pulpit promulgates. I understand all that I must provoke ;

but equally do I understand the urgency of the duty which has already led me to expose the fact, that the teachers of the public mind are, by the very circumstance of their situation, constrained to conciliate every prejudice, and gainsay every truth.

Nor rests the fatal necessity to which I called your attention, in my opening discourse, only with our public teachers. Each member of the public feels something of the same. Trained as we all are, more or less, in the ways of hypocrisy —constrained by fear or by policy, to assume the semblance of such opinions, whether we hold them secretly or not, as rule the ascendant, because they command the wealth of the country ; or, should we forbear from expressing what is false, obliged, at the least, to withhold what is true ;—constrained, I say, in very self-defence, to keep silence, lest the bread be taken from our mouths, or peace from our firesides ; the inutility, or worse, the mischief of our ordinary public instruction, is apparent, both in its effects and in its cause.

Far be it then from me, in exposing the evil, to reflect upon individuals, who are rather its passive agents than its authors. If some there are, so depraved by reigning corruptions, as to volunteer their increase, and fight their way to false honour and foul wealth, by falsehoods uncalled for, dishonesty and defamation as unmanly as they are gratuitously wicked, still are there others who mourn in secret, while they conciliate ruling prejudices, and who ask pardon of truth while they bow themselves in the house of Rimmon. Well do I know this to be widely true, with respect to the press—widely true, also, with respect to the teachers of our youth in schools and colleges—and, disposed am I to believe it partially true, with respect to the clergy. But for these last, more especially, the railroad is marked out, and that they have to tread. Should they depart from it, the very flock would rise up against the shepherd; or let us observe, that if the flock should be convinced by the shepherd, the very calling of the shepherd were destroyed, the craft by which he lives overthrown.

I have seen an honest teacher of religion, born and bred within the atmosphere of sectarian faith, and whose hairs have grown white in the labours of sectarian ministries, open his mind to more expanded views, his heart to more expanded feelings, and as the light dawned upon his own reason, steadily proclaim it to his followers. And what hath been the reward of his honesty? They who should blessed, have risen up against him; the young in years, but the old in falsehood, even among his followers, have sought their own popularity, by proclaiming his heresy; nor rested from plots and persecutions until they drove him from his own pulpit, and shut the doors of his own church, upon his venerable person.

Such being the reward of sincerity, who then shall marvel at its absence. For myself, in exposing the duplicity of the clergy, I neither marvel at, nor judge it in severity. Hypocrisy is the vice of the age, and hypocrites are made to be its teachers!

Not then in satire of the clergy, but in good will to my fellow creatures, have I attempted the exposure of that craft, which is necessary to the very existence of the clerical profession. And not from indifference to the feelings of my hearers, but from deep sympathy with their vital interests shall I venture, now and hereafter, to probe their secret thoughts, and expose their most cherished errors. In so doing, never will it be my intention to offend. I would not wound one conscientious prejudice; not deal a rough word against one feeling of a fellow creature. But I am here to speak what I believe the truth. I am here to speak that for which some have not the courage and others not the independence. I am here, not to flatter the ear, but to probe the heart; not to minister to vanity, but to urge self-examination; assuredly, therefore, not to court applause, but to induce conviction. Must it be my misfortune to offend? bear in mind only that I do it for conscience sake—for *your* sakes. I have wedded the cause of human improvement; staked it on my reputation, my fortune, and my life; and as, for it, I threw behind me in earliest youth the follies of my age, the luxuries of ease and European aristocracy, so do I, and so will I, persevere, even as I began; and devote what remains to me of talent, strength, fortune, and existence, to the same sacred cause—the promotion of just knowledge, the establishing of just practice, the increase of human happiness.

Such being my motives, such my object, I must intreat you to inquire what the knowledge is, that you learn from your spiritual teachers. "The knowledge by faith," they will answer for you. "And faith," they will add, "is the knowledge of things unseen." Can there be any such knowledge? I put it to your reason. Knowledge we have shown

to be ascertained facts. Things unseen! Can human understanding know any thing about them? More I will ask:
could it be of any utility were even such knowledge possible?
And do ye hire teachers to teach you non-existent knowledge,
impossible knowledge, and knowledge which, even under the
supposition of its possibility, could serve no conceivable
purpose? We are on the earth, and they tell us of heaven;
we are human beings, and they tell us of angels and devils;
we are matter, and they tell us of spirit: we have five senses
whereby to admit truths, and a reasoning faculty by which to
build our belief upon them; and they tell us of dreams
dreamed thousands of years ago, which all our experience
flatly contradicts.

Again I must intreat your patience—your gentle hearing.
I am not going to question your opinious. I am not going to
meddle with your belief. I am not going to dictate to you
mine. All that I say is, examine, inquire. Look into the
nature of things. Search out the grounds of your opinions,
the *for* and the *against*. Know *why* you believe, understand
what you believe, and possess a reason for the faith that is in
you.

But your spiritual teachers caution you against inquiry—
tell you not to read certain books; not to listen to certain
people; to beware of profane learning; to submit your reason,
and to receive their doctrines for truths. Such advice renders
them suspicious counsellors. By their own creed, you hold
your reason from their God. Go! ask them why he gave it.

Be not afraid! If that being which they tell us of exist, we
shall find him in his works. If that revelation be his which
they tell us to revere, we shall find all nature and its occurrences, all matter and its phenomena, bearing testimony to its
truth. Be not afraid! In admitting a creator, refuse not to
examine his creation; and take not the assertions of creatures
like yourselves, in place of the evidence of your senses and
the conviction of your understanding.

But you will say, the clergy are moral teachers no less than
religious. They form and amend our practice as well as
dictate our belief.

My friends! we have ascertained the contrary. We have
seen that from Maine to Missouri—from hence each way to
our antipodes—the hired preachers of all sects, creeds, and
religions, never do, and never can, teach any thing but what
is in conformity with the opinions of those who pay them.

We have substantiated the fact, that they never did, and never can, touch the master-vice, whatever it be, and wherever found. We know that they ever have, and ever must, persecute truth, by whomsoever discovered—by Galileo, or by Leslie and Lawrence; we know that they have stifled enquiry, wherever started, in every age and every nation on the globe; and that hardly a fact in science or a truth in philosophy, but has been purchased with the blood, or the liberty, or the domestic peace of a martyr. We have traced this conduct of your teachers to its cause. Remove the cause, and the effect shall cease. Give premiums for the discovery and revelation of knowledge, not for its repression! Take for your teachers experimental philosophers, not spiritual dreamers! Turn your churches into halls of science, and devote your leisure day to the study of your own bodies, the analysis of your own minds, and the examination of the fair material world which extends around you! Examine the expenses of your present religious system. Calculate all that is spent in multiplying churches and salarying their ministers; in clothing and feeding travelling preachers, who fill your streets and highways with trembling fanatics, and your very forests with frantic men and hysterical women. Estimate all the fruits of honest industry which are engulfed in the treasuries of Bible societies, tract associations, and christian missions; in sending forth teachers to central Africa and unexplored India, who know not the geography of their own country; and, hardly masters of their native tongue, go to preach of things unseen to nations unknown; compassing the earth to add error to ignorance, and the frenzy of religious fanaticism to the ferocity of savage existence. See the multitude and activity of your emissaries! Weigh the expenses of your outlay and outfit, and then examine if this cost and this activity could not be more usefully employed. By a late estimate, we learn the yearly expenses of the existing religious system, to exceed in these United States twenty millions of dollars. Twenty millions! For teaching what? Things unseen, and causes unknown! Why, here is more than enough to purchase the extract of all *just* knowledge—that is, of things *seen* and causes *known*, gathered by patient philosophy through all past time up to the present hour. Things unseen sell dear. Is it not worth our while to compare the value with the cost, and to strike the balance between them?

If we consider that there is no arriving at just practice but through just opinions, and no arriving at just opinions but through just knowledge, we must perceive the full importance of the proposed inquiry. Twenty millions would more than suffice to make us wise; and, alas! do they not more than suffice to make us foolish? I entreat you, but for one moment, to conceive the mental and moral revolution there would be in this nation, were these twenty millions, or but one half—but one third of that sum, employed in the equal distribution of accurate knowledge. Had you, in each of your churches, a teacher of elementary science, so that all the citizens, young and old, might cultivate that laudable curiosity without which the human animal is lower than the brute, we should not then see men staggering under intoxication, nor lounging in imbecile idleness; nor should we hear women retailing scandal from door to door, nor children echoing ribaldry in the streets, and vying with the monkey in mischief.

"But" you will say, "the clergy preach against these things." And when did mere preaching do any good? Put something in the place of these things. Fill the vacuum of the mind. Awaken its powers, and it will respect itself. Give it worthy objects on which to spend its strength, and it will riot no more in wantonness. Do the clergy this? Do they not rather demand a prostration of the intellect—a humbling and debasing of the spirit? Is not their knowledge that of things unseen, speaking neither to the senses, nor to the faculties? Are not their doctrines, by their own confession, incomprehensible? Is not their morality based upon human depravity? Preach they not the innate corruption of our race? Away with this libel of our nature! Away with this crippling, debasing, cowardly theory! Long, long enough hath this foul slander obscured our prospects, paralyzed our efforts, crushed the generous spirit within us! Away with it! such a school never made a race of freemen. And, see! in spite of the doctrine, to what heights of virtue and intelligence hath not man attained! Think of his discoveries in science—spite of chains, and dungeons, and gibbets, and anathemas! Think of his devotion to principle! Even when in error, great in his devotion! Think of the energy stronger than power, the benevolence supreme over selfishness, the courage conquering in death, with which he fought, and endured, and persevered through ages, until he won his haven of liberty in America! Yes! he has won it. The noble creature has proved his birthright. May he learn to use and to enjoy it.

But how shall he do this? Sons and daughters of America! 'tis for you to answer. When will ye improve the liberty for which your fathers sought an unknown world? When will ye appreciate the treasure they have won? When will ye see, that liberty leans her right arm on knowledge, and that knowledge points you to the world ye inhabit?

Consider that world, my friends! Enable yourselves, by mastering the first elements of knowledge, to judge of the nature and importance of all its different branches. Fit yourselves for the examination of your opinions, and then *examine your opinions.* Read, inquire, reason, reflect! Wrong not your understandings by doubting their perception of moral, any more than of physical, truth. Wrong not the God ye worship by imagining him armed with thunders to protect the tree of knowledge from approach. If ye conceive yourselves as holding from one great being your animate existence, employ his first best gift—your reason. Scan with your reason that which ye are told is his word, scan with your senses those which ye are told are his works. Receive no man's assertion. Believe no conviction but your own; and *respect not your own* until ye *know* that ye have examined both sides of every question; collected all evidence weighed, compared, and digested it: sought it at the fountain head; received it never through suspicious channels— altered, mutilated, or defaced; but pure, genuine, from the authorities themselves. Examine ye things? look to the fact. Examine ye books? to the text. And when ye look and when ye read, be *sure that ye see, and be sure that ye understand.* Ask *why* of every teacher. Ask *why* over every book. While there is a doubt, suspend judgment; while one evidence is wanting, withhold assent.

Observe here the advantage of material science. Does the physician—(I use the word here, as I shall often have occasion to use it hereafter, to signify the student of physics, or the observers of nature)—does the physician tell you that water is compounded of gases? He perform the experiment. That the atmosphere is another compound? The same. That more of or less of sctivity is in all matter? He shows you the formation of crystals in their bed, and composes and decomposes them before ye. Does he tell you that matter is ever changing, but never losing? He analyzes the substance before your eyes, and gives you its elements with nothing wanting. Do the anatomists and physiologist describe the structure and texture of your bodies? They shew you their hidden arcana, dissect their parts, and trace their relation; explain the mechanism of each organ, and observe, with you its uses and functions. Do the geologist and mineralogist speak to us of the structure and component parts of this globe? They explain to us the strata of earths; the position of rocks; the animal remains they envelope: the marks they exhibit of convulsion or of rest—of violent and sudden, or of gradual and silent, phenomena. See, then, the superiority of physical science! The proof comes with the assertion; the fact constitutes the truth.

But, you will say, there is other evidence than the physically tangible—other truths than those admitted through the senses. There is the more *immediate* and the more *remote* testimony of our senses; nothing more, nothing less. Will you appeal to numerical and geometrical truth? Had we no senses, could we know any thing of either? Were there no objects, no substances and existences around you, how could you conceive of number or of form? If the child see not *four things,* how shall he understand the meaning of *four?* If he see not two halves, put them together, divide them, compare them, measure, weigh them, how shall he *know* that two halves are equal to a whole? or a whole greater than its part? These are the simple truths conceived by the philosopher of nature, Pestalozzi. Here are the leading beauties of that system of experimental instruction which he so long strove to put in practice, and which time may enable others successfully to develope.

But, I hear you again object, that there are truths appealing only to the mind, or directly to the feelings: such are *moral truths.* The varying degree of sensibility evinced by individuals towards the joys and sorrows of others is apparent to every observer. This sensibility forms the basis of virtue; and, when by means of experience we have distinguished painful from pleasurable sensations in our own case, this sensibility assists us to estimate them in the case of others. Yet have we no doors by which to admit knowledge but the senses. We ascertain what is good or evil by experience. The beneficial or injurious consequences of actions make us pronounce them virtuous or vicious. The man of cultivated sensibility then refers his sensations and

E

applies his experience to others, and sympathisies in the pain
or the pleasure he conceives them to feel. But, here are our
moral truths also based upon fact. There is no test of these
but experience. That is good which produces good; that
evil, which produces evil; and, where our senses different
from what they are, our virtue and our vice would be
different also. Let us have done with abstractions! Truth
is fact. Virtue is beneficial action; vice, mischievous action;
virtuous feelings are those which impart pleasure to the
bosom; bad feelings, those which disturb and torment it.
Be not anxious in seeking your rule of life. Consult experience; your own sensations, the sensations of others. These
are surer guides than laws and doctrines, and when the law
and the doctrine coincide not with the evidence of your
senses, and the testimony of your reason, be satisfied that
they, that is, the *law* and the *doctrine,* are false.

Think of these things! Weigh the truth of what I advance!
Go to your churches with your understandings open. Inquire
the meaning of the words ye hear—the value of the ideas.
See if they be worth twenty millions of dollars! And, if they
be not, withhold your contributions. But—ye will be afraid.
Afraid! of what?—of acting conscientiously? of acting
reasonably? Come! learn, then, of a stranger and a woman!
Be bold to speak what ye think and feel; and to act in accordance with your belief. Prefer your self respect to the
respect of others. Nay! *secure* your own respect, and
command that of others.

I speak with warmth. I *feel* warmly. The happiness, the
honour, the dignity of man, are dear to my heart. His ignorance afflicts me; his cowardice afflicts me; his indifference
afflicts me. He feels not for himself, he feels not for his
race.

But—ye will wipe off this stain Ye will awake to the
uses of things. Ye will inquire. Ye will collect just knowledge. Ye will cultivate your reason. Ye will improve your
nature.

Many are the societies, associations, treasury funds, among
you. Organize a society for the promotion of just knowledge. Raise an edifice, sacred to national union and national
instruction, capable of holding from three to five thousand
individuals, where the citizens of all ages may assemble for
the acquisition of useful knowledge, and for the cultivation of
that social feeling and brotherly fellowship, without which no

real republic can have an existence. Select good instructors, masters of science, and capable of developing it easily and agreeably. Attach to the institution your museums and your public libraries. These are of little use single, detached, and unassisted by the elucidations of experienced instructors. Such an institution as that I have now sketched, should be open to as many as possible free of all charge. The rent of *a portion* of the seats might be devoted to the remuneration of such individuals as could not bestow their labours gratuitously. The building itself, I am disposed to hope, could be raised for such a purpose by voluntary contributions.

As soon as possible, there should be attached to this hall of science, a school of industry, which, in time, might be made to cover its own expenses by the labour of the children. Here, besides the imparting of useful trades, would be held also, the earlier classes in intellectual knowledge: and, when sufficiently advanced, the young people could perfect their studies in the hall of science. In the commencement, the school of industry might be conducted on the plan of a day school only, where, at successive hours, the teachers in the various branches of knowledge, mechanical and intellectual, might hold their classes.

Nor let the rich imagine that such a plan of education would not advantage *them* equally with the poor. What is the education they now command? At once false, imperfect, and expensive. Nor let them imagine that *any* can be well trained until *all* are well trained. Example is more than precept. While the many are left in ignorance, the few cannot be wise, for they cannot be virtuous. Look to your jails, your penitentiaries, your poor-houses! Look to your streets, your haunts of vice, your hovels of wretchedness! Look to the unhappy victims of poverty, of passion, gambling, drinking. Alas, the heart turns sick, and the tongue falters, under the enumeration of all the shapes and sounds of suffering which affright the eye and the ear of humanity!

And what is the cause of all this? Ignorance! Ignorance! There is none other. Oh! then, be up and be doing! Rich and poor, be up and be doing. Are ye not all fellow creatures? Are ye not all of one form, of one nature? Have ye not all the same wants? Oh! then, why have ye not the same interests? And ye have—ye have. Oh that ye could believe it! Oh that ye could see it! Oh that ye would unite under the wings of liberty as brothers, as equals, as fellow men! Oh that ye would

E 2

enter as one family, the courts of knowledge, and cast down at her feet your prejudices, your dissensions, your jealousies, your fears! Whenever the people of all the larger towns shall begin the good work of popular and equal instruction, the same may soon become a state concern; and instead of endowing, as is now the custom, colleges for the erroneous education of the few, we shall see spread throughout the land, national institutions for the rational education of the many. To this primary object will be then directed the legislation of all the states; to the same object the taxation of all the states; to the same, also, those contributions which are now devoted to the building of sectarian churches, even frowning defiance at the other, and sectarian preachers all flourishing the torch of discord, and fighting each his own battle for wealth and supremacy, against common sense and the common weal.

But the tree which hereafter shall shadow the land, must grow from a small seed. Plant ye that seed now, that ye may see it shoot and blossom, and that your children may reap of its fruits. Look around upon each other as upon fellow citizens and fellow creatures, interested alike in the discovery of the true and the useful, for the common advantage of all. Unite—unite for the promotion of knowledge? Exchange the spirit of sectarianism for that of universal love, charity, and toleration. Turn from the teachers of strife, and seek ye out inquirers after truth. Look around first among yourselves. Seek out the talent that is at home, and when ye find it not, invite it from afar. Encourage the wise to come among ye instead of the foolish; the peaceful and enlightened instead of the noisy ignorant; the reasoner instead of the declaimer; the child of science who will give you all he knows, and seek with you what he knows not, instead of the master by right divine, who promulgates doctrines without advancing evidence, and who stuns our human reason, as our human ears, with absurdities which, *he says*, come from heaven.

With such guides, and engaged in such investigations and undertakings, as I have ventured to recommend, you will all meet on common ground. You will no longer see in each other Calvinists, Baptists, Catholics, Lutherans, Methodists, and I know not what; you will see only human beings. The halls of science are open to all; her truths are disputed by none. She says not to one, " *eat no meat on Fridays;*"

to another, "*plunge into the river;*" to a third, "*groan in the spirit;*" to a fourth, "*wait for the spirit;*" to a fifth, "*eat bread in the Lord;*" to a sixth, "*eat the Lord in bread;*" to a seventh, "*dance in divine praise;*" to a eighth, "*dance not at all;*" to a ninth, "*perceive in things visible the shadows of things unseen;*" to a tenth, "*there is for you salvation;*" and to nine hundred and ninety-nine thousandths of the human race, "*ye were born for eternal fire.*" Science says nothing of all this. She says, only, "observe, compare, reason, reflect, understand:" and the advantage is, that we can do all this without quarrelling.

I have now attempted to substantiate, with you, the nature, object, and consequences of just knowledge; the means proper for its attainment, and the measures requisite for securing those means to yourselves and your children.

Considering the investigations we have held together in our meetings of Tuesday, Thursday, and this evening, as introductory to the examination of existing opinions, and the present mode of spending the leisure time and surplus money (which I pray you to bear in mind is the surplus industry) of the nation, I propose that we investigate, at our next meeting, more closely the subject which now engages your weekly attention in your churches.

The acquisition of knowledge being essential to our happiness, as being the only means by which we can attain to truth in opinions, and wisdom in practice, it is important that we bestow on every branch of it, an attention exactly proportionate to its utility. We have observed upon the importance of some now entirely neglected. It is well that we weigh accurately the value of that which now engrosses twenty millions per annum of the national wealth, and that we hereafter apportion to it, liberally and readily, so much of both as we may discover it to deserve—*and no more.*

LECTURE IV.

Religion.

I have selected for our consideration this evening a subject which we are generally accustomed to consider as of vital importance; which is usually made to occupy the human mind from the cradle to the grave, and which, however varying in the views and interpretations of its expounders, is conceived to constitute the polar star of human conduct; to be our only guide towards virtue, our only bar from vice, our source of comfort, our anchor of hope, and at once the alarming deterrer from crime and its terrific avenger. My hearers will already have divined that our subject is RELIGION.

To those who may already have substantiated with me those first premises, which I am ever desirous should be seen and understood before I enter on the discussion of isolated topics, or approach the tests of reason and experience to all or any of the multiform tribe of human opinions—to those, I say, among this audience, who may have attended the three preliminary discourses on knowledge, closed last evening, I might consider all prefatory observations on the present occasion unnecessary. But, as in all probability, I am addressing a portion of this audience for the first time, I feel unwilling to launch with undue precipitancy into a discussion calculated perhaps to alarm the fears of some, and the honest prejudices of others.

Myself a scholar, not a teacher, who have purchased such knowledge as I possess, by years of self-directed study, persevering observation, and untiring reflection, I can well conceive, for I myself have experienced, the doubts, difficulties, hopes, fears, and anxieties, which beset the awakening mind in the early stage of inquiry; the indistinct and, often, evanescent perceptions which encourage, and then check, and then again encourage, again to intimidate its advance; the conflicting thoughts and feelings with which it has to struggle ere it can vanquish early impressions, and consent to receive new ones, admit ideas subversive of those which had grown with its growth, and which, associated with tender recollections, cling to the heart as well as the head, or not unfrequently, grafted on the imagination of childhood, by an education as cruel as erroneous, continue to alarm the fancy and agitate the nerves even after the judgment has pronounced them chimeras. All this I can understand, for all this I have either felt or observed in others. Anxiously, therefore, would I temper my words to the timid, and, if possible, the truths themselves, which we are met to search out and investigate.

If, then, in manner or in matter, I should touch too harshly on the opinions of some, or the feelings of any, I will pray them to absolve me of every desire but that of eliciting truths important to the well-being of man ; of every intention but that of administering to the instruction, and consequently, to the happiness of those I may address. But, will it be asked, why I conceive myself fitted to impart instruction, and increase the sum of human happiness? For I must observe, that the individual who should successfully attempt the one, *must* succeed in the other; error and misery being inseparable companions, and knowledge and happiness the same. If I have thus conceived of myself, it has been neither (as I at least believe) through too high a valuation of my own acquirements, nor too eager a desire to assume that tone of dictation which I am accustomed to deprecate in others. I have advanced just too far in knowledge to overrate my attainments ; just far enough at once to understand my own deficiencies, and to have detected the false pretensions of many self-called wise. It is to render apparent the simplicity of real, and the charlatanism of false learning, that I have volunteered—not, I request you to believe, without due reflection, and a thorough understanding of all the criticism, censure, and, I may say, unseemly abuse, which I was about to encounter :—that I have volunteered, I say, to impart to others, what I myself know, and, more than all, to enlighten them as to what can *really be known.* This has been the more especial object of my previous discourses on knowledge : and, as we then observed, so must I now repeat, that until we see clearly what *knowledge is,* we cannot perceive truth, detect error, nor possess one really accurate, reasoned, and consistent opinion.

Knowledge, we ascertained to consist in an accumulation of facts. The doors by which we admit these facts, are our senses ; and the means we possess, for judging, comparing, analyzing, and arranging these facts, are supplied by our faculties, intellectual and moral. Had we *only* senses, each impression would disappear with the object which excited it ; in which case, no knowledge, or accumulation of facts, could exist for us. But, having memory, we can retain each impression, by whichsoever of our senses received ; having judgment, we compare and arrange these impressions ; having imagination, we ingeniously combine impressions, however removed as to time, distant as to place, or slightly assimilated by affinity or resemblance. And, having moral feelings, we consider all occurrences with a reference to the good or evil they may induce to our race.

By these cursory remarks, it is my object to lead to the observation, that nothing can be known where there is nothing to operate on our senses; or, to place more accurately the position, *where we have no primary sensations to constitute elementary facts.*

In my opening discourse upon the nature of knowledge, I had occasion to insist especially on this truth; reminding my then audience, that the sciences but too generally taught on the erroneous principle of *assumed* instead of *substantiated* data, (we here instanced arithmetic, geometry, and morals,) were in reality based upon demonstrations supplied by positive sensations. I will not say that the teachers of unreal science, and dogmatical declaimers upon imaginary subjects and un-meaning words, are aware of the stumbling-block thrown in the way of the human intellect by the old ; and, alas, still the customary method of imparting these most important branches of knowledge; but I will say, that whether awake or blind to the consequences, those consequences are as favourable to the reign of their errors, as they are fatal to the progress of truth and the vital interests of man. Were every teacher called upon to substantiate the elementary facts upon which he builds the fabric of his science, how would the number of our dogmatical assertions and unsubstantiated doctrines—ay ! and the list of our sciences themselves, be curtailed !

In that dawn of intellect, however brilliant, which broke on ancient Greece, when the range of human observation was circumscribed within the limits imposed by a clumsy and imperfect system of navigation, and by a world of unbroken forest, and widely-extended barbarism, and farther circum-scribed within the limits of the human vision, unaided by telescope or microscope, and all the ingenious material which now aids the labours of the physician, and has revealed to us the anatomy of matter, with all its wonder working qualities —such as we are accustomed to distinguish by the names of attraction, electricity, resistance, form, colour, motion, rest, and we may add, feeling, thought, and life. In that bright, but only opening dawn of human inquiry, science had hardly an existence. Facts were wanting; the means for accu-mulating these were not devised, and therefore, while excelling in all the arts for which the state of his knowledge, the form of his government, and his exquisite physical organization combined to fit him, (we may here more especally particularize painting, sculpture, architecteture, poetry, and oratory,) we observe the ingenious Athenian to have been invariably a false logican, and an absurd physician. Physician indeed was a word inapplicable to him, for he knew nothing of physics. With him, all was theory and nothing fact; and knowledge, let it ever be remembered, is all fact, and never theory.

But, before we leave the interesting people to whom we have alluded, I would request you to observe, that while the moderns have opened a field of inquiry unknown to the ancients—while they have substantiated facts subversive of all their dreams—we are still in the habit of employing in our seminaries of learning, such of their elementary books, as the devastation of time and of early Christian fanaticism have spared to us, and of following out their method of instruction wherever it was most defective. Thus are we still in the habit of imparting to a child a first idea of number through the medium of allegorical ciphers, instead of tangible and visible objects; thus do we still persist in substantiating solely by a process of abstract reasoning, based upon verbal sophisms, the truths involved in geometrical science, instead of first submitting those truths in the form of facts to the eye; and thus also are we wise enough to persecute such teachers as have judgment sufficient to distinguish the better method, and courage sufficient to attempt its adoption. We might here further observe, that the logic of Aristotle, with its text additionally obscured and confounded by the labours of puzzle-headed commentators, was, till within a few years, held in vulgar respect, and vulgar use, throughout the seminaries of the world. And, should we examine, we might find, in spite of the labours of a Locke and a Condillac, and others, wiser yet, because aided by the light previously thrown on the path of knowledge by a succession of giant intellects, that the erroneous mode of reasoning admired in ancient Greece, yet lives, under modified but, perhaps therefore, more dangerous forms, in the schools, colleges, and churches in modern Europe, and revolutionized America.

I may be alluding here to subjects unfortunately foreign to the apprehension of a large portion of this audience. Unfortunately, say I? ay! and most inconsistently and unjustly: inconsistently, if we consider the nature of the national institutions which secure equal rights, and consequently, equal instruction, (necessary, as I have formerly shown, to the understanding, protection, and just exercise of those rights,) to all the citizens; and unjustly, if we consider the great principle of liberty, which proclaims to the enlightened

mind the equal rights of all humankind. If the prefatory
observations which I have felt necessary for the elucidation
of our subject, should prove difficult of apprehension to any
present, may it serve as an additional stimulus towards the
adoption of some measures for the popular instruction, by
devoting some of the now mispent time, and mispent money
to this desirable object. Now, as on all other occasions, my
utmost ingenuity is applied as well to simplify my words as
my arguments ; and I wish the least informed of my hearers
could believe that all the facts to which I refer, and all the
learning to which I find myself constrained to allude, are of
most easy attainment : far, far easier than are the errors over
which they are now perhaps weekly stumbling in the
churches of this city.

But, to return from our digressions, and to point out more
distinctly the conclusions towards which my previous observations have aimed :—it is a fact well known to the really
enlightened, and well known also, I believe, to the designing,
who live by the ignorance of the multitude, that every thing
depends upon the *manner* of conveying instruction, and upon
the first premises from which subsequent arguments are
deduced, and thus final conclusions established.

It is not many years, since a native of Switzerland, whose
opportunities were confined within the limits prescribed by
poverty, and to the society of a simple mountain peasantry,
but whose native intellect and unsophisticated observation,
led him to distinguish some first principles, which the more
learned have been accustomed to overlook ; and, above all
whose beautiful moral feelings, led him to see in every human
being, a brother—it is only as it were yesterday, that this
simple philosopher, among a simple people, caught a first
glimpse of a true and rational method of instruction ; namely
by first addressing the senses, and through them, awakening
the faculties commanding the attention, and convincing the
reason. Led by his example, other generous minds have
laboured to improve the idea he had originated ; and the
day must be fast approaching, when the same correct principle will be applied to every branch of knowledge, and
prevail throughout the civilized world.

And yet, hitherto, the enemies of human improvement,
have shown a quicker scent to the consequences of the radical
reform, suggested by Pestalozzi, than have the nations who
are to profit by it. Even the leaden faculties of the despot of

Austria, quickened by the imperial anxiety, as he himself expressed it, to possess within his dominions, *not wise men but obedient subjects*, could perceive the danger to kingcraft, and its coadjutor priestcraft, in a mode of instruction which taught the opening mind to see through the eye, and hear through the ear, and believe only upon the testimony of fact experiment, and experience. The young Pestalozzian schools started by the patriots of Italy, in the short dawn of of liberty which so lately broke on their unhappy country, only to close in darker night, were overthrown, and their very foundations ploughed up, by the soldiers of the holy ally. In Spain, similar efforts met of course with a similar fate. In Switzerland, Pestalozzi's native Switzerland, the aristocratic cantons saw the threatened danger to the pretensions of the few in the simple labours of the friend of the many. In France, the Jesuits, resuscitated for a while by the imbecile Bourbons, persecuted alike all instruction but that patronized by the servants of religion: and, even here, in republican America, such has been the influence of superstition, and of the teachers of superstition, that the efforts of Pestalozzian disciples, have been for the most part paralized, and invariably impeded.

And why in all countries—why in either world this persecution?

Because educators of youth, who speak to the mind, by tangible objects presented to the senses, and who encourage their disciples to look to things, and to seek the proof in the fact, have been supposed to prepare unmanageable subjects for kings, and troublesome disciples for priests. And most wise this apprehension on the part of those who would command the blind obedience, or the blind belief of their fellow men! Most wise this apprehension on the part of those whose power lies in the weakness of those they rule, or in the ignorance of those they lead! They alone, who have justice on their side, fear not to have to do with free minds; they alone, who have truth on their side, fear not to encounter knowledge.

But, would *we* not have truth and justice on our side? What interests have *we* inconsistent with either? What have *we* to fear from the bold inquiry of free intellects? Why should *we* shrink from the fulness and from the universality {knowledge?

But what is knowledge? Again must we put the question.

Again must we repeat the answer: for on this answer, my friends, depends the truth or the falsehood of evey opinion we hold, the reality or unsubstantiality of every subject presented for our investigation.

Knowledge signifies *things known.* When there are no *things known*, there is no *knowledge.* Where there are no *things to be known*, there *can be* no *knowledge.* We have observed that every science, that is, every branch of knowledge, is compounded of certain facts, of which our sensations furnish the evidence. Where no such evidence is supplied, we are without *data;* we are without first premises; and when, without these, we attempt to build up *a science,* we do as those who raise edifices without foundations. And what do such builders construct? *Castles in the air.*

Having now, I trust, substantiated the nature of knowledge, and the basis of all true science, I would suggest the propriety of examining into the reality of the science, current among us under the varying name of religion, theology, or divinity. As this science now draws from the surplus industry of the American nation, twenty millions per annum, and as it is legally authorised to consume all the leisure days of the industrious classes, and farther recommended to consume all the leisure hours snatched from their days of labour, I think we must admit the examination to be not uncalled for.

It will be conceded that religion engulfs more money and more time, than any subject which ever agitated the inquiring mind of man. You will reply, that it is because it involves his most important interests. Such indeed ought to be the case, judging from all that is expended upon it.

Admitting religion to be the most important of all subjects, its truths must be the most apparent; for we shall readily concede, both that a thing true, must be always of more or less importance—and that a thing essentially important, must always be indisputably true. Now, again, I conceive we shall be disposed to admit, that exactly in proportion to the indisputability of a truth, is the proof it is capable of affording; and that, exactly in proportion to the proof afforded, is our admission of such truth and belief in it.

If, then, religion be the most important subject of human inquiry, it must be that also, which presents the most forcible, irrefragable, and indisputable truths to the enquirer. It must be that on which the human mind can err the least, and where all minds must be the most agreed. If religion be at

once a science, and the most true of all sciences, its truths
must be as indisputable as those in any branch of the mathematics—as apparent to all the senses, as those revealed by
the chemist, or observed by the naturalist, and as easily
referred to the test of our approving or disapproving sensations, as those involved in the science of morals.

To ask if this be the case, might seem putting a question
in satire. And it is not I who will use a weapon of ridicule,
where the opinions and feelings of my fellow creatures are
concerned. Against designing teachers of error, I will use
any and every weapon within the compass of my talents and
acquirements to wield; and against error itself, considered
apart from those who may misconceive of its nature, the
same. But ill-fitted were I for the the task I have volun-
tered, ill-fitted to assist in letting down the barrier which
holds back the many from the courts of knowledge—ill-
fitted, I say, were I to address the popular mind, if I could
idly wound the popular feeling;—ill-fitted and unworthy,
to approach the tests of reason and experience, to human
practice and opinion, if I should treat with levity one honest
error, or make truth a cause of offence to one conscientious
bosom. Far be such consequences from my words, as they
are from my heart, while we weigh in the balance that—
must we call it science?—whose value is now estimated at a
yearly tax of twenty millions.

Must we call it science, I asked? Is religion a science?
Is it a branch of knowledge? Where are the *things known*
upon which it rests? Where are the accumulated facts of
which it is compounded? What are the human sensations to
which it appeals?

I request your undivided attention to the present investiga
tion. I request you to keep in view what we have ascertained
all knowledge to be, and how we have observed all knowledge
to be acquired. Unless these simple primary truths be ever
present to the mind, it is without a standard by which to
judge any fact or any opinion; and reflection or reasoning,
to any useful purpose, with any chance of rational results, is
absolutely impossible to it.

Knowledge then, (my hearers will forgive the reiteration,)
is compounded of *things known*. It is an accumulation of
facts gleaned by our senses, within the range of material
existence, which is subject to their investigation. As I
observed on a former occasion, the number of objects com-

prised within the circle of human observation is so multiplied, and the properties or qualities of these objects so diversified, that, with a view to convenient and suitable divisions in the great work of inspecting the whole, and also with a view to the applying more order and method in the arrangement of the facts collated in the wide field of nature, they have been placed under different heads, each of which we may call *a branch of knowledge*, or, more succinctly, *a science*. Thus, do we consider the various living tribes which people the elements? we class our observations under the head of natural history. Do we direct our attention to the structure and internal mechanism of their bodies? we designate the results of our inspection under the heads anatomy and physiology. Do we trace the order of occurrences and appearances in the wide field of nature? we note them under natural philosophy. Do we analyze substances, and search out their simple elements? chemistry. Do we apply ourselves to the measurement of bodies, or calculate the heights and distances of objects? geometry. And so on through all the range of human observation, extending from the relative position of the heavenly bodies, and accurate calculation of their courses, to the uses, habits, structure and physiology of the delicate plant which carpets our earth.

It may be here suggested, in accordance with the vague notions still current respecting the nature of knowledge, that there is yet a science, which rests not upon the evidence of common individual sensations, namely, history, which is supplied by the recorded sensations of others.

I have already observed, in my opening discourses upon knowledge, that history is not, properly speaking, *knowledge*, only *probability*. This probability is less or greater, according to the proximity or remoteness of the circumstances it relates; according to the style of the narrator, the accuracy and extent of the knowledge he displays, the consistency of his statements one with another, and, above all, with the result of our (the reader's) own observation and experience. Human tradition, written or spoken, is only *history* so long as it relates probabilities; when it relates improbabilities, it is *fable*. Even the histories best authenticated by the testimonies of concurring probabilities, living witnesses or surviving monumental remains, are doubtless filled with erroneous statements; and the judicious reader, in admitting the general outline or thread of the relation, is well aware that his acquaintance with the whole must be very imperfect, and his conceptions of the details both confused and mistaken.

The knowledge, then, supplied by history, is not positive, but only relative. It cannot be admitted as knowledge, until it is corroborated by all the knowledge accumulated by our experience; and, whenever our observation of the phenomena of nature refutes the assertions of the historian, we distinguish the latter immediately for erroneous. History, therefore, can only testify to itself; that is, to its own probability. If it relate circumstances in accordance with the nature of man, and the nature of things, we receive it as credible; if it relate circumstances in violation of these, we discard it as spurious. We may here remark as a consequent, that no history can be received in testimony of any occurrence opposed to the established course of natural phenomena; since this would be to receive the reported or traditionary experience of others in preference to our own, which, in the case of a rational being, would be impossible.

Now let us see where, in the table of knowledge, we may class religion. Of what part or division of nature, or material existence, does it treat? What bodies, or what properties of tangible bodies, does it place in contact with our senses, and bring home to the perception of our faculties.

It clearly appertains not to the table of human knowledge, for it treats not of objects discoverable within the field of human observation. "No," will you say? "but its knowledge is superhuman, unearthly—its field is in heaven."

My friends, the knowledge which is not human, is of slippery foundation to us human creatures. Things *known*, constitute knowledge; and here is a science treating of things unseen, unfelt, incomprehended! Such cannot be *knowledge*. What then is it? Probability? possibility? theory? hypothesis? tradition? written? spoken? by whom? when? where? Let its teachers—nay, let all earth reply!

But what confusion of tongues and voices now strike on the ear!

From either Indies, from torrid Africa, from the frozen regions of either pole, from the vast plains of ancient Asia, from the fields and cities of European industry, from the palaces of European luxury, from the soft chambers of priestly ease, from the domes of hierarchal dominion, from the deep cell of the self-immolated monk, from the stony cave of the self-denying anchorite, from the cloud-capt towers, spires, and minarets of the crescent and the cross, arise shouts, and hosannas, and anathemas, in the commingled names of Brama, and Veeshnu, and Creeshna, and Juggernaut; heavenly kings, heavenly queens, triune deities, earth-born gods, heaven-born prophets, apotheosized monarchs, demon-enlightened philosophers, saints, angels, devils, ghosts, apparitions, and sorceries!

But, worse than these sounds which but stun the ear and confound the intellect, what sights, oh humankind! appal the heart! The rivers of earth run blood! Nation set against nation! Brother against brother! Man against the companion of his bosom; and that soft companion, maddened with the frenzy of insane remorse for imaginary crimes, fired with the rage of infatuated bigotry, or subdued to diseased helplessness and mental fatuity, renounces kindred, flies from social converse, and pines away a useless or mischievous existence in sighings and tremblings, spectral fears, uncharitable feelings, and bitter denunciations! Such are thy doings, oh religion! Or, rather, such are thy doings, oh man! While standing in a world so rich in sources of enjoyment, so stored with objects of real inquiry and attainable knowledge, yet shutting thine eyes, and, worse, thy heart, to the tangible things and sentient creatures around thee, and winging thy diseased imagination beyond the light of the sun which gladdens thy world, and contemplation of the objects which are here to expand thy mind and quicken the pulses of thy heart!

"But," say the teachers of that which is not knowledge, which may not be called a science, but which devours the treasure of nations and maddens the intellects of men, "that which we teach, unseen, unknown, unfelt by others, is revealed to us: incomprehended of others, is understood by us; unknown to others, is by us ascertained."

Ha! has their God of justice children of preference? Does their God of wisdom open worlds to the observation of a few especial ministers, who have not senses to investigate the objects presented to them, or, at the least, faculties to describe those objects intelligibly to others? Does their God of beneficence reveal his nature to those who can neither comprehend nor pourtray it? his will, to creatures who, in expounding it, convulse human society to its centre? Are we to believe this? Oh, my fellow-beings! have we believed this so long?

Sisters and brothers! ye more especially, who, knowing the least of things, believe the most in doctrines; who, rocked perhaps in the cradle by fond but mistaken mothers, closed nightly your infant eyes to troubled sleep, upon tales of wicked angels, and tempting devils; and opened them, to shrink under the blessed light of morning, from the imaginary frown of a revengeful God—on ye, more especially, do I call, to arouse the faculties which superstition may have benumbed ; and to put the question to your reason, if all the doctrines of the servants of religion are not inconsistent with their own assumed first premises ? Could a Being of Wisdom demand of ye to spend your time and torture your faculties in imagining things which ye never saw ? worlds beyond the reach of human ken, and existences of whose nature ye can form no conception ? Could a Being of Justice command ye to prostrate the reason he should have given, and swear credence to doctrines, which they even who teach, pretend not to understand? Could a Being of Beneficence visit in anger the errors of the children of his hand, and delight in the torment of those, whose ignorance he could enlighten, and whose sorrows he could heal?

Oh, my fellow beings ! let us leave these inconsistences to those who teach them ! Let us leave things unseen and causes unknown, to those who vend them in this land for twenty millions of dollars; and, in other lands less free and more benighted than ours, for that sum twenty times told. Let us turn from that which is *not* knowledge, to all which *is* knowledge. Let us leave theory for fact; the world of the imagination for that of the eye; laws graven on stones for those graven on the heart ! Let reason be our guide, observation our teacher, our own bosoms our judges !

But, alas ! ere this may be done, our reason must be exercised, our observation awakened, our feelings quickened, by that spirit of charity and brotherhood, which jarring creeds have through ages stifled, and which just knowledge can alone impart !

It has been my object in this, as in my previous discourses, to develope with you the nature of knowledge, to substantiate in what it consists, and where and how it may be found. I have farther, on the present occasion, attempted to prove that you are now engaged in the pursut of what is *not* knowledge. That you are now paying your quota of the twenty millions per annum towards the support of a system of error, which from the earliest date of human tradition, has filled the earth with crime, and deluged its bosom with blood, and which, at

F

this hour, fills your country with discord, and impedes its progress in virtue, by lengthening the term of its ignorance.

The conclusions I am desirous should be drawn from our investigations of this evening, are the same which our judgments must draw from observation of, and reflection upon, the events passing before our eyes in the walks of life. How do these events exhibit the danger of looking out of our own nature and our own world for subjects of inquiry! How do these admonish us of the errors of our ways, and check the impotent presumption of our perverted curiosity, which, aiming at things beyond our vision and so beyond our comprehension, neglects the fair field of nature it is ours to admire ; the human duties and charities it is ours fo fulfil; and the human delights it is ours to administer and to enjoy.

I will pray ye to observe how much of our positive misery originates in our idle speculations in matters of faith, and in our blind, our fearful forgetfulness of facts—our cold, heartless, and, I will say, *insane* indifference to visible causes of tangible evil, and visible sources of tangible happiness ? Look to the walks of life I beseech ye—look into the public prints—look into your sectarian churches—look into the bosoms of families—look into your own bosoms, and those of your fellow-beings, and see how many of our disputes and dissensions, public and private—how many of our unjust actions—how many of our harsh judgments—how many of our uncharitable feelings—spring out of our ignorant ambition to rend the vail which wraps from our human senses the knowledge of things unseen, and from our human faculties the conception of causes unknown ? And oh, my fellow beings! do not these very words *unseen* and *unknown*, warn the enthusiast against the profanity of such inquiries, and proclaim to the philosopher their futility ? Do they not teach us that religion is no subject for instruction, and no subject for discussion ? Will they not convince us, that as beyond the horizon of our observation, we can *know* nothing, so within that horizon is the only safe ground for us to meet in public ?

I know how far from this simple conviction we now are. Perhaps at this very moment, the question, *what does she believe*, is uppermost in the thoughts of two-thirds of my hearers. Should such be their thoughts, I will reply to them.

With respect to myself, my efforts have been strenuously directed to ascertain what *I know*, to understand what *can be known*, and to increase my *knowledge* as far as possible. In the next place, I have endeavoured to communicate my *knowledge* to my fellow-creatures; and strictly laid down to myself the rule, never to speak to them of that of which I have *not* knowledge. If beyond the horizon of things seen—without the range of our earthly planet, and apart from the nature of our human race, any speculations should force themselves on my fancy, I keep them to myself, even as I do the dreams of my nightly sleep, well satisfied that my neighbour will have his speculations and his dreams also, and that his, whatever they may be, will not coincide precisely with mine.

Satisfied by experience, no less than observation, of the advantage to be derived from this rule of practice, viz. to communicate with others only respecting my knowledge, and to keep to myself my belief, I venture to recommend the same to my fellow creatures; and, in conformity with this rule, would urge them, as soon as possible, to turn their churches into halls of science, and exchange their teachers of faith for expounders of nature. Every day we see sects splitting, creeds new modelling, and men forsaking old opinions only to quarrel about their opposites. I see three Gods in one, says the trinitarian, and excommunicates the socinian, who sees a godhead in unity. I see a heaven but no hell, says the universalist, and disowns fellowship with such as may distinguish less. "I see a heaven and a hell also, beyond the stars," said lately the orthodox friend, and expelled his shorter-sighted brethren from the sanctuary. I seek them both in the heart of man, said the more spiritual follower of Penn, and straightway builded him up another temple, in which to quarrel with his neighbour, who perhaps only employs other words to express the same ideas. For myself, pretending to no insight into these mysteries, possessing no means of intercourse with the inhabitants of other worlds, confessing my absolute incapacity to see either as far back as a first cause, or as far forward as a last one, I am content to state to you, my fellow creatures, that all my studies, reading, reflection, and observation, have obtained for me no knowledge beyond the sphere of our planet, our earthly interests, and our earthly duties; and that I more than doubt, whether, should you expend all your time and all your treasure in the search, you will be able to acquire any better information respecting unseen worlds, and future events, than myself. Whenever you shall come to the same conclusion, you will probably think the many spacious edifices which rear their heads in your city, are somewhat misapplied, and the time of the individuals who minister therein, somewhat misemployed: you will then doubtless perceive that they who wish to muse, or pray, had better do it after the manner designated by the good Jesus, namely, by entering their closet and shutting the door ; and farther perceive, that the true Bible is the book of nature, the wisest teacher he who most plainly expounds it, the best priest our own conscience, and the most orthodox church a hall of science. I look round doubtless upon men of many faiths, upon calvinists, unitarians, methodists, baptists, catholics, and I know not what beside, and yet, my friends, let us call ourselves by what names we will, are we not creatures occupying the same earth, and sharing the same nature ? and can we not consider these as members of one family, apart from all our speculations respecting worlds, and existences, and states of being, for which, in ages past, men cut each other's throats, and for which they now murder each other's peace ?

And now, if among my hearers there should be one, whose opinions I have too rudely jarred, or, worse, whose feelings I have wounded, more deeply than he will I lament the offence, and lament it the rather because of its necessity. Had your public teachers employed their twenty millions in shedding peace on earth, and knowledge among men, I had not been here to startle the flock nor alarm the shepherd ; I had not stept forth from the studies and retirement which I love, into a world distracted with dissension and profaned with vice ; I had not thus ventured, and thus endured, in the cause of human reason, happiness, and tranquillity, if the teacher had done his duty, and the people had grown wise under his tuition.

At our next meeting, I purpose to call your attention to a subject of vital importance. I purpose to develope with you that just rule of life, which no system of religion ever taught, or can ever teach ; which exists apart from all faith, all creeds, and all written laws, and which can alone be found by following, with an open eye, a ready ear, and a willing heart, the steps of knowledge ; by exercising the senses, faculties, and feelings, which appertain to our nature ; and, instead of submitting our reason to the authority of fallible books and fallible teachers, by bringing always the words of all books and all teachers to the test of our reason.

LECTURE V.

Morals.

In my previous discourses, I have chiefly laboured to sub-stantiate with you the nature of knowledge. The importance of the object, may have led me to insist even to tediousness. on those primary truths which, once perceiving, the mind wonders could ever be unseen, and which, but for the errors inherent in our education, could never fail to be brought by the opening senses to the opening mind. But, as it is, our instincts supplanted, stifled, annihilated, instead of actively exercised, and widely guided; our faculties perverted, tortured, neglected; the most useful cramped or misled; the least useful unduly forced, prematurely exercised, and fed from a wrong source; our feelings led astray from the first moment of their blossoming; the canker of fear blighting their freshness, and visionary thoughts usurping the place of realities: nothing more difficult, sometimes more hopeless, than to awaken the mind to a perception of first principles, by simply calling on the eye to see, the ear to hear. all the senses to feel, and the understanding to admit, arrange, compare the facts so ascertained. Aware at once, both of the necessity and the difficulty of clearing the simple threshold of knowledge, of the thorns and branches heaped on it, by unbridled imaginations; I ever hesitate in our progress to make a step in advance, without appealing to the first simple premises which we have so laboured to establish. At our last meeting, therefore, we carefully recapitulated the result of our previous observations, respecting the nature and the limits of the field of human inquiry; and, having first con-vinced ourselves of what real knowledge consists, we pro-ceeded to try, by the test thus obtained, the reality of a subject which now absorbs the leisure, sways the feelings, and engulfs the surplus industry of mankind.

The result of these investigations, placed religion *without* the field of knowledge. Based upon assertion, hypothesis, tradition, we found it wanting in substantiated and ever enduring data to which the senses of each individual might appeal, and by which the faculties of each individual might be convinced. We remarked, that in consequence, no minds were agreed upon the matter : that while none disputed the truths of real science, consisting of *things known,* all disputed the lessons of religion, treating of things unknown, and things imagined. We remarked farther, that what is unreal in its nature, vague and ever varying in its lessons, could afford no safe guide to human reason, no just rule to human conduct; but that, on the contrary, all the experience supplied by tradition as well as by the observation of existing generations, combined to attest, that, so far from entrenching human conduct within the gentle barriers of peace and love, religion has ever been, and now is, the deepest source of contentions, wars, persecutions for conscience sake, angry words, angry feelings, backbitings, slanders, suspicions, false judgments, evil interpretations, unwise, unjust, injurious, inconsistent actions.

But shall we be told that these consequences are the result of false religions. Alas, my friends! and who has the true? Ask the Mahometan, the Jew, the Pagan, the Deist, the Christian, in all his multiform varieties, under all his multiplied appellations—each has the right, all others possess the wrong. And where, among these contradictory and confounding faiths, is one whose *ipse dixit* truths are compounded of facts; whose first premises are demonstrable to the human eye, the human ear, the human touch; whose proofs are sought and found in the nature of man and the nature of things, and whose conclusions are sanctioned by our own confirming sensations and assenting reason?

No, my friends, we have seen that no religion stands on the basis of *things known*; none bounds its horizon within the field of human observation; and, therefore, as it can never present us with indisputable facts, so must it ever be at once a source of error and of contention.

If, then, that which we have followed for a true light, be proved a meteor—if, instead of leading us into safe and pleasant paths, it have enticed us into swamps and quagmires—if, instead of informing the mind, warming and gladdening the heart, it have clouded and confounded the one, chilled and bruised the other, are we then without a guide in the path of life? Are our barks launched upon the ocean, without rudder or compass? Is there no star by which to steer, no rule-directed skill wherewith to trim our sails, and point an unerring course through the rocks and whirlpools of our passions and appetites, and the fogs and deceiving *mirage* of our deluding and deluded imaginations? Wo to man, should the answer be a negative! Wo to our race should we be—I say not without a rule, but without an *unerring* rule, by which to shape our course safely, steadily, usefully, happily, justly ; by which to regulate our actions, frame our opinions, chasten our feelings, and render the term of our existence, one of utility and delight. Were not this rule within our power to substantiate, idle were every other human inquiry, idle were every fact gathered in every science ; yea, idle were all human researches, if their results combined not to aid us in the establishing of that golden rule, which conducts by one and the same path to virtue and happiness.

And what then is this rule? Where in the field of knowledge must we seek it? Under what science shall we find it written ? In casting onr eye over the table of just knowledge, we shall find the rule we seek, under the head of " MORALS" —it being the science of human actions or of human life.

In earlier ages, however removed from the simple view of things to which the clearer lights of physical science are now leading civilized man, we perceive him always to have had some general ideas respecting this important branch of human inquiry ; nor, however it may administer to our vanity to believe the contrary, might we find upon minute investigation, that we have greatly advanced this science beyond the point to which the sages of Greece and Rome, or of Persia and China, had placed it before the date of our modern era. The cause of this remissness on our part, I conceive to be, that we have lost sight, even more than did the ancients, of the true basis of the science, and substituted one even more false than did the legislators of Greece, or the patriots of Rome.

The usual motive principle in Athenian ethics, and invariably of Spartan and Latin virtue, was the good of country, but that good always more or less unwisely interpreted ; military glory the means, and national greatness. instead of national happiness, the object. Still, if in something, or even in much, mistaken, the MORALS of the ancients was a soul-stirring science, encouraging a generous, if even an exaggerated forgetfulness of self, and calculated to form, as we read that it did form, commanding nations, and self-respecting men. Among the Athenian schools, indeed, were some models of practical virtue, and teachers of moral science, whose lessons and whose lives seem to have equalled all that we can show in modern generations of good and wise. Such appears to have been the modest and benevolent Socrates: such, more especially, appears to have been the mild, unpresuming, reasonable Epicurus, in whose ethics, as imperfectly conveyed to us, we find the science first based upon its just foundation—*the ascertained consequences of human actions.*

The moderns, whether we look to the numerous family of Christian nations, or to the equally numerous family who have followed the standard of Mohammed, have unfortunately based their morals upon their religion, or, where that was impracticable, have so mingled the truths of the science with the dogmas of the faith, that, while the vulgar mind has been unable to conceive of them as separate, even more enlightened minds, yielding to the force of education, have found it difficult not to conceive of them as related. The more effectually to detect the error of this persuasion, let us examine first what we understand by the term MORALS, and them what we understand by that of RELIGION. First, then, what is the meaning attached to the word MORALS. It is a word often in our mouths, and the first step towards acquiring a knowledge of any science, is so possess an accurate idea of the subject of which it treats, or of the meaning of the term employed for its designation.

What then is MORALS ?

A rule of life.

How formed ? from what deduced ?

From the consequences of actions as ascertained through our sensations, and our observations of the sensations of others.

Actions which produce good, we call moral actions; actions which produce evil, immoral actions. Revolve the matter as we may, we can come to no other rational conclusion. The word MORALS, then, is employed to designate a course of actions, whose effects are beneficial to ourselves and others. In other words, they constitute a rule of life drawn from the ascertained consequences of actions The rule is simple. If we never look out of it, we can never go wrong in morals.

Let us now inquire what is RELIGION? We have seen what religion *is not.* Our present object will be to ascertain what *it is,* and thus to establish a correct definition of the word applicable to it, by whatever religious sect, in whatever country, employed.

Were each individual in this assembly to answer the question in turn, I am somewhat doubtful if there would be two who would agree in their replies. Some would place religion in the intellectual admission of certain dogmas; others, in that of dogmas directly opposed to the first enumerated. Others would see it in the observation of certain days, fasts, and festivals; some in certain prayers offered up in certain places; others in songs and hymns, or in meditations, and visions, and ablutions, and all manner of ceremonies. There are doubtless some present, who would say all external rules and abstract creeds are of no importance; and who would direct us to see religion in the just actions of men.

I wish you here to observe, that such religionists as the last mentioned, are in fact no *religionists* at all; they are only *good men.* Either religion is something distinct from morals, or it is the same thing. If it be distinct, what is it? I believe there is one definition which will embrace all religions, from the Laplander's to the Hottentot's; from those of this city, round the world, until we land here again in the same.

Religion, as distinguished from morals, may be defined thus: *a belief in, and homage rendered to, existences unseen and causes unknown.* This definition will apply equally to the Hindoo, Mahommedan, Jew, Christian, Pagan, Theist, and every variety of religionist existing or imaginable. Of religion, as used to express *a just practice,* nothing can be said, but that it is a misapplication of terms. If religion mean good morals, let us call it good morals, that we may understand each other. I had occasion, during the course of our preliminary investigations on knowledge, to insist much on the importance of accurate language. Without it there can be no accurate ideas.

We perceive then that religion and morals are words bearing distinct significations. The one implies a mode of belief; the other a just mode of practice. These may indeed be occasionally conjoined, but there is no necessary relation between them; and I must request you to 'observe, that it is exceedingly difficult for them to be placed in contact, without the one, more or less, neutralizing the other. A necessary consequent of religious belief is the attaching ideas of merit to that belief, and of demerit to its absence. Now here is a departure from the first principle of true ethics. Here we find ideas of moral wrong and moral right associated with something else than beneficial action. The consequence is, we lose sight of the real basis of morals, and substitute a false one. Our religious belief usurps the place of our sensations, our imaginations of our judgment. We no longer observe effects; we lay down laws. We no longer look to actions, trace their consequences, and *then* deduce the rule; we first make the rule, and then, right or wrong, force the action to square with it.

But, methinks I hear you observe—that Religion, if not the source, may be at least the coadjutor of virtue; if not the parent, she may be at least the companion Far be it from me to say that such may not be—that such never is. I have crossed in the path of life some lovely minds and lovely hearts, of which no harsh and narrow creed could mar the beauty; and which could enfold in their own gentleness, and expand with their own warmth, the chilling and censorious faith, which drove less kindly natures to angry uncharitableness or morose fanaticism.

Religion I have observed to take its complexion from that of the bosom which harbours it. Where the disposition is gentle, its inmate will soften her temper, modify her doctrines, and sink to whispers the thunder of her denunciations. Where the character has more vigour, and firmness of purpose, and ardent imagination unite with scrupulous conscientiousness, we find the ardent zealot and sincere fanatic ready to sacrifice life, friends, country, aye, and the whole human race on the altar of his idolatry, and to make his existence one long scene of denial to himself, and of infliction upon others. On such temperaments as the last adverted to, we perceive the most fatal effects of religion on the moral character of the man. Such as we have here depicted, should be the enlightened benefactors of their race; the leaders of improvement, the firm defenders and fearless advocates of truth. Such would they be if led by wise guides into the field of real knowledge, and there taught by observation and experience, to base their opinions upon ascertained facts, and to seek in their own unsophisticated sensations, the rules of temperance, justice. toleration. and humanity. But led by error into the stony ground of religious faith, all the qualities of their noble nature are perverted to evil. Their eye no longer fixed on this world, nor their hearts on their fellow creatures, they are transformed into the enemies of true science, the scourgers of society, the persecutors of reason and of sane morality. It may be, as we have observed, that religion will borrow the

the fair robes of virtue, and speak in the tones of love caught from lovely hearts, but never did she herself originate, however she may sometimes pervert to her own purposes, that human sympathy with human weakness, that gentle patience with human error, that untiring perseverance in the cause of human improvement, which the study of human nature, and acquaintance with the reforming, enlightening power of human knowledge, impart to the reflecting observer of the world without and of the world within.

Let us not mistake causes! Let us not misconceive of effects! Let us not so wrong the heart of man, as when we see the turbaned follower of Mohammed, invoking Allah, while he spreads the carpet for the weary traveller, and shares with him his bread—let us not, I say, so wrong the human heart, as to believe, that but for the written law of his Koran he would shut his door against the houseless, the friendless, and the hungry; or that when he opens it, he obeys not a law nobler and purer than that cried by his priest from the minaret—even that which is entwined and incorporated with his being, and which teaches him to pity in others the wants which he feels within himself! The simple African, whose desires are bounded by his grove of cocoa nuts and bread fruits, and whose superstitions extend not beyond the charms and whimsical ceremonies of nurses and conjurors over the bodies of the sick, yields his mat, and shares his fruits with the fainting white man whom the love of science, or the madness of superstition, leads to his peaceful hut; and, unlearned in all of truth as of error, beyond what his simple experience has taught him, binds up the wounds of the suffering stranger, and lulls him to sleep with his pitying songs. Or, who that has visited the native sons of America's forest, where the vices of civilized and christian nations are yet unknown, but has eat of the venison prepared by the gentle squaw, where there was no priest to bless, or written law to teach; and farther seen the son of nature lay him down to his last sleep with the dignity of a mind which had followed virtue up to its knowledge, and knew as little to fear possibilities beyond the grave, as realities here.

And must we be told that unnerving fears and disgracing penalties are requisite to drive man into the path of virtue? Must he be made a coward ere he can be innocent? Must he be sold to folly ere he can be saved from crime? Little have such moralists studied the latent powers inherent in our nature—the beautiful faculties and emotions which need but to be awakened and exercised, for us to distinguish good from evil, even as we distinguish pleasure from pain. Little know they of the satisfaction imparted to the bosom by a course of gentle feeling and generous actions; little conceive they of the pain and disquiet consequent on feelings of uncharitableness and deeds of violence, who imagine temptations of heavenly rewards requisite to incline the well taught mind to the one, or threats of ugly fiends, and phantoms, and torments, first conceived and accurately realized in the earthly dungeons of Christian inquisitors, necessary to turn the human heart from the other.

Alas, my friends! we have tampered with imaginary demons through all the ages of human ignorance up to the present hour—we have quailed the human heart with fear —we have shaken reason from her throne with the agues of superstition—we have broken down the self-respecting spirit of man with nursery tales and priestly threats, and we *dare* to assert, that in proportion as we have prostrated our understanding and degraded our nature, we have exhibited virtue, wisdom, and happiness, in our words, our actions, and our lives!

Time it is, that we awake to a better knowledge of things —a more just appreciation of our own powers and capabilities, a more accurate observation of consequences and causes, and that we fit ourselves wisely to enjoy the life which is ours, and wisely to instruct the rising generation to avoid the errors which have led our minds astray, and to seek the truths which we have neglected.

Conceiving us, my friends, to have sufficiently discussed the tendency of those doctrines and assertions which were never made to stand an encounter with reason, we will now recal our attention to the consideration of the science which is to supply the unerring rule of human conduct.

Morals we defined to be *a rule of life drawn from the ascertained consequences of human actions.* You will observe that here, as in every other branch of knowledge, our own sensations, accurately observed, supply us with the facts of which the science is compounded.

Morals, thus considered, is a wide and spacious field: as spacious as human life and human action. There is a wrong and a right way of doing every thing; a wrong and a right way of feeling every thing; a wrong and a right way of saying every thing. We are therefore moral or immoral at every moment of our conscious existence.

What is required for the securing of our moral rather than our immoral state? Attention. Attention to the consequences of our actions; attention to the nature of our feelings; attention to the meaning, and the bearing, and the effects of our words. Look to these! Look around ye! Look within! Ye need no other rule; ye need no other law. Would ye ascertain what of your rules are just? Put them to this test. Examine where they run; what they hit, and what they miss. Trace them *through* all their consequences, *to* all their results. Believe not they are right *because they are your rules*, but test them by the actions they produce, and these actions again by the simple good or evil of their results.

Permit me here to recapitulate a few observations presented at our last meeting. We then remarked, that had we only senses, each impression would disappear with the object which excited it; in which case, no knowledge, or accumulation of facts, could exist for us. But, having memory, we can retain each impression by whichsoever of our senses received; having judgment, we compare and arrange these impressions; having imagination, we ingeniously combine impressions, however removed as to time, distant as to place, or slightly assimilated by affinity or resemblance; and, having moral feelings or emotions, we consider all occurrences with a reference to the good or evil they may induce to our race.

In that most important branch of knowledge which we are now considering, all these properties of our nature are called into action. Our sensations supply the facts which our faculties treasure up and arrange; and, aided by our emotions enable us to judge and to feel for others: out of which sympathy springs all the bright family of the virtues.

In considering the science of morals, it might seem, at the first glance, to divide itself into two distinct heads: as our conduct affects ourselves, and as it affects others. This distinction, however, is more apparent than real, since it is barely possible for us to consider any action, much less any course of actions, without a reference to their effects, either immediate or more remote, by example, on the sentient beings around us; which effects must ever again react upon ourselves, and influence, pleasurably or painfully, our state of being. Still are there some actions involving more peculiarly our own selfish interests; and upon which, in cases where no

counter interest of others is presented, prudence, or a just
calculation of consequences to ourselves, may be allowed
solely to decide.   Such are the actions incidental to the
gratification of the appetites appertaining to our nature.   The
rules by which to restrain these within just and healthy
propriety are peculiarly simple ; and, when carefully substantiated by observation, and habitually followed, supply us with
the virtues of temperance and sobriety. Were the habit
induced from infancy upwards, of closely observing all our
sensations, and distinguish the moment when healthy indulgence passes into unhealthy excess, there would not be
(except in cases of defective organization) one being in
existence afflicted with those unreasoned, self-tormenting
habits, which are now, in vulgar parlance, more especially
distinguished by the name of *vices*.

But let us here observe, that to secure for ourselves that
seemly propriety which constitutes the rule of temperance,
we must as little incline to the extreme of fanatical self-
denial as to that of indulgence. We must govern and not
crucify the appetites which, forming a part of our being, can
as little be stifled as palled, without injury to our physical,
moral, and mental health. It has been the requiring the
annihilation instead of the just government of the human
passions, which has nourished the belief, so slanderous to our
nature, that they were beyond the control of our reason.
Oh! let but reason be appealed to, and we shall acknowledge,
for we shall see and feel her power.

In the day that reason shall be consulted, we shall study
ourselves with a reference to the world about us, and that
world again with a reference to ourselves ; and, applying all
external things wisely to their uses, apply also all our organs,
physical and intellectual, wisely to theirs. Then may we
find that the error lies not in our nature, but in the false
usages, opinions, laws, habits, and customs, which have
originated in our ignorance and in the superstitions which
that ignorance has engendered.

In considering our conduct with relation to the world,
without us, we find the science under our immediate review
associated with every other ; extending its ramifications through
the whole field of knowledge, turning to profit every fact
drawn from the rich stores of nature, and calming and expanding the human heart in proportion as the human mind
becomes enlightened.

The sciences have ever been the surest guides to virtue, because, demanding calm observation, obtaining all their results by means of dispassionate investigation, they bring into action our noblest faculty, the judgment, and submit the imagination to its guidance; dispose us by the previous accurate observation of things to an equally accurate observation of men, and, confirming us in the habit of tracing effects to causes in the world without, prepare us to follow attentively the train of occurrences in the world within.

In seeking that principle of our nature which leads the heart of man to sympathise with that of his fellow; to extend the hand in succour, or to drop the tear in sympathy, philosophers have strangely disputed. But, without adverting to the various arguments and speculations which have more frequently tended to confuse the intellect than to develope the fact, we may remark, that the many who have agreed in referring all our noblest actions and most beautiful feelings to the single desire of attaining our own individual good, present at the least, an immutable basis of morals; since even self-love and self-interest, rightly understood, would always lead to justice, beneficence, gentleness, truth, candour, and indulgent toleration. And such doubtless is the truth. A simple but accurate calculation of selfish consequences, would lead invariably to the cultivation of every amiable feeling, and practice of every action beneficial to society. For, as we have previously inquired, how come we at a knowledge of virtue? By our sensations. What constitutes moral good? A course of actions producing beneficial results. What moral evil? A course of actions whose results are injurious. Now most true it is, as I trust the experience of each and all of us can testify, that never does the human breast throb with purer delight, than when man has been instrumental to the happiness of his fellow man. The pleasure derived from any selfish enjoyment, dies with the immediate sensation; but that shared with others, or that imparted to others, even with temporary loss or inconvenience to ourselves, will live in the memory to the latest period of existence, and thrill the bosom with pleasure each time it is recalled. Certain it is, therefore, that the pursuit of our own happiness would alone suffice to induce the cultivation of that tone of thinking and feeling, which tends to promote that happiness. But we have still something within us, better than any process of reasoning, which prompts us to spring forward to the relief of suffering; and which we have only to cultivate, in conjunction always with the cultivation of our judgment, (or we may sadly err) to become the active and enlightened friends of our race. When, having distinguished beneficial from injurious actions, in the consequences resulting to ourselves, and observed similar effects to result from similar actions to others, we distinguish an emotion within us, varying indeed in strength in each individual, which prompts to the conferring of benefits to our brother man, and even, occasionally, to the preferring of his advantage to our own. In this preference of others to self, or, to put it according to the views of the moralists before quoted, *in this seeking of our own pleasure through the pleasure of others*, consists the highest degree of active virtue.

Great is the difference between what I have here denominated *active virtue*, and what we may call *negative virtue*— albeit, in the present unfortunate state of society, we are often but too happy when we find the latter, and have not to encounter *active mischief*.

By the negatively virtuous, I understand those who regulating judiciously their passions and appetites with a view to their own healthy existence, and forbearing from all words and actions which might disturb their tranquillity by attracting the hostility of others, yet are deficient in that generous sensibility to the feelings of others, which we have distinguished as the source of active virtue; and which dictates the ready sacrifice of selfish enjoyment, whenever such sacrifice will purchase a greater enjoyment to a fellow creature, or stimulates to voluntary exertions in favour of suffering, or in the cause of human improvement.

This cultivated sensibility, variously called by philosophers, the moral principle, emotion, faculty, or sympathy, and in the figurative language of Friends, *the light within, the spirit of truth*, or *God within the breast*, may, I think, be distinguished by every self observer, as existing apart from the purely intellectual powers, though always demanding their guidance. When not under the guidance of our noblest intellectual faculty, the judgment, it may place ourselves, and involve others, in the worst difficulties; when under the direction of a well-balanced and discriminating intellect, it leads to every good, and constitutes a man of virtue.

Now the object of all education should be the active development and cultivation of the generous emotion we are now

now considering, and which is but too often allowed to remain dormant in the bosom, until it is absolutely choked and annihilated by vicious examples and equally vicious lessons. First comes false parental indulgence, teaching the young creature to seek its little pleasures at expense of the comfort and convenience of others, by passionate cries and obstinate peevishness; to seek them, too, without a reference to its companions and playmates, if not often at their cost. Next comes erroneous instruction, to frighten the opening mind from innocent truth, to unfit it for observation of the interesting realities around it, and to poison the sweet pleasures of its age, by tales of unseen things and revengeful beings—these also armed, like their earthly governors, with whips and scourges. Then comes worldly policy, with selfishness, censoriousness, and avarice, in her train, to perfect an education whose motive principle is FEAR, and whose fruits are hard-heartedness and hypocrisy !

What, my friends, and do we charge to our organization what springs from our ignorance of its powers. Do we libel the nature of man, while we are violating instead of guiding its instincts, perverting its faculties, and feeding it with error instead of truth ? That which we sow, must we reap. The infant mind is a virgin soil. While we plant tares, shall we gather tares. While, in pursuit of things unseen and causes unknown, we waste our surplus time and our surplus industry, and while we neglect or pervert the powers of the human mind, must idleness and error, with their offspring violence and profligacy, distract and afflict all the nations of the earth.

But let us adopt measures for wisely developing and directing the faculties which distinguish our nature. Let us seek out patient and enlightened guides, instead of angry and dogmatical teachers, who will encourage the lively observation of childhood, foster its better feelings, remove from its eye, and its ear, and its imagination, all that can awaken unkindly emotions, impart painful sensations, provoke angry passions, suggest false ideas, and judiciously surround it with such impressions as shall turn all its faculties to good.

To prepare such a system of education for the young, we must begin with ourselves. We must purge our own hearts of evil, and our own minds of error, ere we can distinguish those just rules of conduct, which, as parents, as citizens, as

G

human beings, it is our common duty and common interest to discover for the rising generation.

In this imperfect discourse, I have but sketched the outline and laid down the first principles of that beautiful science of which all others should be but the handmaidens, to which the whole field of knowledge should lend its accumulated facts, and a succession of enlightened generations supply their accumulated experience.

My object here, as in all our previous investigations, has been to elucidate the simple nature of the science. To show that its truths are discoverable by observation, and supplied by our sensations; that all lessons which depart from the premises of our sensations, are but idle declamation; that the seeds of all excellence are within ourselves—that is, in the senses and the faculties which enlighten and adorn our nature; that the source of all vice is ignorance, and that of virtue, knowledge; that the field of human inquiry is the world we inhabit; the field of human duty that of human action; the only rational pursuit of human beings that of human happiness; that happiness, to be experienced by *any*, must be shared by *all*; that the real interests of the the whole human family are one, even as their nature is in itself the same; that comprising in our being physical, moral, and intellectual organs, it is only in and by the judicious exercise of all these organs that we can secure to ourselves the health of any; that unless our limbs and muscles be exercised, our whole frame must be weak or diseased; unless our intellectual faculties be fairly developed and exercised, we cannot regulate wisely our passions or our actions, and unless all our sensibilities be wisely cultivated and regulated, we can never experience that highest enjoyment proceeding from the practice of active virtue, which we have seen to flow from a ready sympathy in the wants and feelings of others.

I shall now close our investigations by the remark, that MORALS, OR THE SCIENCE OF HUMAN LIFE, may for better convenience, and with a view to the presenting in order all the relations it involves, be divided into several heads.

These divisions may, in some cases, be rather supplied by existing errors than by inherent truths. It being indispensable, however, in the actual state of society, to develope all truth with a reference to existing error, I purpose, as leisure and my more regular engagements may permit to consider the conduct of human beings under the three great relations in which we may observe them to stand.

First. *Their relation to each other, and to the mass.* This will embrace a review of all our duties, public and private. It will lead us also to inspect the principles of national government, law, and social economy.

Secondly. *The mutual relation of the two sexes ;* in which we shall be called upon to examine the principles that should direct the social intercourse of men and women.

Thirdly. *The relation of the old to the young ; of the existing to the rising generation, viewing us in the character of human beings, free born, and self-governing.* Also, *the relation of parents to children ;* examining *the duties and responsibilities of the being who gives life to the being who receives it.* This will lead to the discussion of the important subject of education, and elicit suggestions respecting a plan of national education. Until some measures shall be adopted for the judicious and equal instruction and protection of every son and daughter born to the Republic, ye cannot be (as I conceive) Republicans. Until exclusive colleges, paltry common schools, ignorant Sunday schools, and sectarian churches, be replaced by state institutions, founded by a general tax, and supported by the same, (so long as it shall be necessary—that is, till the well regulated industry of the children shall meet the expenses of their education;) and until, in these national institutions, the child of your Governor shall be raised with the child of your farmer, and the child of your President with that of your mechanic, ye cannot be (as I conceive) Republicans. And farther, until ye have good libraries and good teachers of elementary science in all your towns, for the mental improvement of the existing generation, and popular halls of assembly, where all adults may meet for the study and discussion of their social and national interests, as fellow creatures, and fellow citizens ye cannot be (as I conceive) Republicans.

To attempt the satisfactory development of the important subjects to which I have here alluded, it would be necessary for us to meet under other circumstances than those at present existing. On my part would be necessary, the conviction that I was devoting my time and labour, not to satisfy the unmotived and momentary curiosity of a public indifferent to its noblest interests, but that I was employed with and for a public anxious to substitute knowledge for error, and virtue for superstition.

To inspire that conviction in me, would be necessary on your part some active measures, for which the desire or the courage, or both, may be at present wanting.

For the time being, I shall confine my exertions to the simple elucidation of the first principles of the science; to the sketching of that great outline within which all truth must be sought, and where, I trust, you may yet be induced to seek it. To complete the general survey in which we are considerably advanced, I shall endeavour, at our next meeting, to elicit the nature of opinions, and the manner of their formation; with a view to the correction of that spirit of proselytism, which now transforms us all into angry combatants, for each whimsey of our brain, and of that spirit of censoriousness, which is now ever interfering with the mental liberty and moral peace of society, and rendering the life of man one continued scene of strife and of hypocrisy.

LECTURE VI.

Formation of Opinions.

THE subject to which I shall call your attention this evening *the formation of opinions,* is one of the utmost practical importance; one which thoroughly understood, would remove uncharitableness from the heart of man, and shed the placid rays of peace and truth upon the path of life.

For eighteen centuries and upwards, the nations styled civilized, have waged a war of opinion, dying the altars of their faith with each other's blood, or, in their gentlest mood, in this freest country, and in this (compared with all the past) enlightened age, judging in severity, sentencing in bitterness, and persecuting, by angry word and oppressive deed, each his fellow creature. For eighteen centuries and upwards, sword and fire, chains, dungeons, tortures, threats and curses, or (scarcely less severe) public scorn and private censure, the

falling back of friends and setting on of foes, the whisperings
of detraction, the surmises of folly, the misapprehensions and
misrepresentations of ignorance, have conspired to wreak vengeance upon the mind and body of man, constraining the
sacrifice, impossible to force, of honest opinion, and commanding the assent to truth or error, as it may be, of that noblest
property of our being—even our free-born intellect. For
eighteen centuries and upwards, the human family, estranged
from each other, albeit pinned within the fold of one faith,
have striven in deadly feud like the fierce beasts in the Roman
arena, or like the iron knights of crusading chivalry within the
fatal lists of cruel ordeal, where *might* alone did constitute *the
right*, and the fall of the weak substantiated the justice of the
strong.

Such, to look no farther than the date of the modern era,
hath been the fate of the nations. The weak have been trampled on, the bold in spirit have been crushed, the conscientious
have been martyrized, the honest have been silenced, the
stigmatized for liberty, mercy, and charity, have been hunted
through the earth by the bloodhounds of superstition, until the
heart of philanthropy hath drooped even to despair, and the
hope of philosophy in a better and fairer future hath given
way. Such droopings and faintings must have been experienced by every generous mind, when, in contemplating the
face of society, it loses sight of the generating cause of the
evil which it mourns; and, again, when it ceases to compare
the present with the past, and so marks not the slow and
silent progress of our race from the foul night of barbarous
ignorance towards the fulness of civilizing knowledge. But
let us clearly distinguish the cause, and we may hasten the
application of the remedy; let us trace the advance already
made and now making, and we may calculate with cheerful
confidence on our future destinies.

Persecution for opinion is the master vice of society. It
was this raised the gloomy walls and dug the foul caverns of
the Inquisition. It was this invented the rack, and the
wheel, and the faggot, and the death-pang, and the dungeon,
where the Moor, and the Jew, and the philosopher, and the
suspected heretic expired, unpitied, unremembered, before
thanksgiving, heaven-invoking bigotry. It was this but-
chered the simple Waldenses, in the valleys of their mountains. It was this mowed down the Huguenots in the palace of
the Gallic king. It was this dyed the rivers of either Indies

with the blood of their peaceful children. It was this reared
the horrid pile round the gentle Servetus, by the hand of
presbyterian Calvin. It was this drave from their native isle
the forefathers of this nation ; and it has been, and yet is, the
same scourger of human peace, and bridler of human liberty,
PERSECUTION FOR OPINION, which ruffles the whole surface
of this fair republic, nurtures the harsh spirit and pride of
sectarianism, hardens the heart of man towards his brother,
sours the disposition of woman, and drops gall and aloes into
the cup of human life. Surely, then, are we called, in our
character of reasoning beings, to pierce to the source of this
poisonous fountain of woe ! Surely then, are *ye* doubly called,
in your character of a self-governing people, to arrest the
flow of its deadly waters, and to seek the ways and the means
for refreshing the land with the soft dews of love !

In developing the cause of the vice to which we have reference, we must first examine what *an opinion is ;* establish the
meaning of the word, and the nature of the intellectual state
it is employed to designate.

The chief aim of my previous efforts in this place, has been
directed to the attaining a just apprehension of the nature of
knowledge. The result of those elementary inquiries, I conceive to be present to your minds. Now, as we established
knowledge to be an accumulation of facts, so are all just
opinions, intellectual conclusions drawn from those facts. It
follows, therefore, that exactly in proportion to the extent and
accuracy of our knowledge, must be the justice of our opinions ;
and *vice versa,* that in equal proportion to our remissness in
collecting, and carelessness in weighing, examining, comparing, and arranging facts, must be the error of our opinions.
Here then we see ignorance, or the absence of facts from the
mind, to be the primary cause of all error.

I must now call your attention to a very curious inconsistency in human feeling. Men are seldom disposed to be
angry with each other on account of the more or less knowledge they may possess, while they are incessantly angry
with the varying opinions, which are as necessary conse-
quents upon this varying knowledge, as we conceive light
or darkness to be upon the rising or setting of the sun.
That one should know more than another appears simple
and pardonable; but, that one knowing more, should think
differently from others, is stamped for a mortal offence, without hope of pardon or benefit of clergy. The absurdity of

applying the torture to the physiological anatomist, who should simply discover such and such to be the structure of our corporeal machine, would appear too gross for the human imagination, and yet the no less gross absurdity of resenting the conclusions generated by his discoveries appear to it quite facile of admission. The facts themselves, if deprived of all their consequences and so of all their utility, would be tolerated, but let them generate, as they must inevitably generate, their own conclusions in the mind, and the unfortunate explorer of science is hunted down by the dogs of persecution. When the observations of Lawrence associated the phenomena of life, thought, and motion, inseparably with the living, thinking, and moving organs of our frame, instantly awoke the cry of Infidel! Sceptic! Materialist! Atheist! As if with these unmeaning words, which those who employ usually understand no more than did Aristotle the rules of his own logic or the causes of the influent and refluent tides—as if, I say, by these unmeaning words, coupled with insulting vituperations, we could overthrow nature herself, annihilate the facts, in her own bosom, or stifle the conclusions which the inspection of those facts necessitate in the perceiving mind. When the inquiring Galileo observed that the phenomena of the celestial bodies substantiated the motion of the planets in lieu of that of the sun, why was he dragged before the tribunal of death? Because the facts he proclaimed started in the mind of bigotry itself the inevitable conclusion, that if he was right, the astronomy of the Jews was wrong? and that, " Sun, stand thou still," argued an error in the pen that wrote, or in the voice that spake. And we may farther ask, why in in these or our own times, why at the present hour, if a bold inquirer unclasp the book of knowledge, and simply proclaim its simple truths, the trump of alarm sounds throughout the land, and threats, outrage, and abuse, are heaped even on the head of a woman? Why, but because the facts which she, strong in her love to man, has the courage to reveal, generate in the minds of her very opponents conclusions inimical to existing systems and existing expenditures, and proclaim aloud to the teacher as well as the scholar, the clergy as well as the people, the designing as well as the ignorant, that if knowledge be true, superstition is false, and that if inquiry be prosecuted, church and hierarchy must fall.

But in discovering the propelling motives of this inconsistency, the inconsistency remains the same. Unless we can annihilate facts themselves how can we annihilate the conclusions, that is, the opinions, which those facts suggest? When we employ our eyes, and when we see, or when we stretch forth our hand, and when we feel, must we not acknowledge the presence of the objects before us and can we resist the intellectual assent which follows upon their perception?

Whenever, then we hear an opinion startling from its novelty, what, in modesty, should we say? "Perhaps the individual is possessed of facts which have not fallen under our observation, or attracted our attention. Let us inquire of him what they are, and then examine the facts for ourselves." And what upon such a course of proceeding, would be the result? One of three consequences. Either we should find the opinion corroborated by facts, in which case it would be true, and compel our own minds to its admission; or it would appear insufficiently substantiated by facts, in which case we should leave it for doubtful; or we should find it in contradiction with facts, in which case we should discard it for spurious.

But now, in any or all of these cases, what rational ground can we find for anger against the individual who may think otherwise than we think? He is right, he is credulous, he is wrong. What then? If he be right, it is for us to agree with him; if credulous, we are not obliged to be the same; if wrong, he is mistaken—and, in so far as this may be a source of evil, the loss must be to him. For that he thinks as he thinks, and as we think not. it is convincing that some evidence is present to his mind which is not present to ours; and, albeit upon examination we should pronounce that evidence false, so long as it exist in his mind for true, must he think as he thinks. And shall we stigmatize his honest opinion for a crime? By treating him as a felon we may indeed force him into hypocrisy, but cannot convince his understanding. To do the latter, we must present some other and better evidence to his mind—some incontrovertible facts, out of which a more correct opinion may arise. Opinions are not to be learned by rote, like the letters of an alphabet, or the words of a dictionary. They are conclusions *to be formed*, and formed by each individual in the sacred and free citadel of the mind, and there enshrined beyond the arm of law to reach, or force to hake; ay! and beyond the right of impertinent curiosity to

violate, or presumptuous arrogance to threaten. Alas, for
consistency! Alas, for reason and happiness! Hath man
fought and bled for political liberty, and will he violate the
liberty of the mind? When he has broken the bars and bolts
of corporeal dungeons, will he essay to clip and stretch the
thoughts of his fellow beings to the measure of his own?
Must all see just as far and no farther than we see? If this be
civil liberty, better the wild freedom of the wild hunter! Nay,
better the honest slavery of oriental despotism, where at least
the wretch is warned to choose between unmuttering obedience and the bowstring!

I speak warmly, my friends, for truly my heart is moved in
the cause of that holy principle, whose name is on every lip,
on every badge, on every coin of the land, but whose vital
spirit is profaned in our high places and our private ways,
in house and chamber, in book and converse, in hall and
church, and oh, more than all profaned in the secret heart of
man!

Could we but obliterate all the false lessons imbibed
during a pernicious education—could we but arrive at the
perception of those primitive truths, which it is now the
object, because the interest, of all our teachers to stifle—
could we but engage in the investigation of the operations of
our own intellect—could we understand the nature of an
opinion, and the manner of its formation, never could we
be guilty of persecution for the involuntary conclusions of the
mind.

And yet simple ignorance, as we have seen, is not the only
cause of the irrational anger elicited by the varying opinions
of men. Ignorance, unbacked and unspurred, would not
suffice to breed such tempests in the human bosom as we see
engendered against so gentle, so unintentional an offence
as a difference in opinion. The untutored Indian lifts not
his tomahawk against his brother because he thinks not
with him respecting the attributes of their Great Spirit,
or the nature of their expected hunting ground in the
shadowy world of the dead. No! ignorance of the powers
of the human mind will not alone explain the existence
of the deadly evil, albeit knowledge of those powers would
suffice to dispel it.

The unhappy circumstances which combined to organize
a system of instruction in speculations of faith instead of
objects of knowledge, and to set apart a body of men for

the express purpose of expounding inexplicable creeds, and chaining the intellects of their hearers down to written points of doctrine, unintelligible mysteries and verbal quibbles, first originated the monsterous absurdity and lamentable evil to which we have reference. Were it not absolutely made the occupation of a part of the community to set the rest by the ears, never could human beings have disputed for ages, and shed rivers of blood, for establishing and protecting the dogma of a trinity in unity, predestination to salvation or damnation, the divine presence or absence in a wafer of bread or the liquor in a wine cup, the saving efficacy of the sign of the cross, or the sprinkling of cold water on the forehead of an infant. Never could they have wasted their lives and their treasure in squabbles about hair-drawn distinctions in fantastic ideas and unimportant possibilities, had not the custom been originated of employing *teachers of opinions,* instead of *teachers of facts.*

That we have here suggested the main cause of the irrational disputes which up to this hour have corroded the peace of society, is abundantly substantiated by observation, and corroborated by history.

In whatever country there has existed a priesthood, *there* opinionative persecution has prevailed, and there, and there only, has the popular superstition been profaned by blood, expiatory atonements, and never slumbering opinionative dissensions.

Let us look back to Egypt, to India, to Judea, to Carthage, to Greece, to Rome—in all, tradition presents us with a priesthood, and exactly in proportion to the power of that priesthood, with less or more of religious butcheries or opinionative persecutions. We find the same, in a ratio exactly proportionate to the power of the priesthood, among all Christian nations; while among savages, however ignorant, or even in their ignorance revengeful, but whom we find without religious teachers, the popular superstition is ever harmless. Witness the gentle South Sea Islander, or the fierce Indian of this Northern hemisphere, whose faith, simple in itself, and entirely devoid of ceremonial, has never once been found a cause of war, or even of dissension; while in Mexico, when first explored by the Spaniards, the blood of victims streamed from altars sanctified by officiating ministers, whose butcheries only ceased, to give place to those of their Christian conquerors.

And among ourselves, my friends, what feeds the angry spirit which is abroad? Even that which first originated it among men: the exalting the dreams of our ignorance into a science; the setting apart times and places for its especial study, and the ordaining a body of men to propound its mysteries, and to protect them from the power of that principle which is inherent alike in matter and in mind—improvement. Let us leave Religion to herself, and she will work no evil. Let us leave her single and alone, without the adjunct of priest or temple, to measure weapons with knowledge. If true, she will stand; if false, she will fall. Let us store the human mind with the truths of science; and, what ever opinions these may confirm or may generate, neither time nor changes, power, wealth, violence nor corruption, the vicissitudes of fortune, nor the fall of empires, can overthrow.

I have already attempted to show that an opinion, properly so called, is a conclusion of the mind, spontaneously elicited upon the admission of facts, or upon the admission of evidence which it receives for fact. On the accuracy of the evidence received must then depend the accuracy of the opinion elicited therefrom. Wheresoever we are in possession of facts, well examined, well substantiated, arranged, and compared, are our opinions just; whenever we receive for fact what is not fact, or whenever we are careless in our examination of facts, must our opinions be erroneous.

But how are we to designate those states of the mind, when in the absence of all facts, and all evidence, it is tortured to receive ideas? Ideas they cannot be called, for these are suggestions derived from sensations. Opinions they cannot be called, for these are conclusions spontaneously elicited by evidence. The teacher who begins by essaying to instil opinions, attempts an impossibility. He may engraft prejudices, suggest fantasies, distort the feelings, put the mind in confusion, but he cannot *teach opinions.*

Oh, when will men perceive what it is possible to impart, and desirable to acquire? When will they look to KNOWLEDGE as the subject matter of instruction, and dropping its pleasant truths in the fertile soil of the mind, leave OPINIONS to spring up themselves, as the plant from the seed!

But, look ye, my friends! what are ye or your agents now labouring to teach, not in your own land only, but in the remotest regions of the globe? Opinions. About what are ye disputing yourselves, and assaying to make all tribes and nations dispute? Opinions. For what pour ye forth your treasures? For what endow seminaries and churches? For what plant spies and eves-droppers in every establishment, charitable, philosophical, or humane, founded in your cities? For what are the gentle and the wise driven from superintendence in your jails, your bridewells, your houses of refuge, your asylums, your schools? For what all this but for opinions.

But ye will say, "It is not *we*, it is not we, the people—it is the Clergy, it is the American Jesuit, it is more than all, the Presbyterian." With permission, my friends, but it *is* you—it *is* the people. Why give ye the rein to ambition? Why gold to rapacity? Why stay ye not the strife of tongues, the battle for supremacy, the fever of proselytism, the *persecution for opinions?* True, the teacher hath led the way. True, the false shepherd hath beguiled you. But when ye see the error of the path, will ye not tread back your steps? Will ye madly drive on when your eyes are open to the pit and your ears warned of destruction?

But say that ye be willing to foster strife within your own borders—under what plea, by what right, by what authority, scatter ye its seeds in lands not yours, among people neither acknowledging your supremacy, nor subject to your laws? I will not follow your missions across Atlantic and Pacific, athwart other zones, and one half of the world's meridians, to the banks of Senegal and Ganges; I will not track your emissaries to the Isles of the Southern Sea, and note the peace of their simple children profaned by dogmas, and their innocence by intoxicating liquors. I will not look beyond the borders of this Union, nor will I invoke other testimony than that supplied by the native sons of the land. I will summon my witnesses and your accusers from the deep forests of the Mobile, the sweet springs of the pleasant Yazoo, and the shores of your own fresh water seas. I will call upon the Creek and the Choctaw, the Cherokee and the Seneka, to denounce the folly and mischief of your emissaries, and the madness of your zeal. Or it shall suffice, to array against ye the words of the venerable chief, the expostulations of the father of his people, who in this city, so lately, in the ears of its citizens, denounced the intriguing spirit, the feud-breeding faith, the *honey-lipped* but *bitter-hearted* hypocrisy (I employ his own epithets) of your proselytizing missionaries.

Oh, when ye afflict strange people and other races with the curse which rests upon yourselves—when, despite their expostulations, and presuming upon your power, ye add the feuds of opinions to the hatred of tribes, and send forth retailers of spirituous and spiritual poison to the dusky children of nature—Oh, think well of the liberty ye outrage, the rights of nations that ye violate, the awful responsibility that ye assume!

Could ye send to your red brethren peaceful instructors in the useful arts of life, enlightened observers of nature, respecters of human feeling, who, without questioning their reverence for the benign spirit whose presence they acknowledge in the heart, would travel with them in peace the paths of life, and exchange with them all the offices of human love; could ye send to the feeble remnant of that race, whose decay has been the price of your greatness, such instructors as these, ye might cancel the remembrance of injury, and preserve in your bosom a happy relic of a people, interesting from your own history, their character, and their wrongs. But, until such ye can send, (and, alas, such how rare!) oh, my friends, *send not at all.*

Another remark here suggests itself; that as in the existing state of human knowledge, an uncommon opinion is always unpopular, so does it afford strong evidence of the honesty of the individual who expresses it.

If the observations now presented, in conjunction with our previous investigations should have satisfied you of the involuntary birth of opinions in the mind, the impossibility of changing opinions but by supplying other and stronger evidence than that which generated the existing opinions, and the impossibility of teaching opinions as we teach words to a parrot, you will perceive the absurdity, no less than the injustice, of all displeasure on account of the intellectual conclusions generated in our fellow-creatures, and the equal absurdity of devoting your time and money to the acquisition and propagation of opinions, instead of the acquisition and propagation of facts. You will admit also, I think, that an honest opinion, even when erroneous, merits always the respect of a good mind, and that an uncommon opinion merits always the investigation of an inquiring mind.

These considerations will appear to you of the highest moral importance should you examine, as it is your duty to examine, the harsh feelings and ungentle dealings springing daily and hourly out of intolerance and censoriousness. Lamentably has the list of the human virtues been curtailed by our inobservancy of the occurrences passing around us, our inattention to the effects of our words and actions on the happiness of our fellow beings, our ignorance of the powers of our own minds, and our indifference to the gentle dictates of human sympathy. While our thoughts have been wandering in the limbo of theological speculations, our eyes have been prying with impious curiosity into those of our neighbour, our lips have been outraging the liberty of man, by challenging his right to the utterance of his opinions, and so perverted has been our reason, so corrupted our hearts, that while thus engaged in murdering our own peace, and the peace of others, we have called our censoriousness by the name of virtue, and sanctified our orthodox intolerance by the name of religion. Alas! when shall we see that our business is with our *own* doings, our *own* feelings, our *own* opinions; and that with a view to the formation of the one, and the regulation of the other, we must patiently observe all things, and gently hear all things, even that we may be fitted in all things to choose that which is best!

One observation, not without its practical importance, yet occurs to me on the subject of opinions. While our first duty is correctly to form our own, it is doubtless our farther duty to assist in the formation of those of others. How this may alone be done we have seen; namely, by presenting facts to the mind; in other words, by organizing a plan of uniform and universal instruction in all the branches of positive knowledge, by which means all men, being gradually put in possession of the same correct evidence, may be gradually led to the formation of just and coinciding opinions.

It needs not to ask if such a consummation be desirable. It needs not to ask if disputing and quarrelling be advantageous or agreeable. It needs not to ask if the employment of twenty millions per annum in feeding sectarian jealousies, bitter feelings, persecuting creeds, and contradictory conclusions, be injudicious or profitable. I care not what opinions or what fantasies we profess. I care not under what standard we have ranged ourselves—I care not how ignorant or how positive we may be in our errors, still am I persuaded that *all*, however differing as to the point of union, are agreed that union would be desirable. All? Said I that *all* are agreed? Yes, all; save those who live by existing divisions and confusion.

But it will be asserted, in the present confused state of the human intellect, that, however desirable, what we have suggested is impossible. We shall be told that men can never agree in opinion. They certainly never can, until they understand *what an opinion is, and what knowledge is;* then will they perceive how, when we shall be all informed in the knowledge of things, and shall consent to restrict our inquiries within the range of our observation, we must all agree in the other.

I know we shall be asked tauntingly, whether we expect all men to become philosophers. Certainly not all those now living, and *most* certainly few of those who put the question. Generations may pass away, ere, even in this comparatively free country, all men attain to their birth-right, equal privileges of instruction. I incline not to gigantic hopes respecting our contemporaries. Much they certainly may do—much more I wish them to do. And though it be ill-planting the best seed in the summer and autumn of life, and though the spring time be past in our own minds, could we but learn sufficient to remove some weeds, and but to lop away that one poisonous wide-spreading tree of evil, *persecution for opinion,* the paths of life, even in our day, might be made smooth, and the children of men travel through them in peace.

Nor should we omit to notice one fact, sufficient if observed, even in the absence of all other knowledge, to turn men from the idle warfare in which they are engaged. Let us look to the consequences of persecution. Did it ever convince? did it ever convert? Violence indeed may overthrow empires, may slaughter nations, may assassinate individuals, may harrass the mind, crucify the feelings, but it cannot controvert opinions. Persecution will suffice even to establish error, and hath ever proved omnipotent in advancing truth. They who have recourse to it are blind to all facts, blind to the noblest principle of our nature, to the strongest instinct in all sentient existence. Where doth violence not provoke resistance from the lowest animal up to man? Wound the bear, and he will turn on the hunters; press on the noble stag, and he will give battle to his murderers; nay! injure the gentle and faithful dog, and we find the spirit of the lion.

And is it man—man, strong in every noble energy, powerful in every faculty, rich in all the resources, and sublime in all the dignity of intelligence—is it man whom we would frighten into tame surrender of his loftiest powers? whom we would cudgel out of his own free thoughts, and crush under the chariot-wheels of intolerance? Let us look into past history—let us mark on the human mind, through all ages, in all nations, the effects of persecution. When the justice of Aristides turned admiration to envy, what restored him to the love of his countrymen? Persecution. When the lessons of Socrates fell powerless on the giddy ears of the Athenians, what graved his name and his precepts on their hearts? His death by persecution. What revenged all the patriots of Rome of a misguided multitude? Persecution. And what rooted Christianity in the hostile soil of heathenism? Persecution. What fostered the heresy of Luther? Persecution. What built up the church of Calvin? Persecution. What hath given a substance and a name to all the distinctions, real or imagined, of each religious reformer? Persecution. What hath preserved the Jew pure and entire in his faith, in his blood, in ceremony and feature, through ages of time, and while lost and scattered amidst nations opposed in every custom, law, feeling and creed? Why hath he stood a noble monument of patient endurance, conscientious pertinacity, scrupulous fidelity, long-suffering and uncomplaining, yet unyielding resistance? Why, like a column in the desert, wearing its capital, and tracery, and all the form and ornament stamped by the genius of forgotten artists and forgotten nations, stands he to this hour a wondrous relic of empire departed and grandeur overthrown? Why, but because of persecution?

Or, say again, what hath provoked vengeance on the head of kings? What hurried English Charles to the scaffold? What threw down the royalty and nobility of France from their antique thrones, and long-established supremacy? Or, yet once more, what turned the people from the prostituted name of liberty and the insignia of a republic drooping with gore, to reconcile them again to detested sceptres and the name and style of king? And, oh say, people of America! descendants of English puritans, French huguenots, Irish catholics, condemned regicides, outlawed patriots, and sanctified martyrs! what, driving your fathers from European realms, hath built up the noble frame of this republic? Oh say, torturers of the human mind! what hath done this save persecution?

And will ignorance never cease from troubling, and error

never be at rest? Will persecution take her stand even at the fane of freedom, denouncing alike socinian, universalist, Jew, sceptic, and philosopher, yea! denouncing every profession, employment, discovery and recreation which squares not with the rule of orthodoxy, or diverts dollars from its treasury?

I point here to no particular sect; I point here to no individuals: I point to the spirit of persecution arising out of written creeds, and authorizing ambition to make religion its stalking horse, and to say to every man within or without the pale of the declaration of faith, "*so far shalt thou go, and no farther.*"

I am said to make war upon the clergy, and to hold them up to the hatred and derision of the people: it is not so. I have denounced the system, not the men. I have denounced the system which splits this nation into parties, which encourages and authorizes individuals, under the plea of serving God and teaching faith, to injure what I believe the interests of man, and darken what every mind blessed with intelligence *knows* to be the light of truth. I have not denounced the clergy as men. I have denounced them as an organized body. As a body, set apart from the people, with other interests, other duties, other feelings. I have not denounced them as men—so help me that spirit of charity which I trust by my lip or my pen hath never been profaned! but I *have* denounced. and (so help me the spirit of truth which arms me to fight this battle in its cause!) so *will* I denounce them, as the organs and ostensible representatives of a pernicious system, which is driving the moral character, and shaking the political frame of this nation, to its dissolution.

But I will say no more. So far from essaying to stigmatize the mass of any clergy, I have held in private esteem and respect individuals among all. The catholic, the episcopal, the baptist, the methodist, the unitarian, the universalist, the most rigid as the most benign expounders of the christian law, may doubtless show among them men who wear their religion less on the lip than in the heart, and who, more citizen than sectarian, present to their fellows a creed made up of gentleness and love. But such as these could echo if I mistake not the denunciations I pronounce. Yea! such as these, if I mistake not, writhe under the fanacticism they are constrained to tolerate in their brethren, and both lament the error of the system with which they are associated, and blush for the

H

OPIOIONS.

arrogance of those martinets in orthodoxy, whose noise drowns all gentler voices, and whose assumption of authority, awes the timid and the ignorant into submission.

Say I too much of the spirit that is abroad? Denounce I too warmly a system, which in a land professing liberty, is the more dangerous because the less suspected? There is other persecution than that by fire and faggot; other weapons than the bayonet and the sword; other restraints than those of law and arrest; other ways to coerce contributions than by tithes and taxation: yea! and those other, and those worse, because less alarming while equally effectual and vexatious— those other, and those worse, are here. In this land, cunning does the work of violence. Persecution wears her shafts close hid: they are not winged in the broad sun-shine for every eye to see and every spirit to resent: silently, and from the covert, are they sped; unseen the aim, and unheeded the mischief. There is a secret influence at work, which all feel and none distinguish. It infects all society, taints every institution in the land, poisoning alike human instruction, human laws, and human recreation. In your schools—it diseases the infant mind with superstitious terrors, and with reason-confounding, heart-distorting creeds. In your colleges —it stifles the breath of your teachers of science, and constrains the entanglement of their simple facts with the dreams of theology. In your books and periodicals—but it matters not to speak of the press. In your courts of law—it tempts to perjury, sitting in judgment on the religious creed of witnesses, and reflecting even on that of the prisoner. In your legislatures—it dictates unconstitutional ordinances, and unconstitutional disposals of money and of lands. Nay! at this moment, it is outraging the ear of your national congress, with presbyterian Sabbath law petitions.* In your amusements—alas! there its influence hath been mortal! Your amusements, which under wise direction and judicious encouragement, should elevate the mind and humanize the heart— your amusements, I say, it has degraded, it has perverted, and so led the mind astray from pleasure to vice, from healthy recreation to mind-debasing, life destroying licentiousness.

* This discourse was first delivered in the Second Universalist Church, New-York, (by request of its pastor and the majority of the trustees,) during the season of the presentation of those petitions at Washington. which produced the celebrated report of the committee of the senate, already familiar to every American citizen.

Have I charged orthodoxy with too much? Look to your stage! see what it is; then look back to ancient Greece, and judge what it might be. Listen on every hand to the denunciations of fanaticism against plearures the most innocent, recreations the most necessary to bodily health, and conducive to social fellowship and mental improvement. See it make of the people's day of leisure, a day of penance! Thus, in the absence of innocent diversion, or improving study, driving men to intoxication, women to scandal, or to silly, sentimental, reason-confounding novels, half filled with romance and half with superstition, and by dint of fatiguing the mind with irrational doctrines, and tedious exhortations, disgusting youth with all instruction, and turning it loose upon a corrupt world with no light for its reason, no rein for its passions, no prop for its integrity.

We hear of Sabbath breakers. And who are they that break the Sabbath of the mind? Even such as, it would seem, taxed with Sabbath breaking the poor man's friend and rich man's reprover, Jesus; who, instead of frequenting temples made with hands, where the Scribes and Pharisees expounded their written laws, and acted the outer ceremonies of their superstition, sought the world of nature and the fields of human industry, and, as he gathered the ears of corn on the day sanctified to superstition, sentenced by practice as well as precept, those observances which, at this day, in a country styled Christian, cost to the nation twenty millions per annum. "Many things," said the mild reformer, whose mildness saved him not from martyrdom—"many things have I to say to ye, but ye cannot bear them now." And alas, could his followers bear them yet? Are they not still led as were the Jews of old by Scribes and Pharisees, who make broad their phylacteries, devour widow's houses, and for a pretence, make long prayers? Are they not still sitting in judgment on their neighbour; questioning his faith, instead of looking to their own doings; and, content with idle observances of days and seasons, neglecting all that could improve their own hearts and add to the happiness of their fellow creatures?

What think ye my friends? If Jesus, or his likeness, should now visit the earth, what church of the many which now go by his name would he enter? Or, if tempted by curiosity, he should incline to look into all, which do you think would not shut the door in his face? "He despises the law," would sound from one; "He breaks the Sabbath," would echo from another;."He makes no prayers and professes no creed," would mutter a third; "He would exalt the low, bring down the mighty, and revolutionize society," would cry a fourth; "He keeps company with publicans and sinners," from a fifth; "He is no better than an infidel," would shout the whole, since he lets pass the Sadducees without reproach who profess no knowledge out of this world and this life, and denounces the Pharisees who holds the keys of heaven and hell, and know all that is passing in both regions.

It seems to me, my friends, that as one who loved peace, taught industry, equality, union, and love, one towards another, Jesus were he alive at this day, would recommend you to come out of your churches of faith, and to gather into schools of knowledge. Methinks he would inquire into the use of all the large buildings you are now raising, for the only purpose of collecting there once a week in groups of sectarians, and this again, for the only object of learning what we are all too much disposed to believe already—viz: that we are each of us in the right, and that all others are in the wrong. Methinks, I say, that Jesus would recommend you to pass the first day of the week rather otherwise than you pass it now, and to seek some other mode of bettering the morals of the community than by constraining each other to look grave on a Sunday, and to consider yourselves more virtuous in proportion to the idleness in which you pass one day in seven, and to the length of the doctrinal creed you allow your spiritual instructors to sign for you.

The importance attached to opinions and formal observances of days and ceremonies by all Christian sects, is truly surprising, when we consider that Jesus, so far as tradition informs us, never wrote a line, never framed a creed, condemned all prayers in public, and taught his disciples to "love one another," which was as much as to say—*never discuss opinions.* Now those who profess to follow him, discuss little else, but opinions, and therefore do little else but quarrel. To think this way, or to think that way, constitutes the whole duty of man.

My friends, I am no Christian, in the sense usually attached to the word. I am neither Jew nor Gentile, Mahomedan nor Theist; I am but a member of the human family, and would accept of truth by whomsoever offered—that truth which we can all find, if we will but seek—in things, not in words; in nature, not in human imagination; in our own hearts, not in temples made with hands.

Fain would I see my fellow creatures in pursuit of that truth which is around, and about, and within us. Fain would I see them burying their opinions in their own bosoms, and uniting for the study of facts and a knowledge of themselves. Many evils are abroad on the earth, and never did supineness threaten greater dangers than at the present moment. Old superstitions are shaken to their foundation. The false restraints imagined in ages of primeval ignorance are loosened from the mind. Men have grown out of the fear of devils and eternal brimstone, and, applying their ingenuity to evade the laws of earth, laugh in secret at the hobgoblin tales of hell. What then must ensue, if, while old things are passing away, we seek not to discover new? If, while the chains of superstition are falling from the mind, we build not up therein a moral bulwark, nobly to replace the Gothic barriers that are withdrawn, nor apply ourselves to lead by persuasion and conviction that nature which may be no longer cowed by superstition, nor mastered by force? Man is no longer in leading-strings, nor submissive to the rod. He is at this hour too knowing to be driven, and too ignorant to walk alone. Let a free people look to it in time, nor waiting, until law and religion are alike under foot, they shall have to devise remedies in the midst of confusion, and to school the human mind and the human heart in the depths of their corruption. Enough hath been said—the path lies clear. Virtue and truth dwell only with knowledge, and as, when a people shal possess knowledge, they will form on all subjects just opinions so will they also, in all the relations of life, as citizens, parents and fellow creatures, discover and pursue a just practice.

LECTURE VII.

Of Existing Evils, and their Remedy.

[As delivered in Philadelphia, June 2, 1829.]

HAVING now traced with you what knowledge is in matter and in mind; what virtue is in human conduct, where its rules are to be sought, and how they may be found; tested, by the standard thus supplied, the ruling topic of discussion and instruction throughout this country; shown that, while this topic subtracts from the wealth of the nation twenty millions per annum, and from the hearts and minds of the people social fellowship and common sense, it has in nature no real existence—is not knowledge, but only imagination—is not fact, but only theory; and, having shown, moreover, that theory can supply no subject matter of instruction; that the teaching of opinions is as erroneous in principle as it is dangerous in practice; that the duty of the instructor is simply to enrich the mind with knowledge, to awaken the eye, and the ear, and the touch, to the perception of things, the judgment of their comparison and arrangement, and to leave the free unbiassed mind to draw its own conclusions from the evidence thus collected,—I shall now present a few observations on the necessity of commencing, and gradually perfecting, a radical reform in your existing outlays of time and money—on and in churches, theological colleges, privileged and exclusive seminaries of all descriptions, religious Sabbath schools, and all their aids and adjuncts of Bibles, tracts, missionaries, priests, and preachers, multiplied and multiplying throughout the land, until they promise to absorb more capital than did the temple of Solomon, and to devour more of the first fruits of industry than did the tribe of Levi in the plentitude of its power;—on the necessity, I say, of substituting for your present cumbrous, expensive, useless, or rather pernicious, system of partial, opinionative, and dogmatical instruction, one at once national, rational, and republican; one which shall take for its study, our own world and our own nature; for its object, the improvement of man; and for its means, the practical depelopment of truth, the removal of temptations to evil, and the gradual equalization of human condition, human duties, and human enjoyments, by the equal diffusion of knowledge without distinction of class or sect—both of which distinctions are inconsistent with republican institutions as they are with reason and with common sense, with virtue and with happiness.

Time is it in this land to commence this reform. Time is it to check the ambition of an organized clergy, the demoralizing effects of a false system of law; to heal the strife fomented by sectarian religion and legal disputes; to bring down the pride of ideal wealth, and to raise honest industry to honour.

Time is it to search out the misery in the land, and to heal it
at the source. Time is it to remember the poor and the
afflicted, ay! and the vicious and the depraved. Time is it
to perceive that every sorrow which corrodes the human
heart, every vice which diseases the body and the mind, every
crime which startles the ear and sends back the blood affrighted
to the heart—is the product of one evil, the foul growth from
one root, the distorted progeny of one corrupt parent—IGNO-
RANCE.

Time is it to perceive this truth; to proclaim it on the
housetop, in the market place, in city and forest, throughout
the land; to acknowledge it in the depths of our hearts, and
to apply all our energies to the adoption of those salutary
measures which this salutary truth spontaneously suggests.
Time is it, I say, to turn our churches into halls of science,
our schools of faith into schools of knowledge, our privileged
colleges into state institutions for all the youth of the land.
Time is it to arrest our speculations respecting unseen worlds
and inconceivable mysteries, and to address our inquiries to
the improvement of our human condition, and our efforts to
the practical illustration of those beautiful principles of liberty
and equality enshrined in the political institutions, and, first
and chief, in the national declaration of independence.

And by whom and how, are these changes to be effected?
By whom! And do a free people ask the question! By
themselves. By themselves—*the people.*

I am addressing the people of Philadelphia—the people of
a city where Jefferson penned the glorious declaration which
awoke this nation and the world—the city, where the larum
so astounding to tyranny, so fraught with hope, and joy,
and exulting triumph to humankind, was first sounded in
the ears of Americans. I speak to the descendants of those
men who heard from the steps of their old state house the
principles of liberty and equality first proclaimed to man.
I speak to the inhabitants of a city founded by the most
peaceful, the most humane, and the most practical of all
Christian sects. I speak to mechanics who are uniting for
the discovery of their interests and the protection of their
rights. I speak to a public whose benevolence has been long
harrowed by increasing pauperism, and whose social order
and social happiness are threatened by increasing vice. I
speak to sectarians who are weary of sectarianism. I speak
to honest men who tremble for their honesty. I speak to the

*dis*honest whose integrity has fallen before the discouragements waiting upon industry; and who, by slow degrees, or in moments of desperation, have forsaken honest labour, because without a reward, for fraudulent speculation, because it promised one chance of success to a thousand chances of ruin. I speak to parents anxious for their offspring—to husbands who, while shortening their existence by excess of labour, foresee, at their death, not sorrow alone, but unrequited industry and hopeless penury, involving shame, and perhaps infamy, for their oppressed widows and unprotected children. I speak to human beings surrounded by human suffering—to fellow citizens pledged to fellow feeling—to republicans pledged to equal rights and, as a consequent, to equal condition and equal enjoyments; and I call them—oh, would that my voice were loud to reach every ear, and persuasive to reach every heart!—I call them to UNITE; and to unite for the consideration of the evils around us—for the discovery and application of their remedy.

Dreadful has been the distress exhibited during the past year, not in this city only, but in every city throughout the whole extent of this vast republic. Long had the mass of evil been accumulated, ere it attracted attention; and, would we understand how far the plague spot is to spread, or what is to be its termination, we must look to Europe.

We are fast travelling in the footsteps of Europe, my friends; for her principles of action are ours. We have in all our habits and usages, the same vices, and, with these same vices, we must have, as we see we have, the same evils.

The great principles stamped in America's declaration of independence, are true, are great, are sublime, and are *all her own*. But her usages, her law, her religion, her education, are false, narrow, prejudiced, ignorant, and are the relic of dark ages—the gift and bequeathment of king-governed, priest-ridden nations, whose supremacy, indeed, the people of America have challenged and overthrown, but whose example they are still following.

A foreigner, I have looked round on this land unblinded by local prejudices or national predelictions; a friend to humankind, zealous for human improvement, enamoured to enthusiasm, if you will, of human liberty, I first sought this country to see in operation those principles consecrated in her national institutions, and whose simple grandeur had fired the enthusiasm and cheered the heart of my childhood, disgusted as it

was with the idle parade and pride of unjust power inherent
in European aristocracy. Delighted with the sound of political liberty, the absence of bayonets and constrained taxation,
I spake and published, as I felt, in praise of American institutions; and called, and, I believe, first generally awakened, the
attention of the European public to their study and appreciation.

Disappointed, in common with all the friends of liberty in
Europe, by the issue of the well-imagined, but ill-sustained,
revolutions of the old continent, which closed, as you will
remember, by the triumph of France and the holy alliance
over the bands of Riego and Mina in Spain. I returned to
this republic as to the last hope of the human family, anxious
to inspect it through its wide extent, and to study it in all its
details.

The result of my observation has been the conviction, that
the reform commenced at the revolution of '76 has been but
little improved through the term of years which have succeeded; that the national policy of the country was then
indeed changed, but that its social economy has remained
such as it was in the days of its European vassalage.

In confirmation of this, I will request you to observe, that
your religion is the same as that of monarchical England—
taught from the same books, and promulgated and sustained
by similar means, viz. a salaried priesthood, set apart from the
people; sectarian churches, in whose property the people
have no share, and over whose use and occupancy the people
have no control; expensive missions, treasury funds,
associations, and, above all, a compulsory power, compounded
at once of accumulated wealth, established custom, extensive
correspondence, and a system of education imbued with its
spirit and all pervaded by its influence.

Again, in proof of the similarity between your internal
policy and that of monarchical England, I will request you to
observe that *her law is your law.* Every part and parcel of
that absurd, cruel, ignorant, inconsistent, incomprehensible
jumble, styled the common law of England—every part and
parcel of it, I say, not abrogated or altered expressly by
legislative statutes, which has been very rarely done, is at this
hour the law of revolutionized America.

Farther, in proof of the identity of your fabric of civil polity
with that of aristocratical England, I will request you to
observe that the system of education pursued in both countries

is, with little variations, one and the same. There you have endowed universities, privileged by custom, enriched by ancient royal favour, protected by parliamentary statutes, and devoted to the upholding, perpetuating, and strengthening the power and privilege to which they owe their origin. There, too, you have parish schools under the control of the parish priest, and a press every where coerced by law, swayed, bribed, or silenced by ascendant parties or tyrannous authority. And *here* have we not colleges with endowments still held by the royal charters which first bestowed them, and colleges with lands and money granted by American legislatures—not for the advantage of the American people, but for that of their rulers; for the children of privileged professions upon whom is thus entailed the privilege of their fathers, and that as certainly as the son of a duke is born to a dukedom in England. *Here* have we not also schools controlled by the clergy; nay, have we not all our public institutions, scientific, literary, judicial, or humane, ridden by the spirit of orthodoxy, and invaded, perverted, vitiated, and tormented by opinionative distinctions? And *here* have we not a press paralized by fear, disgraced by party, and ruled by loud-tongued fanaticism, or aspiring and threatening sectarian ambition. And more, my friends, see we not, in this nation of confederated freemen, as many distinctions of class as afflict the aristocracies of Britain, or the despotism of the Russias; and more distinctions of sect than ever cursed all the nations of Europe together, from the preaching of Peter the hermit, to the trances of Madame Krudner, or the miracles of Prince Hohenlohe?

Surely all these are singular anomalies in a republic. Sparta, when she conceived her democracy, commenced with educational equality; when she aimed at national union, she cemented that union in childhood—at the public board, in the gymnasium, in the temple, in the common habits, common feelings, common duties, and common condition. And so, notwithstanding all the errors with which her institutions were fraught, and all the vices which arose out of those errors, did she present for ages, a wondrous sample of democratic union, and consequently of national prosperity?

What, then, is wanted here? What Sparta had—*a national education.* And what Sparta, in many respects, had not—*a rational education.*

Hitherto, my friends, in government as in every branch of

morals. we have but too much mistaken words for truths, and forms for principles. To render men free, it sufficeth not to proclaim their liberty; to make them equal, it sufficeth not to call them so. True, the 4th of July, '76, commenced a new era for our race. True, the sun of promise then rose upon the world. But let us not mistake for the fulness of light what was but its harbinger. Let us not conceive that man in signing the declaration of his rights secured their possession ; that having framed the theory, he had not, and hath not still, the practice to seek.

Your fathers, indeed, on the day from which dates your existence as a nation, opened the gates of the temple of human liberty. But think not they entered, nor that you have entered the sanctuary. They passed not, nor have you passed, even the threshhold.

Who speaks of liberty while the human mind is in chains? Who of equality while the thousands are in squalid wretchedness, the millions harrassed with health-destroying labour, the few afflicted with health-destroying idleness, and all tormented by health-destroying solicitude ?   Look abroad on the misery which is gaining on the land ! Mark the strife, and the discord, and the jealousies, the shock of interests and opinions, the hatreds of sect, the estrangements of class, the pride of wealth, the debasement of poverty, the helplessness of youth unprotected, of age uncomforted, of industry un-rewarded, of ignorance unenlightened, of vice unreclaimed, of misery unpitied, of sickness, hunger, and nakedness unsatisfied, unalleviated, and unheeded. Go ! mark all the wrongs and the wretchedness with which the eye and the ear and the heart are familiar, and then echo in triumph and celebrate in jubilee the insulting declaration—*all men are free and equal !*

That evils exist, none that have eyes, ears, and hearts can dispute. That these evils are on the increase. none who have watched the fluctuations of trade, the sinking price of labour, the growth of pauperism, and the increase of crime, will dispute. Little need be said here to the people of Philadelphia. The researches made by the public spirited among their own citizens, have but too well substantiated the suffering condition of a large mass of their population. In Boston, in New-York, in Baltimore, the voice of distress hath, in like manner, burst the barriers raised, and so long sustained, by the pride of honest industry, unused to ask from charity what it hath been wont to earn by the sweat of the brow. In each and every city necessity has constrained inquiry ; and in each and every city inquiry has elicited the same appalling facts: that the hardest labour is often without a reward adequate to the sustenance of the labourer ; that when, by over exertion and all the diseases, and often vices, which excess of exertion induces, the labourer, whose patient, sedulous industry supplies the community with all its comforts, and the rich with all their luxuries—when he, I say, is brought to an untimely grave by those exertions which, while sustaining the life of others, cut short his own—when he is mowed down by that labour whose products from the boasted wealth of the state, he leaves a family, to whom the strength of his manhood had barely furnished bread, to lean upon the weakness of a soul-stricken mother, and hurry her to the grave of her father.

Such is the information gleaned from the report of the committee lately appointed by the town meeting of the city and county of Philadelphia, and as verbatim reiterated in every populous city throughout the land. And what are the remedies suggested by our corporation, our newspaper editors, our religious societies, our tracts, and our sermons? Some have ordained fasts, multiplied prayers, and recommended pious submission to a Providence who should have instituted all this calamity for the purpose of fulfilling the words of a Jewish prophet, " the poor shall never cease from the land." Some, less spiritual-minded, have called for larger jails and more poor houses ; some, for increased poor rates and additional benevolent societies; others, for compulsory laws protective of labour, and fixing a *minimum*, below which it shall be penal to reduce it ; while others, and those not the least able to appreciate all the difficulties of the question, have sought the last resource of suffering poverty and oppressed industry in the humanity and sense of justice of the wealthier classes of society.

This last is the forlorn hope presented in the touching document signed by Matthew Carey and his fellow labourers.

It were easy to observe, in reply to each and all of the palliatives variously suggested for evils, which none profess to remedy, that to punish crime when committed is not to prevent its commission ; to force the work of the poor in poor houses is only farther to glut an already unproductive market; to multiply charities is only to increase pauperism ; that to fix by statute the monied price of labour would be impossible in itself, and, if possible, mischievous no less to the labourer than to the employer ; and that, under the existing state of things, for human beings to lean upon the compassion and justice of their fellow creatures, is to lean upon a rotten reed.

I believe no individual, possessed of common sense and common feeling, can have studied the report of the committee to which I have referred, or the multitude of simililar documents furnished elsewhere, without acknowledging that reform, and that not slight nor partial, but radical and universal, is called for. All must admit that no such reform —that is, that no remedy commensurate with the evil, has been suggested, and would we but reflect, we should perceive that no efficient remedy *can* be suggested, or if suggested, applied, until the people are generally engaged in its discovery and its application for themselves.

In this nation, any more than in any other nation, the mass has never reflected for the mass ; the people, as a body, have never addressed themselves to the study of their own condition, and to the just and fair interpretation of their common interests. And, as it was with their national independence, so shall it be with their national happiness—it shall be found only when the mass shall seek it. No people have ever received liberty *in gift*. Given, it were not appreciated ; it were not understood. Won without exertion, it were lost as readily. Let the people of America recal the ten years of war and tribulation by which they purchased their national independence. Let efforts as strenuous be now made, not with the sword of steel, indeed, but with the sword of the spirit, and their farther enfranchisement from poverty, starvation, and dependence, must be equally successful.

Great reforms are not wrought in a day. Evils which are the accumulated results of accumulated errors, are not to be struck down at a blow by the rod of a magician. A free people may boast that all power is in their hands; but no effectual power can be in their hands until knowledge be in their minds.

But how may knowledge be imparted to their minds ? Such effective knowledge as shall render apparent to all the interests of all, and demonstrate the simple truths—that a nation to be strong, must be united ; to be united, must be equal in condition ; to be equal in condition, must be similar in habits and in feeling ; to be similar in habits and in feeling, *must be raised in national institutions, as the children of a common family, and citizens of a common country.*

Before entering on the development of the means I have here suggested for paving our way to the reform of those evils which now press upon humanity, and which, carried, perhaps, to their acme in some of the nations of Europe, are gaining ground in these United States with a rapidity alarming to all who know how to read the present, or to calculate the future—I must observe, that I am fully aware of the difficulty of convincing all minds of the urgency of these evils, and of the impossibility of engaging all classes in the application of their remedy.

In the first place, the sopular suffering, great as it is, weighs not with a sufficiently equal pressure on all parts of the country ; and, in the second, affects not equally all classes of the population, so as to excite to that union of exertion, which once made, the reform is effected and the nation redeemed.

While the evil day is only in prospect, or while it visits our neighbour but spares ourselves, such is the selfishness generated by existing habits, and such the supineness generated by that selfishness, that we are but too prone to shrink from every effort not absolutely and immediately necessary for the supply of our own wants or the increase of our own luxuries. Yet, would the most spoiled child of worldly fortune but look around him on the changes and chances which ofttimes sweep away the best secured treasures, and bring in a moment the capitalist to bankruptcy, and his family to want, he could not feel himself entirely removed in sympathy from the suffering portion of his fellow creatures. But let us take the case of the thriving artizan, or successful merchant—on what security does he hold that pecuniary independence which puts the bread into the mouths of his children, and protects from destitution the companion of his bosom ? On sustained industry and unremitting exertions, which sickness may interrupt, a fall in the market reduce to half its value, or a few casualties or one miscalculation in a moment annihilate. Or what if death finally interrupt the father's care or the husband's tenderness— where is the stay for his orphan children ? where succour for their widowed mother, now charged alone with all the weight of their provision ? I have taken no extreme cases ; I have taken such as may, in the course of events, be the case of every man who hears me.

Were it my disposition, which, I think, it is not, to exaggerate evils, or were I even disposed to give a fair picture of those really existing among a large mass of the American population, more especially as crowded into the cities and manufacturing districts, easy it were to harrow the feelings of the least sensitive, and, in the relation, to harrow my own.

But as the measure it is my object this evening to suggest to the people of Philadelphia, and my intention hereafter to submit to the whole American nation, must, at the first sight, win to its support the more oppressed and afflicted, I am rather desirous of addressing my prefatory arguments to that class from whence opposition is most to be apprehended.

I know how difficult it is—reared as we all are in the distinctions of class, to say nothing of sect, to conceive of our interests as associated with those of the whole community. The man possessed of a dollar, feels himself to be, not merely one hundred cents richer, but also one hundred cents *better*, than the man who is pennyless ; so on through all the gradations of earthly possessions—the estimate of our own moral and political importance swelling always in a ratio exactly proportionate to the growth of our purse. The rich man who can leave a clear independence to his children, is given to estimate them as he estimates himself, and to imagine something in their nature distinct from that of the less privileged heirs of hard labour and harder fare.

This might indeed appear too gross for any of us to advance in theory, but in feeling how many must plead guilty to the prejudice ! Yet is there a moment when, were their thoughts known to each other, all men must feel themselves on a level. It is when as fathers they look on their children, and picture the possibility which may render them orphans; and then calculate all the casualties which may deprive them, if rich, of their inheritance, or, if poor, grind them down to deeper poverty.

But it is first to the rich, I would speak. Can the man of opulence feel tranquil under the prospect of leaving to such guardianship as existing law or individual integrity may supply, the minds, bodies, morals, or even the fortune of their children? I myself was an orphan : and I know that the very

law which was my protector, sucked away a portion of my
little inheritance, while that law, insufficient and avaricious
as it was, alone shielded me from spoliation by my guardian.
I know, too, that my youth was one of tribulation, albeit
passed in the envied luxuries of aristocracy. I know that the
orphan's bread may be watered with tears, even when the
worst evil be not there—*dependence.*

Can, then, the rich be without solicitude, when they leave
to the mercy of a heartless world the beings of their creation?
Who shall cherish their young sensibilities? Who shall stand
between them and oppression? Who shall wisper peace in
the hour of affliction? Who shall supply principle in the
hour of temptation? Who shall lead the tender mind to
distinguish between the good and the evil? Who shall fortify
it against the corruptions of wealth, or prepare it for the day
of adversity? Such, looking upon life as it is, must be the
anxious thoughts even of the wealthy. What must be the
thoughts of the poor man, it needs not that we should picture.

But, my friends, however differing in degree may be the
anxiety of the rich and the poor, still, in its nature, is it the
same.   Doubt, uncertainty, apprehension, are before all.
We hear of deathbed affliction. My friends, I have been
often and long on the bed of mortal sickness: no fear had the
threatened last sleep for me, for *I was not a parent.*

We have here, then, found an evil common to all classes,
and one that is entailed from generation to generation. The
measure I am about to suggest, whenever adopted, will blot
this now universal affliction from existence ; it will also, in
the outset, alleviate those popular distresses whose poignancy
and happy increase weigh on the heart of philanthropy, and
crush the best hopes of enlightened patriotism. It must further,
when carried into full effect, work the radical cure of every
disease which now afflicts the body politic, and built up for
this nation a sound constitution, embracing at once, public
prosperity, individual integrity, and universal happiness.

This measure, my friends, has been long present to my
mind, as befitting the adoption of the American people ; as
alone calculated to form an enlightened, a virtuous, and a
happy community ; as alone capable of supplying a remedy
to the evils under which we groan ; as alone commensurate
with the interests of the human family, and consistent with
the political institutions of this great confederated republic.

I had occasion formerly to observe, in allusion to the efforts already made, and yet making, in the cause of popular instruction, more or less throughout the Union, that, as yet, the true principle has not been hit, and that until it be hit, all reform must be slow and inefficient.

The noble example of New-England has been imitated by other states, until all not possessed of common schools blush for the popular remissness. But, after all, how can *common schools*, under their best form, and in fullest supply, effect even the purpose which they have in view?

The object proposed by common schools (if I rightly understand it) is to impart to the whole population those means for the acquirement of knowledge which are in common use: reading and writing. To these are added arithmetic, and occasionally, perhaps, some imperfect lessons in the simpler sciences. But I would ask, supposing these institutions should even be made to embrace all the branches of intellectual knowledge, and, thus, science offered gratis to all the children of the land, how are the children of the very class, for whom we suppose the schools instituted to be supplied with food and raiment, or instructed in the trade necessary to their future subsistence, while they are following these studies? How are they, I ask, to be fed and clothed, when, as all facts show, the labour of the parents is often insufficient for their own sustenance, and, almost universally, inadequate to the provision of the family without the united efforts of all its members? In your manufacturing districts you have children worked for twelve hours a day; and in the rapid and certain progress of the existing system, you will soon have them, as in England, *worked to death*, and yet unable, through the period of their miserable existence, to earn a pittance sufficient to satisfy the cravings of hunger. At this present time, what leisure or what spirit, think you, have the children of the miserable widows of Philadelphia, realizing, according to the most favourable estimate of your city and county committee, sixteen dollars per annum, for food and clothing? what leisure or what spirit may their children find for visiting a school, although the same should be open to them from sunrise to sunset? Or what leisure have usually the children of your most thriving mechanics, after their strength is sufficiently developed to spin, sew, weave, or wield a tool? It seems to me, my friends, that to build school houses now-a-days is something like building churches. When you have them, you need some measure to ensure their being occupied.

I

But, as our time is short, and myself somewhat fatigued by continued exertions, I must hasten to the rapid development of the system of instruction and protection which has occurred to me as capable, and alone, capable, of opening the door to universal reform.

In lieu of all common schools, high schools, colleges, seminaries, houses of refuge, or any other juvenile institution, instructional or protective, I would suggest that the state legislatures be directed (after laying off the whole in townships or hundreds) to organize, at suitable distances. and in convenient and healthy situations, establishments for the general reception of all the children resident within the said school district. These establishments to be devoted, severally, to children between a certain age. Say, the first, infants between two and four, or two and six, according to the density of the population, and such other local circumstances as might render a greater or less number of establishments necessary or practicable. The next to receive children from four to eight, or six to twelve years. The next from twelve to sixteen, or to an older age if found desirable. Each establishment to be furnished with instructors in every branch of knowledge. intellectual and operative, with all the apparatus, land, and conveniences necessary for the best development of all knowledge ; the same, whether operative or intellectual, being always calculated to the age and strength of the pupils.

To obviate, in the commencement, every evil result possible from the first mixture of a young population, so variously raised in error or neglect, a due separation should be made in each establishment; by which means those entering with bad habits would be kept apart from the others until corrected. How rapidly reform may be effected on the plastic disposition of childhood, has been sufficiently proved in your houses of refuge, more especially when such establishments have been under *liberal* superintendance, as was formerly the case in New-York. Under their orthodox directors, those asylums of youth have been converted into jails.

It will be understood that, in the proposed establishments, the children would pass from one to the other in regular succession, and that the parents who would necessarily be resident in their close neighbourhood, could visit the children at suitable hours, but, in no case, interfere with or interrupt the rules of the institution.

In the older establishments, the well directed and well protected labour of the pupil would, in time, suffice for, and, then exceed their own support; when the surplus might be devoted to the maintenance of the infant establishments.

In the beginning, and until all debt was cleared off, and so long as the same should be found favourable to the promotion of these best palladiums of a nation's happiness, a double tax might be at once expedient and politic.

First, a moderate tax per head for every child, to be laid upon its parents conjointly, or divided between them, due attention being always paid to the varying strength of the two sexes, and to the undue depreciation which now rests on female labour. The more effectually to correct the latter injustice, as well as to consult the convenience of the industrious classes generally, this parental tax might be rendered payable either in money, or in labour, produce, or domestic manufactures, and should be continued for each child until the age when juvenile labour should be found, on the average, equivalent to the educational expenses, which, I have reason to believe, would be at twelve years.

This first tax on parents to embrace equally the whole population; as, however moderate it would inculcate a certain forethought in all the human family; more especially where it is most wanted—in young persons, who before they assumed the responsibility of parents, would estimate their fitness to meet it.

The second tax to be on property, increasing in per centage with the wealth of the individual. In this manner I conceive the rich would contribute, according to their riches, to the relief of the poor, and to the support of the state, by raising up its best bulwark—an enlightened and united generation.

Preparatory to. or connected with, such measures, a registry should be opened by the state, with offices through all the townships, where on the birth of every child, or within a certain time appointed, the same should be entered, together with the names of its parents. When two years old, the parental tax should be payable, and the juvenile institution open for the child's reception; from which time forward it would be under the protective care and guardianship of the state, while it need never be removed from the daily, weekly, or frequent inspection of the parents.

Orphans, of course, would find here an open asylum. If possessed of property, a contribution would be paid for its revenue to the common educational fund; if unprovided, they would be sustained out of the same.

In these nurseries of a free nation, no inequality must be allowed to enter. Fed at a common board; clothed in a common garb, uniting neatness with simplicity and convenience; raised in the exercise of common duties, in the acquirement of the same knowledge and practice of the same industry, varied only according to individual taste and capabilities; in the exercise of the same virtues, in the enjoyment of the same pleasures; in the study of the same nature; in pursuit of the same object—their own and each other's happiness—say! would not such a race, when arrived at manhood and womanhood, work out the reform of society— perfect the free institutions of America.

I have drawn but a sketch, nor could I presume to draw the picture of that which the mind's eye hath seen alone, and which it is for the people of this land to realize.

In this sketch, my friends, there is nothing but what is practical and practicable: nothing but what you yourselves may contribute to effect. Let the popular suffrage be exercised with a view to the popular good. Let the industrious classes, and all honest men of all classes, unite for the sending to the legislatures those who will represent the real interests of the many, not the imagined interests of the few—of the people at large, not of any profession or class.

To develope farther my views on this all important subject at the present time, would be to fatigue your attention, and exhaust my own strength. I shall prosecute this subject in the periodical of which I am editor.* which in common with my public discourses, have been, and will ever be, devoted to the common cause of human improvement, and addressed to humankind without distinction of nation, class, or sect. May you, my fellow beings, unite in the same cause, in the same spirit! May you learn to seek truth without fear! May you farther learn to advocate truth as you distinguish it; to be valiant in its defence, and peaceful while valiant; to meet all things, and bear all things, and dare all things for the correction of abuses, and the effecting, in private and in public, in your own minds, through the minds of your children, friends, and companions, and, above all, *through your legislatures*, a radical reform in all your measures, whether as citizens, or as men!

* The Free Enquirer, Published in New-York.

ADDRESS I.

[Delivered in the New Harmony Hall, on the Fourth of July, 1828.]

THE custom which commemorates in rejoicing the anniversary of the national independence of these states, has its origin in a human feeling, amiable in its nature, and beneficial, under proper direction, in its indulgence.

From the era which dates the national existence of the American people, dates also a mighty step in the march of human knowledge. And it is consistent with that principle in our conformation which leads us to rejoice in the good which befals our species, and to sorrow for the evil, that our hearts should expand on this day;—on this day, which calls to memory the conquest achieved by knowledge over ignorance, willing co-operation over blind obedience, opinion over prejudice, new ways over old ways, when, fifty-two years ago, America declared her national independence, and associated it with her republican federation. Reasonable is it to rejoice on this day, and useful to reflect thereon; so that we rejoice for the real, and not for any imaginary good, and reflect on the positive advantages obtained, and on those which it is ours farther to acquire.

Dating, as we justly may, a new era in the history of man from the Fourth of July, 1776, it would be well, that is, it would be useful, if on each anniversary we examined the progress made by our species in just knowledge and just practice. Each Fourth of July would then stand as a tide mark in the flood of time, by which to ascertain the advance of the human intellect, by which to note the rise and fall of each successive error, the discovery of each important truth, the gradual melioration in our public institutions, social arrangements, and, above all, in our moral feelings and mental views. Let such a review as this engage annually our attention, and sacred, doubly sacred, shall be this day: and that not to one nation only, but to all nations capable of reflection.

The political dismemberment of these once British colonies

from the parent island, though involving a valuable principle, and many possible results, would scarcely merit a yearly commemoration, even in this country, had it not been accompanied by other occurrences more novel, and far more important. I allude to the seal then set to the system of representative government, till then imperfectly known in Europe, and insecurely practised in America, and to the crown then placed on this system by the novel experiment of political federation. The frame of federative government that sprung out of the articles signed in '76, is one of the most beautiful inventions of the human intellect. It has been in government what the steam engine has been in mechanics, and the printing press in the dissemination of knowledge.

But it needs not that we should now pause to analyse what all must have considered. It is to one particular feature in our political institutions that I would call attention, and this, because it is at once the most deserving of notice, and the least noticed. Are our institutions better than those of other countries? Upon fair examination most men will answer *yes*. But why will they so answer? It is because they are republican, instead of monarchical? democratic, rather than aristocratic? In so far as the republican principle shall have been proved more conducive to the general good than the monarchical, and the democratic than the aristocratic—in so far will the reasons be good. But there is another and a better reason than these. There is, in the institutions of this country, one principle, which, had they no other excellence, would secure to them the preference over those of all other countries. I mean—and some devout patriots will start—I mean the principle of *change*.

I have used a word to which is attached an obnoxious meaning. Speak of *change*, and the world is in alarm. And yet where do we not see change? What is there in the physical world *but* change? And what would there be in the moral world *without* change? The flower blossoms, the fruit ripens, the seed is received and germinates in the earth, and and we behold the tree. The aliment we eat to satisfy our hunger incorporates with our frame, and the atoms composing our existence to day, are exhaled to morrow. In like manner our feelings and opinions are moulded by circumstance, and matured by observation and experience. All is change. Within and about us no one thing is as it was, or will be as it is. Strange, then, that we should start at a word used to

signify a thing so familiar ?   Stranger yet that we should fail
to appreciate a principle which, inherent in all matter, is no
less inherent in ourselves; and which as it has tracked our
mental progress heretofore, so will it track our progress
through time to come.

But will it be said *change* has a bad, as well as a good
sense ?   It may be for the better, and it may be for the worse?
In the physical world it can be neither the one nor the other.
It can be simply such as it is.   But in the moral world—that
is, in the thoughts, and feelings, and inventions of men, change
may certainly be either for the better or for the worse, or it
may be for neither.   Changes that are neither bad nor good
can have regard *only* to trivial matters, and can be as little
worthy of observation as of censure.   Changes that are from
better to worse can originate only in ignorance, and are ever
amended so soon as experience has substantiated their mischief.   Where men then are free to consult experience they
will correct their practice, and make changes for the better.
It follows, therefore, that the more free men are, the more
changes they will make.   In the beginning, possibly, for the
worse ; but most certainly in time for the better ; until their
knowledge enlarging by observation, and their judgment
strengthening by exercise, they will find themselves in the
straight, broad, fair road of improvement.   Out of change,
therefore, springs improvement ; and the people who shall
have imagined a peaceable mode of changing their institutions, hold a surety for their melioration.   This surety is worth
all other excellences.   Better were the prospects of a people
under the influence of the worst government who should hold
the power of changing it, than those of a people under the
best who should hold no such power.   Here, then, is the
great beauty of American government.   The simple machinery of representation carried through all its parts, gives facility for its being moulded at will to fit with the knowledge of
the age.   If imperfect in any or all of its parts, it bears within
it a perfect principle—the principle of improvement.   And, let
us observe, that this principle is all that we can ever know of
perfection.   Knowledge, and all the blessings which spring out
of knowledge, can never be more than progressive ; and
whatsoever *sets open the door* does all for us—does every
thing.

The clear-sighted provision in the national constitution, as

in the constitutions of the different states, by which the frame
of government can be moulded at will by the public voice,
and so made to keep pace in progress with the public mind,
is the master-stroke in constitutional law. Were our institutions far less enlightened and well digested than they are—
were every other regulation erroneous, every other ordinance
defective—nay, even tyrannous—this single provision would
counterbalance all. Let but the door be opened, and be fixed
open, for improvement to hold on her unimpeded course, and
vices. however flagrant, are but the evils of an hour. Once
lanch the animal man in the road of inquiry, and he *shall*—he
must—hold a forward career. He may be sometimes checked ;
he may seem occasionally to retrograde ; but his retreat is
only that of the receding wave in the inning tide. His master
movement is always in advance. By this do we distinguish
man from all other existences within the range of our observation. By this does he stand pre-eminent over all known
animals. By *this*—by his capability of improvement : by his
tendency to improve whenever scope is allowed for the development of his faculties. To hold him *still*, he must be
chained. Snap the chain, and he springs forward.

But will it be said. that the chains which bind him are more
than one ? That political bonds are much, but not all; and
that when broken, we may still be slaves? I know not, my
friends. We tax our ingenuity to draw nice distinctions. We
are told of political liberty—of religious liberty—of moral
liberty. Yet, after all, is there more than one liberty ; and
these divisions. are they not the more and the less of the same
thing ? The provision we have referred to in our political institutions, as framed in accordance with the principle inherent
in ourselves, insures to us all of free action that statutes *can*
insure. Supposing that our laws, constitutional, civil, or
penal. should in any thing cripple us at the present, the power
will be with us to amend or annul them so soon (and how
might it be sooner?) as our enlarged knowledge shall enable
us to see in what they err. All the liberty therefore that we
yet lack will gradually spring up—*there,* where our bondage
is—in our minds. To be free we have but to see our chains.
Are we disappointed—are we sometimes angry, because the
crowd or any part of the crowd around us bows submissively
to mischievous usages or unjust laws ? Let us remember,
that they do so in ignorance of their mischief and injustice, and

that when they see these, as in the course of man's progressive state they must see them, these and other evils will be
corrected.

Inappreciable is this advantage that we hold (unfortunately)
above other nations? The great national and political revolution of '76 set the seal to the liberties of North America.
And but for one evil, and that of immense magnitude, which
the constitutional provision we have been considering does not
fairly reach—I allude to negro slavery and the degradation of
our coloured citizens—we could foresee for the whole of this
magnificent country a certain future of uniform and peaceful
improvement. While other nations have still to win reform
at the sword's point, we have only to will it. While in Europe men have still to fight, we have only to learn. While
there they have to cope with ignorance armed cap-a-pee, en-
circled with armies and powerful with gold, we have only
peacefully to collect knowledge, and to frame our institutions
and actions in accordance with it.

It is true, that we have much knowledge to collect, and
consequently much to amend in our opinions and our practice.
It is also true that we are often ignorant of what has been
done, and quite unaware that there is yet any thing to do.
The very nature of the national institutions is frequently mistaken, and the devotion exhibited for them as frequently based
on a wrong principle. Here, as in other countries, we hear
of *patriotism ;* that is, of love of country in an exclusive sense;
of love of our countrymen in contradistinction to the love of
our fellow-creatures; of love of the constitution, instead of
love or appreciation of those principles upon which the constitution is, or ought to be, based, and upon which, if it
should be found not to be based, it would merit no attachment at all.

The sentiment here adverted to involves much of importance to us in our double character of human beings and
citizens. That double character it will be also useful that we
examine, as much confusion prevails in the vulgar ideas on
the subject.

It will be conceded, that we do not cease to be human
beings when we become citizens ; and farther, that our happy
existence as human beings is of more importance to us than
our artificial existence as members of a nation or subjects
of a government. Indeed, the only rational purpose for
which we can suppose men congregated into what are called

nations, is the increase of happiness—the insuring of some advantage, real or imagined. The only rational purpose for which we can suppose governments organized, the same. If, upon examination, we should find the object not gained, the experiment, so far as it went, would have failed, and we should then act rationally to break up such national congregations, and to change or annul such governments. Our character as citizens, therefore, must ever depend upon our finding it for our interest as human beings to stand in that relation. What then is patriotism, or the fulfilment of our duties as citizens, but the acting consistently in that way which we conceive it for our interest that we should act? Or what reason might be offered for our consulting the interests of a government, unless its interests are in unison with our own?

The great error of the wisest known nations of antiquity, the Greeks and Romans, was the preference invariably given to the imagined interests of an imaginary existence called *the state* or *country*, and the real interests of the real existences, or human beings, upon whom, individually and collectively, their laws could alone operate. Another error was the opposition in which they invariably placed the interests of their own nation to the interests of all other nations; and a third and greater error, was the elevating into a virtue this selfish preference of their own national interests, under the name of patriotism. The moderns are growing a little wiser on these matters, but they are still very ignorant. The least ignorant are the people of this country; but they have much to learn. Americans no longer argue on the propriety of making all men soldiers, in order that their nation may be an object of terror to the rest of the world. They understand that the happiness of a people is the only rational object of a government, and the only object for which a people, free to choose, can have a government at all. They have, farther, almost excluded war as a profession, and reduced it from a system of robbery to one of simple defence. In so doing, they ought also to have laid aside all show of military parade, and all ideas of military glory. If they have not done so, it is that their reform in this matter is yet imperfect, and their ideas respecting it are confused.

Who among us but has heard, and, perhaps, echoed eulogiums on the patriotism of statesmen and soldiers—not because they have upheld some strict principle of justice, which should rather merit the name of virtue, but because they have flattered the vanity of their countrymen in a public speech, defended their own interests, and the national interests, in some foreign treaty, or their own possessions, and the national possessions, in a siege or a pitched battle? It is not that some of these actions may not be just and proper; but are they justly and properly estimated? It is *virtuous* in a man if a pistol be presented to his breast, to knock down the assailant? The action is perfectly warrantable; but does it call forth admiration? Should the attack be made made on another, and should he defend the life of that other at the risk of his own; the action, though not exceedingly meritorious, might excite a moderate admiration, as involving a forgetfulness of self in the service rendered.

Does not the defence of country afford a parallel case to the first supposition? Insomuch as it be ours, we defend our own. We do what it is fair and proper that we should do, but we do nothing more. What, then, is patriotism, of which we hear so much, and understand so little? If it mean only a proper attention to our own interests, and the interests of the people with whom we stand connected, and of the government instituted for our protection, it is a rational sentiment, and one appertaining to our organization. It is one, in short, with the love of self, and the principle of self-defence and self-preservation. Again; are we to understand by it an attachment to the soil we tread, because we tread it; the language we speak, because we speak it; the government that rules us, merely because it rules us? It means nothing, or it means nonsense. Again; are we to understand by patriotism a preference for the interests of our own nation under all circumstances, even to the sacrifice of those of other nations—it is a vice.

In continental Europe, of late years, the words patriotism and patriot have been used in a more enlarged sense than it is usual here to attribute to them, or than is attached to them in Great Britain. Since the political struggles of France, Italy, Spain, and Greece, the word patriotism has been employed, throughout continental Europe, to express a love of the public good; a preference for the interests of the many to those of the few; a desire for the emancipation of the human race from the thrall of despotism, religious and civil; in short, patriotism there is used rather to express the interest felt in the human race in general, than that felt for any country, or inhabitants of a country, in particular. And patriot, in like manner, is employed to signify a lover of human liberty and human improvement, rather than a mere lover of the country in which he lives, or the tribe to which he belongs. Used in this sense, patriotism is a virtue, and a patriot a virtuous man. With such an interpretation, a patriot is a useful member of society, capable of enlarging all minds, and bettering all hearts with which he comes in contact ; a useful member of the human family, capable of establishing fundamental principles, and of merging his own interests, those of his associates, and those of his nation, in the interests of the human race. Laurels and statues are vain things, and mischievous as they are childish ; but, could we imagine them of use, on *such* a patriot alone could they be with any reason bestowed.

> Is there a thought can fill the human mind
> More pure, more vast, more generous, more refin'd
> Than that which guides the enlightened patriot's toil :
> Not he, whose view is bounded by his soil :
> Not he, whose narrow heart can only shrine
> The land—the people that he calleth *mine;*
> Not he, who to set up that land on high,
> Will make whole nations bleed, whole nations die ;
> Not he, who, calling that land's rights his pride
> Trampleth the rights of all the earth beside ;
> No !—He it is, the just, the generous soul !
> Who owneth brotherhood with either pole,
> Stretches from realm to realm his spacious mind,
> And guards the weal of all the human kind,
> Holds freedom's banner o'er the earth unfurl'd,
> And stands the guardian patriot of a world !

If such a patriotism as we have last considered should seem likely to obtain in any country, it should be certainly in this. In this, which is truly the home of all nations, and in the veins of whose citizens flows the blood of every people on the globe. Patriotism, in the exclusive meaning, is surely not made for America. Mischievous every where, it were here both mischievous and absurd. The very origin of the people is opposed to it. The institutions, in their principle, militate against it. The day we are celebrating protests against it. It is for Americans, more especially, to nourish a nobler sentiment ; one more consistent with their origin, and more conducive to their future improvement. It is for them more especially to know why they love their country, but because it is the palladium of human liberty—

the favoured scene of human improvement. It is for them
more especially, to know why they honour their institutions,
and *feel* that they honour them because they are based on
just principles. It is for them, more especially, to examine
their institutions, because they have the means of improving
them ; to examine their laws, because at will they can alter
them. It is for them to lay aside luxury, whose wealth is
in industry ; idle parade, whose strength is in knowledge ;
ambitious distinction, whose principle is equality. It is for
them not to rest satisfied with words, who can seize upon
things ; and to remember, that equality means, not the mere
equality of political rights, however valuable, but equality
of instruction, and equality in virtue ; and that liberty means,
not the mere voting at elections, but the free and fearless
exercise of the mental faculties, and that self-possession
which springs out of well-reasoned opinions and consistent
practice. It is for them to honour principles rather than men—
to commemorate events rather than days ; when they rejoice,
to know for what they rejoice, and to rejoice only for what
has brought, and what brings, peace and happiness to men.
The event we commemorate this day has procured much
of both, and shall procure, in the onward course of human
improvement, more than we can now conceive of. For
this—for the good obtained, and yet in store for our race—
let us rejoice ! But let us rejoice as men, not as children—
as human beings, rather than as Americans—as reasoning
beings, not as ignorants. So shall we rejoice to good purpose
and in good feeling ; so shall we improve the victory once on
this day achieved, until all mankind hold with us the jubilee
of independance.

ADDRESS II.

[Delivered in the Philadelphia Theatre, on the Fourth of July, 1929.]

[The Declaration of Independence was read, and laid, unrolled, on the table by the speaker, who during the following Address, will be conceived as frequently appealing to the same.]

FELLOW CITIZENS AND FELLOW BEINGS—

THE day we are assembled to commemorate, hath been ushered in by the roar of cannon, and the roll of musketry. Such, in very deed, was the note of war and dreadful preparation it awoke for your fathers. Such, in very deed, had they to hear and to answer, as they might and as they could, when, weak in numbers, unskilled in the art of human butchery, but strong in the courage of a righteous cause, they gave the challenge to tyranny in the name of humankind; and staked life, fortune and honour on the throw. Yea! on that morn, big with the destinies of humankind, prophetic of reforms then even unimagined, of knowledge and liberty, and virtue then even unhoped for and unconceived—yea! on that morn, when freedom's first larum was rung to the world, and despotism's legions sprang to arms at the sound, then, indeed, might the fathers of our peaceful liberties, in proclaiming those truths in which we, now in part, and hereafter in fulness, may live, and move, and have our being as free-men—then, indeed I say, in uttering the words of peace, might they grasp the weapons of war; and while pronouncing the future redemption of the world from violence, injustice, and tyranny, might they array the battle, and mount the cannon, and number the children of the land, who, in the hour of need, might prove them men of war, and forsake the plough and the pruning hook, for the musket and the spear.

But wherefore now sounds the martial reveillie and the clash of steel? Where is the foe who threatens devastation to our borders, fire to our cities, slaughter to our people? Are his fleets on the waters—his armies in the field, that we wake the day as with the thunders of battle, and profane this solemn anniversary with sights and sounds, and pageants, and clamor befitting a sieged city; and awakening thoughts of violence and blood, unhallowed ambition, and more unhallowed murder?

Curse on the crimson'd plumes, the banners flouting,
The stirring clarion, the leaders shouting,
The fair caparisons, the war horse champing,
The array'd legions—pressing, rushing, tramping,
The blazon'd falchions, crests that toss afar,
The bold emprize, the spirit rousing jar,
The martial pæans, thundering acclaim,
The death of glory, and the living fame,
The sculptor's monument, the people's bays,
The historian's narrative the poet's lays—
Oh—curse on all the pageant and the show,
That veileth o'er the fiendish hell below!

Far be such pageantry from our eyes—such sounds from our ears, on this day of hope, and in this land of peace! Let the insignia of death, and the parade of military violence, bespeak the accession of European monarchs to the lawless thrones of lawless power. Let the war note and the cannon's thunder proclaim the success of titled robbers returning from the sack of cities and desolation of empires. Let them follow the steps, and celebrate the deeds, of insane and insatiate ambition. Let them surround the car of bloody conquest, where they may drown the cry of the injured, and the curse of the oppressed. Let them sound in the courts of tyranny, where they may stifle the moan of the captive, and the death-sob of the patriot martyr. Let them swell over the field of carnage where they may drown the sigh of the widow and the shriek of expiring agony. There let them sound; for there they speak the spirit of the hour, and proclaim their own work of robbery and death!

But not the chaste ear of liberty let such sounds profane, where, as in this land, she hath broken her sword to clasp the wand of peace; and waits only for knowledge to extend her dominion and fix her throne in every human breast. No! let the sound of rejoicing, in this land of promise, be heard in the glad voice of an enlightened and united people. Let it breathe from minds wise with truth, and hearts warm with benevolence. Let it rise in songs of joy from fields rich in the treasures of prosperous industry; from dwellings blessed with social happiness; from a land—from a world possessed, improved, enjoyed by a race awakened from ignorance, redeemed from error, reclaimed from vice, and healed from suffering. Yea! let the sun which riseth on this blessed morn—this festival of freedom and anniversary of human independence—be hailed by sounds betokening universal peace and universal prosperity; and welcomed by hearts proud and blessed in the

accomplishment of the gloried and the glorious declaration—
all men are free and equal.

I have said *let this so be.* Let this so be ; for this is not
yet. I am not here, as the custom is, to flatter your pride,
fellow citizens of a common country ! by recounting the deeds
of your ancestors, and applauding you for the truths they
proclaimed, and the conquests they achieved. I am not here,
fellow beings of a common race ! to feed your presumption, by
culling from the annals or humankind the brightest records of
human greatness, and teaching ye that, in wisdom, ye are
wiser than the wisest, and, in virtue, more exalted than the
best. Enough have ye heard of flattery—more than enough
of gratulation. The more honest, the more useful, but the
more ungracious and thankless task be mine to speak the
words of counsel, or, if it must be, of reproof.

The first jubilee of your nation's independence has been
celebrated and ye are advancing towards the second. Fifty-
three years have ye been in possession of the heritage won by
your fathers ; that heritage comprising national independence
and political freedom—the one guarranteeing a free theatre
of action at home; the other presenting security from all
interference from abroad.

Previous to that memorable era which converted these then
colonies into independent states, the North American continent was known to few Europeans, save the business trader,
the daring adventurer, or the political martyr. They only
whom gain allured, or persecution drove to the shores, seemed
aware of their existence. Even their imperious rulers, while
taxing the population, disputing their laws and their constitutions, were ignorant of the extent and geography of the
country, and, possibly, in common with even the better
informed portion of the English community, imagined the
colour of its population to be akin to that of the Moors, and
its language to be a corruption of Iroquois.

The resistance of America first fixed the eyes of the world
upon her. It was at first the gaze of astonishment and curiosity. But when the battle was fought, and that having
sealed her independence with her blood, she sat down to
entrench her liberty within the novel bulwark of novel institutions ; when her act of national independence had been followed by a declaration of rights, and a constitution based upon
and limited by those rights ; and when a term of years had
tried the strength of the daring experiment, she then became,

what she still is—the hope of the nations, and the terror of their oppressors. On her, from that hour, has the eye of human patriotism been fixed. The political reformer in lands the most benighted and enslaved, has seen in the existence of America, the promise of his own country's redemption ; while, in the same, the philosopher hath found a surety for the final and universal enfranchisememt of humankind.

When the European sage hath seen the old continent bowed beneath the yoke—when he hath seen its choicest sons shed their blood on the scaffold, expire in dungeons, or deplore in exile and poverty their degraded country and ruined hopes— when he hath seen the lights of knowledge quenched around him, the tide of time turned, as it were, backward in its course, and the human mind receding into the night of bygone ages— still in this wide spreading scene of desolation could his heart find comfort—still did he behold a nation, strong and established in principle, with whom was the power to roll back the clouds of ignorance, and bid the human intellect " move on!" Then, when the storm gathered darkest around him, hath he said, " Behold liberty hath followed the sun in his path, and called the new hemisphere her own ! and there shall not knowledge kindle her torch, and man, by its light, explore his own world and himself, until error, crime, and wretchedness shall disappear, and truth, in its effulgence, break upon the world ?"

Hath wisdom hoped thus of ye, free born citizens of independent republics ! Hath such, I say, been her hope ? If it have, how have ye fulfilled it ?

Oh, people of America ! weighty is your responsibility ! The destinies of mankind hang upon *your* breath. The fate of all the nations of the earth is entrusted to *your* keeping. On you devolves the task of vindicating our human nature from the slanders heaped on it by superstitious ignorance, and the libels imagined by designing ambition. With you rests the duty, for with you is the power, to disprove the blasphemies of temporal tyrants, and spiritual craftsmen. On you the whole family of humankind turns the eye of expectation. From the Hellespont to the icy sea—from the Don to Atlantic, suffering Europe hopes in your liberty, and waits for the influence of the virtue she dreams must be yours. On the shores of the ravaged Tagus, the ruined Tyber, the barbarous Tanais and Danube, the palace crowned Thames and luxurious Seine, where wealth displays its splendour, and poverty its wretch-

K

edness—there in each varied realm and distant region, does
the oft defeated patriot, and oft disappointed believer, in the
latent excellence and final enfranchisement of trampled humanity, breathe his sighs and wing his hopes to the far off
land, which, on this day, celebrates, not its own, but the
world's festival ; and renews, in the name of humankind, the
declaration of human independence.

Say, will ye disappoint these high expectations? Will ye
prove false to the cause ye have espoused? Will ye belie the
pledge of your fathers and your own ; and make of this day,
and all that it commemorates, a byword and a mockery among
all the nations of the earth?

Let me reason with you fellow beings ! for to develope your
interests, to point to your duties, to detect your negligence,
or, if such there be, to challenge your transgressions, am I
here.

High is the ground you have assumed, people of the United
States ! Pure and sublime are the principles on which you
have based your institutions. Simple and grand are those
institutions themselves. And, in proporton to the greatness
of these, is your responsibility.

Other nations, governed by the loose tide of circumstances,
or by the whim of silly monarchs and their crafty ministers,
may throw from them the folly of their national errors, or
claim but little part in their wiser actions. Not so with you,
people of these United States! You have willed yourselves
free as well as independent. You are proclaimed to the
world for a self-governing people. You have declared liberty
to be the birthright of man. You have purchased it with toil,
and blood, and suffering ; entrenched it within the peaceful
but immutable bulwarks of representative government, and
hold in your hands the power to correct its every error, and to
improve its every good.

Behold, then, every institution, every law, every action, of
your government emanating from yourselves ! Is the spirit of
the national policy enlightened—on you reflects the honour.
Are the public measures wise—to you is traced the wisdom.
Is aught done foolishly—the folly rests with your ignorance.
Is aught neglected—with your negligence lies the omission.
You may not, then, be judged in comparison with other
nations. Your own mouth must supply your sentence. Even
by those principles shall you be tried, which are set forth in
this declaration ; and to the support of which, you, even as

your fathers before you, have pledged your lives, your fortunes, and your honour.

If, then, in your constitutional code, there shall be found one article in violation of the principles herein enshrined, then is your sacred honour impeached in the eyes of the world. If, in one act of your government, at home or abroad, you shall have violated these principles, then is your sacred honour impeached in the eyes of the world. If you shall have harboured within your bosom, and sanctioned by your laws, one practice outraging these principles, then is your sacred honour impeached in the eyes of the world. If ye shall have omitted one measure necessary for the protection and practical illustration of these principles, then is your sacred honour impeached in the eyes of the world.

How stands, then, your account, my fellow-citizens? How have ye fulfilled your promise and redeemed your pledge? Can ye, on this day, when the eyes of the world are upon ye, renew your solemn appeal to all the nations of the earth, and court their scrutiny throughout your borders? Can ye, on this day, challenge the investigation of mankind, and say— " We have improved the heritage bequeathed by our fathers. We have followed the path they traced for our footsteps. We have revealed, in our practice, the excellence of those truths whose theory they proclaimed. We have exercised those rights and powers which they purchased with their blood, and gave us, in peace to enjoy, and in wisdom to improve?"

Can ye, fellow citizens, say this? Oh—would, for the sake of humankind, that ye could answer "Yea!"

Bitter are the words of reproof: nor needs it that my voice should speak them. The cry of misery hath gone up from the land ; and that cry is your condemnation.

And was it for this your fathers raised the standard of rebellion? Was it for this they braved an empire's power, and bare with ten years of war and tribulation? Was it to effect no more of good than we see around us, that they shut their unarmed ports against the navies of Britain, and set at nought the authorities of ancient days and the threats of parliaments and thrones? Was it to exchange the open tyranny of temporal kings for the more subtle dominion of spiritual hierarchs, that the American people first pledged their honour to this sacred instrument? Was it to build up the ascendancy of priests omniscient by the grace of God, that they challenged the prerogatives of monarchs omnipotent by the same? Was

K 2

it to crush down the sons and daughters of your comtry's industry under the accumulated and accumulating evils of neglect, poverty, vice, starvation, and disease. that your fathers
bought your independence with their blood, and decreed, by
this charter, your equality as citizens, and your liberty as
men ? Oh! were this noble instrument to work no more of
practical reform than it hath wrought to this hour, wiser it
were to burn it on the very spot where sages first conceived
and heroes proclaimed it. than longer to mock the ears of this
nation and the hopes of the world with the sound of truths,
man is never to realize, of blessings he is never to enjoy!
Yea! were the rights of conscience, of self-government, of
thought, and of action, as set forth in this declaration, able to
effect no more than we behold, I would tell ye to hasten to
your old state house—and there, where these bold words first
startled the world, to consign them to oblivion. I would tell
ye, I say, to let the same walls which echoed the first cry of
" Liberty and Equality " give back, ere they totter to decay,
the last hollow murmurs of a deceiving sound. I would tell
ye to end in the patriot's breast the sickness of hope long de-
cayed ; to remove from the ear of reason and the eye of philanthropy sights and sounds which should then speak only of
insults and mockery : and to leave the good and the wise, who
now stand expecting at your hands the redemption of our race,
to let go the deceiving anchor of their hope, and nerve their
minds to view with fortitude or apathy evils without remedy.
and submit to a destiny beyond the reach of circumstance to
influence, or knowledge to improve.

I pray ye to observe and well to understand that the fate of
this nation involves that of the world ; and that if man should
here fail to improve his nature and his condition, his nature
must stand demonstrated for innately depraved, his condition
for irretretrievably wretched. No argument is required to
show that, if the human character and position are capable of
improvement, it must be in the country where human exertion
is free. All must perceive that if good sense and right principles of action are to take place of prejudice and corrupt
principles of action, it is in the country whose government, in
its forms as well as its measures, may profit by the lessons of
experience and look to public opinion for its guide and its
corrector.

I have already (in the address delivered on the last anniversary of this day) developed, in full, what I conceive to con-

stitute the excellence of the national institutions, and to which
it is now only necessary to make a passing allusion.

I then observed the great beauty of American government
to be, *that the simple machinery of representation, carried
through all its parts, gives facility for its being moulded at
will to fit with the knowledge of the age; that thus, although
it should be imperfect in any or all of its parts, it bears within it a perfect principle—the principle of improvement.*
And that, therefore, we should distinguish the advantage we
possess over other nations, to be—*not that our form of
government is republican, or democratic, or federative, but
that it possesses the power of silent adaptation to the altering views of the governing and governed people; that it
may ever peacefully be changed with the changing spirit of
the age, and express the sentiments and advance the interests of each successive generation.*

This one distinguishing property of a government, purely
representative in all its parts and modes, is that, in virtue of
which, the era we now celebrate, and this charter of the rights
of humankind, may alone be made instrumental to the happiness of our race.   And so, in like manner, has it been the non-
appreciation and nonperception of this one inherent excellence
which has hitherto neutralized the effect of the American
institutions.

This, with all other errors, may be traced to that defective
instruction, which, teaching words, apart from principles as
from things, makes us ever intent on the sign instead of the
substance, the theory instead of the practice.

Because we find in this instrument the liberty and equality
of man set forth as an abstract truth, we conceive the same to
be practically secured.   Because we have established in the
constitutional code that each male adult, or nearly so, shall
have a voice in the nomination of the public officers, we conceive ourselves to be in effect a self-governing people.   And
yet to what, I pray ye, does the privilege of the elective franchise as now exercised, amount?   To *a choice of men,* and
those men found, and necessarily found, among a class whose
interests are at variance with those of the great body of the
nation.   And what are the results even of this right of choice,
partial and ineffectual as it is?   Let the history of every election declare—from that of a militia colonel to the governors of
your commonwealths; from that of a member of your city
council to the officers of your national senate, or even to the

first magistrate of the republic ! What, I ask, at this hour, are the moral results to the American people of that political right upon which rests the whole frame of their civil liberty ? What does its exercise now generate but a spirit of intrigue and ambition on the one hand—of license, violence, and corruption on the other ? What have your popular elections to office, as yet, produced, but a system of *electioneering ?*— the very word breathing of vice and venality.

How perverted your political institutions from their first intent, let your press declare ? Sold, alternately, to each party and each partizan ; ever silent as respects principles, insolently bold as respects men. Visit not this upon your editors. Let the people take it home unto themselves.

The writers for the public market write for the public taste. To teach the truths they may even distinguish, would be to offend their readers ; to investigate principles—to treat of a subject too novel to interest the attention ; to explore the actual condition of society, and seek the means for its amelioration, would be to rouse the hostility of wealth, alarm the fears of every speculating aspirant after the same, and muster in battle array every priest, every lawyer, and every politician in the land. While, on the other hand, to libel or to eulogise each pretender to public favour is to feed the credulity and curiosity of every mind unawakened to matters of real interest, and, ofttimes, to win credit for courage and patriotism (those prostituted words !) by the very efforts which are more deeply corrupting the feelings and blinding the understandings of the people at home, and bringing into contempt the character of the nation abroad.

When such are the rewards awaiting on the worse and on the better part, are we to marvel that the worse is chosen, and the better left ? When bribes are held out to slander, to intrigue, to folly, and to falsehood, are we to sit in judgment upon those who follow where they are led? So long as the people are blind to principles, will they be deceived by men. So long as they are occupied with trifles, by triflers will they be led So long as they neglect their own interests, will they press, their teachers, and their rulers, do the same.

I said that I was no there to flatter, and you will think that I have kept my word. Doubtless it were more pleasing to you, and less hazardous for me, to echo all the compliments and proud thanksgivings customary on this day, and which to utter is to ensure popularity ; to withhold, to purchase cold looks; while to replace, as I may seem to have done, the honied words of praise by those of censure, may be only to win more of that calumny which my fellow beings have already so bounteously bestowed.

Yet all this am I willing to meet, if haply, I may be instrumental in shortening the term of those errors and that apathy which now pervert your noble institutions, and neutralize the truths enshrined in this sacred heirloom of your revolution.

Your fathers proclaimed, on the day of which this is the fifty-fourth anniversary, your independence as a nation, and your equal rights as members of the human family. To secure these blessings from foreign assault and domestic attainder, you associated for the mutual defence of your lives. your property, the country you inhabit, and that form of government which appeared to present the greatest advantages and the fewest evils. The result of this association was your national constitution, together with the revision of all your state constitutions or old colonial charters: the same being always subject to future alterations, curtailments, or amendments. Within the pale of these constitutions, and in the mode specified, you decreed it should be lawful to legislate for the correction of evil and promotion of good. Of this evil and this good you declared *the people* to be the only judges; deciding, however, that, for the prevention of disorder, the opinion of the majority should stand for that of the whole body; and that the view of that majority should be carried into effect through the medium of representatives, chosen for the express object.

This system, simple in all its parts, evidently rests upon two main positions: first, that the people are enlightened judges of their own interests—or, in other words, *that they are by nature or by education, fitted to distinguish the means by which the greatest happiness may be produced to the whole population;* and secondly, *that the representatives, through whom the people legislate, shall, in all cases, faithfully carry into effect the views of the people whose attorneys they are.*

Now, unless we suppose that all human beings come into the world full grown in intellect and endowed with foreknowledge we should certainly expect to find some provision for the just training of their minds and habits in childhood, with a view to the high character they are destined in after life to

sustain as a self-governing people, and the important duties
they are then to fulfil as citizens, as parents, and as human
beings. I say we should expect the same instrument which
charges the people with the duties of government to suggest
the means by which they may be fitted to fulfil the same.
I say that common sense would lead us to expect that, before
legislation, should come instruction; even as childhood precedes
manhood, and the training of the youth decides the character
of the adult.

It does appear to me, then, that *the right of equal instruction* should have been enumerated among those human rights
which preface your constitutional codes; and that the first
act of a self governing people should have been that of
organizing a plan of rational and republican education, in
unison with the bold declaration we are called on this day to
celebrate, and which, if practically attempted at the close of
your revolutionary struggle would have rendered you, at this
hour, in fact, what you are as yet only in theory—a people
equal in rights, free in the exercise of those rights, and happy
in the result of that exercise.

But if ever we turn the eye on the past, it should be—not
idly to regret, but wisely to reform. The present is ours; the
future is before us. The power that was with your fathers is
with you. What they omitted, you, wise by their experience
and your own, may supply. If they laid the *foundation,* do
you lay the *corner* stone, of the republic. If they brake the
fetters from the limbs, do you break them from the mind. If
they won for their children the right of free action, do you
give to yours the knowledge to use it. If they declared you
equals at the birth, do you prepare the next generation to be
equals through life. Extend to your children the never dying
protection, the never slumbering care, of their country—of
the nation. Make them, in tender infancy, fellow playmates,
fellow learners, fellow labourers; so shall they, when grown
to manhood and womanhood, be, in thought, in feeling, in
affection, fellow citizens and fellow creatures.

Much labour have ye bestowed in law making; much
money have ye expended in the same. Much time, much
temper, have ye wasted in canvassing the merits and demerits
of individuals—in eulogizing and libelling, by turns, the very
men judged most worthy to fill the first office in your gift,
until foreign nations must have been in doubt whether the
people were most void of truth and decency, or their rulers

of honour and honesty. Hot hath been your indignation against vice, and fearful your vengeance against crime. Ye have given your thousands to raise jails and gibbets for punishing sinners in this world, and millions to proclaim their damnation in another. Zealous have ye been to spread your fame in foreign lands, and your faith in the farthest regions of the globe. Ye have covered the seas with your ships, and the earth with your missionaries. Ye have rested not until ye rivalled Britain in her commerce, in competitive labour, in mechanical ingenuity, in the triumph of monied wealth, and in the oppression of industry; nor will ye rest, perhaps, until ye rival her in riches and in want; in luxury, in pauperism, and in misery.

Such have been your doings, oh ye people! under the banner of independence and of equal liberty. Ye have followed the footsteps of aristocratic nations, and their character and their destiny shall be yours.

Wisdom and mercy forbid the fulfilment of the prophecy! Noble charter of the freedom of our race, do thou forbid it! As, in the hands of the past generation, thou brakest the sceptre of transatlantic oppression, so, in the hands of the present, do thou break the chains of our vice, and lighten the darkness of our ignorance! As of yore thou nervest the minds of the fathers of this people to assert their rights before the cannon's mouth, so do thou, in this day, inspire their children with wisdom yet more justly to interpret the same, and with courage to make thy truths the law of their hearts, and the rule of their lives! Not in words let thy truths live alone! Not from this parchment let us learn the equal rights of humankind! Let the spirit which breathes from this instrument animate our thoughts and our exertions! On this day be the pledge of Americans renewed! In the deep solemnity of contrition for past errors and past omissions—in the ardour of hope and generous intent for the future, may they breathe on this day a vow of '76, and earn, by their efforts, for the next generation, yet more than they received from their fathers!

By this charter, oh ye people! your destinies are placed in your own hands. By this charter ye are free to choose between liberty and slavery, knowledge and ignorance, virtue and vice, happiness and misery. Will ye choose the nobler and the better part? Prepare the only means that reason suggests and consistency demands. Add to your institutions what can alone ensure to them permanence, dignity, and utility. Add to your system of republican government one republican instruction. Then, and then alone, shall these United States be a republic, and their citizens republicans. What have been said of other nations is true of this—*to be free you have but to will it.* Legislate for the enfranchisement of the rising generation—you, who are doubly its fathers. Suspend, if needs be, all other measures; curtail all other expenditures, postpone all other improvements, until this first of all duties be fulfilled by a self-governing people!

Enough have we of churches, my friends—enough of bride-wells and jails. Enough of monuments to the dead, and prisons to the living. Enough, and more than enough, of curious inventions, time and labour-saving skill. Let us learn to enjoy the riches we possess; to distribute the wealth we accumulate; to apply to the benefit of man the works of his own genius. We hear of *internal improvement.* Let us have it; let us see it; let us feel it—*in the mind.* Let us, at least, end where we ought to have begun. Let us suspend our refinements in machinery, our canals, and our railroads, which, at the present time, under existing arrangements, only encourage monied speculation and stock-jobbing gambling, farther to crush down productive industry, and to blind the mass to the causes of their ruin. Let us suspend, I say, these labours befitting a race more advanced than ours. Let us turn to the field of human life, rank with every poisonous growth, and thicker sown, from hour to hour, with seeds of corruption! Let us turn to the study of our human condition—to the consideration of our social existence. Let us count all the evils we have there to remedy, all the obstacles to overcome, all the sorrows to alleviate, all the wrongs to redress. To this work of charity and of duty let us apply. Let us give relief to the widow, protection to the orphan, the guardianship of the state to every child in the land. Let us assist oppressed industry in the discharge of the parental duties. Let us form the morals, and advance the happiness of the nation by watching over its education. "These things ought we to do, and, *then*, not to leave the others undone." But, until these duties be accomplished—until this righteous work be achieved—until every son and daughter in this galaxy of commonwealths shall be equally provided with the means of instruction—shall be raised in the habits of healthy industry —be protected equally from the sufferings and the vice attendant on poverty and on riches—be trained as equals to understand and to exercise the rights set forth in this charter —all your laws and your provisions, your preaching and your punishments, your churches, your prisons, your partial colleges and inefficient schools, your asylums and your hospitals, your restricted commerce and protected manufactures, your canals and your railroads, your taxes and your bounties, your inventions and your improvements, multiplied without object and without end, will work no real benefit to man—will do nothing towards the alleviation of one of the weighty evils which now press on the population—will and can, tend to no other consequences than farther to vitiate the feelings, confound the understandings, deprave the habits, and render yet more disproportionate the condition of humankind.

While wealth is considered distinct from enjoyment, and enjoyment is calculated by the luxury of the few instead of the ease of the many—while art and science are applied, not to relieve the labour of industry, but to depreciate its value— while human beings count but as an appendage to the machinery they keep in motion, and the tender strength and dawning intellect of infancy are crippled by forced labour, improper diet, neglect, ill usage, and bad example, think not that canals and railroads are to advance the nation, nor that steamboats and spinning-jennies are to save the world.

The subject now adverted to I have already treated at large in the last discourse delivered in this city "on Existing Evils." But I feel its importance too deeply not to recur to it often—not to recur to it especially on this day, when the past history, present condition, and future prospects of the nation all crowd upon the mind. Conceiving, as I do, rational education to comprise the whole duty of man, to involve the principles of all law, all liberty, all virtue, and all happiness— to present the only possible cure for every vice in our existing practice, error in our opinions, and evil in our condition, I could not, on this day, speak of your national institutions without adverting to an omission which it behoves you to supply, and which, by the light emitted from this charter, you may see to frame in unison with human nature, with human liberty, and with republican equality.

Until this great oversight be rectified, the revolution we this day commemorate will be incomplete and insufficient; the " declaration " contained in this instrument will be void.

Liberty shall exist only for man when it shall reign in the

mind; equality, when it shall exist in our knowledge, in our habits, in our enjoyments; and both these righteous principles, and blessed sources of all individual security and national greatness shall only exist *in practice* when a self-governing people shall *legislate for the equal instruction, the rational education, and the national protection of youth.* The day on which this righteous resolve shall pass the senate of one commonwealth in the Union—that will be for this nation what the Fourth of July, '76, is now for the world.

May the light of knowledge so dawn upon your minds, my fellow citizens! and the spirit of freedom which erst guided your fathers on this day, so quicken your exertions, that, to us now present, it may be given to celebrate the decree which alone can work out the fulfilment of this declaration, and lead to the equal liberty and equal happiness of all human-kind.

ADDRESS III.

[Delivered at the opening of the Hall of Science, New-York, on Sunday April 26, 1829.]

THE object that assembles us here this day is the same for which through all past ages, the wise have laboured, and the good have suffered. This object it imports us well to under-stand, and steadily to keep in view. If misconceived, or if lost sight of, our efforts here will be worse than useless—they will be mischievous; in that while they fail of success, they must bring discredit on the undertaking.

The words engraved over the entrance of this building define its purpose and our object. Raised and consecrated to sectarian faith, it stands devoted this day to universal know-ledge—and we, in crossing its threshold, have to throw aside the distinctions of class; the names and feelings of sect or party; to recognise, in ourselves and each other, the single character of human beings and fellow creatures, and thus to sit down, as children of one family, in patience to inquire—in humility to learn.

What I have here suggested as our single object, may

appear too simple for some, and prove too hard for others. Oh, may it not prove beyond the power, superior to the reason, of us all!

Born and reared as we have been in a world of strife ; fed with horror even from the cradle; encouraged, alike by precept and example, to esteem ourselves wise in our own conceit; to imagine that truth lies only in the opinions we have imbibed; that to be obstinate is to be consistent; to be disputatious is to be zealous; to resent injuries is to show good courage ; to vilify our fellow creatures, to prove our own worthiness ; to reprobate sinners, to substantiate our own morality ; to laugh at the follies of others, to give evidence of our own wisdom—trained I say as we have been, to judge and to be judged in severity; provoked ofttimes by persecution to persecute, and driven by injustice to misanthropy — who among us, the best or the wisest that shall have no rebellious spirit to quell, no watch to set upon his lips, no internal censorship to execute, ere he can enter, at peace with all mankind, the courts of union, and sit down, in simplicity of heart, *a pupil in the Hall of Science!*

I would not seem to counsel where I would rather listen, nor to teach where I would rather learn ; but the views and circumstances heretofore explained, which called me forth to stem the tide of prejudice, and to enter my protest against religious controversies and sectarian hostilities, have necessarily exposed to my individual observation all the worst consequences and tendencies of the evils I have challenged. Few in these days, none in this country, have ventured more, if as much endured, for the great, and good, and solemn cause which assembles us here this day. Let me, then, so far presume as to prefer to my fellow labourers in truth's vineyard, a caution suggested at once by all that I have had occasion to observe and to experience.

There are who apprehend danger to the attempt now made towards national union, and moral and intellectual improvement, from the hostility of constituted authorities and organized bodies. Here lies not my fear. There are, also, who apprehend our failure from the popular indifference, or from the prevailing cowardice and immorality which the existing forms of society are so calculated to generate. I see no such grounds of discouragement. The spirit of inquiry is abroad ; the dawn of a brighter day is kindling in the horizon, and the eyes of *the people* are opening to its observation. I say *of the*

people ; of that large, and, happily, sounder part of the population who draw their subsistence from the sweat of the brow,
and whose industry constitutes at once the physical strength,
and the moral prop of the nation. No ! my fears look not to
the power of the few, nor to the indifference of the many.
They look not, my friends, beyond ourselves. Let the soldiers
of the van preserve at once good courage and good discipline,
and the army of the nation shall follow its lead in confidence
and security.

But what must constitute our courage that it be *good ?*
We may be bold and yet we may be weak. The brave have
been overthrown in the onset and in the breach, when the
pulses throbbed with enthusiasm, and the word was " victory or death." There is a courage better than that of
valour—it is that of wisdom; which, seizing at once on the
post to be defended, plants firm the foot, neither to retreat
from it an alarm, nor to hurry past it in zeal. And what
must supply our discipline? Self government. Firm in
principle, fixed in purpose, we must turn neither to the right
nor to the left. Wise in the choice of means, temperate in
our words, chastened in our feelings, we must pursue truth
in the path of knowledge, and, without disputing with errors,
seek to substantiate facts.

I am tempted on this to speak farther. I am tempted, at
this commencement of our labours, to give utterance to some
anxious thoughts which the importance of our enterprise,
and the circumstances which surround us, are calculated to
inspire. As I have said, I apprehend not the wrath of the
few, nor the indifference of the many. Pride or passion will
ever work their own destruction. The more strenuous the
opposition to truth, the more speedy will be its triumph.
The efforts of a hierarchy, the denunciations of orthodoxy,
or the jealousy of wealth and pretension, can do nought
against free thoughts and free speech in a country *politically
free.* Nor is it in such a country that the many can be
long indifferent to their best interests, nor deaf to those who
would stimulate to their investigation. I see the field open
before us. I see no let nor hindrance in the way of our
rapid progress and final triumph, but such as our own deficient virtue may breed, foster, and perpetuate.

The object we have in view, namely, the acquisition and
diffusion of knowledge, is so noble, so rational, and so pure,
that, in pledging ourselves to its pursuit, we may feel ele-

vated above all unworthy feelings, and not merely willing, but eager, to exchange passion for reason, and to immolate selfishness at the shrine of the public good. But enthusiasm, however ardent and pure, cannot supply the spirit which must sustain our perseverance and effect the extensive reform which we have in view. Zeal may impart energy to our first movements, but will not generate and nourish those steady motives which, by sustaining equal and healthy exertions, can alone ensure success. Anxious, as I feel assured we all are, that the spirit of inquiry now kindled in the public mind should be turned to the best account, and that our efforts in this place should be of lasting benefit to the human race, it seems advisable, that, at this opening of our labours, we well examine, until we distinctly understand, both our object, and the means by which it may be attained.

Our object is simply and singly the acquisition of knowledge, and its diffusion among our fellow creatures. My previous exertions in this city, both as a lecturer and a writer, have been devoted to the developing the nature of all knowledge, physical and moral, and to the distinguishing those first principles which have been so long and so universally obscured by the sophisms of false learning—the words, maxims, dreams, and hypothesis of man's perverted ingenuity. If the general survey of the field of knowledge, as presented in my field of public discourses and the pages of the Free Enquirer, be present to your minds, our object in this place cannot be mistaken. You will understand both what knowledge is, and how it can be acquired ; and you will understand, moreover, what investigations can be useful to man, and, consequently, suitable to be followed in this place, and what others must necessarily be useless, and, consequently, unsuitable. But, far better will you understand our object here, and distinguish between the profitable and profitless in human inquiry, when you shall have entered on the patient development of nature's phenomena, under the guidance of your various scientific instructors. . I have presented you only with an outline of the whole ; a general view of that field of varied interest and untiring beauty, through which masters of more practical experience and minute research will now undertake to lead you.

Under the wise direction of men of science, honest enough to reveal what they know, and bold enough to be silent—

(for alas! in these days of error even silence may be a crime;) bold enough, I say, to be silent where they are ignorant—under the guidance of such friends your steps cannot err, and your minds must gradually expand to the perception of all those truths most important for man to understand.

What, then, I am most anxious we should bear in mind is, *that we have all to be learners.* Ask the most experienced philosopher, whose patient mind has explored all the paths of discovered knowledge, and added new wealth to the stores of the human intellect—ask him, and he will tell you he is yet a pupil. Ask him, and he will tell you that the span of human life sufficeth not to explore the whole even of the observable wonders of nature—wondrous at least to our limited perceptions and finite existence ; while beyond the stretch of our vision, as evinced by the microscope and telescope, he will tell you that the phenomena of nature extend through the infinitely little and the infinitely great, in duration and extension, without limit as without end. Oh, who hath said that science teaches pride, when with her alone is humility! Who hath said, that to study the field of nature can generate self-conceit, when he who should know all that by human senses and faculties can be known, would only best understand that he knew, as it were, *nothing !*

An ingenuous poet hath sung :

A little learning is a dangerous thing ;"

I will not say that, nor will I say :

" Drink deep or taste not of the spring !"

but this I will say—be sure that ye mistake not between what is now *esteemed* learning, and what *is* knowledge. Drink of the right spring, and, drink little or drink much, so far as ye drink ye shall be wise. Yet this, above all things : *speculate not farther than you know.* Endeavour to curb that futile curiosioty, which, fostered by a vicious education, is ever winging the human imagination beyond what the eye hath seen, the touch examined, and the judgment compared. Let us unite on the safe and sure ground of fact and experiment, and we can never err ; yet better, we can never differ. Let us investigate within these walls what are to us all realities, and will yield to us all useful truths. The field of nature is before us to ex-

plore; the world of the human heart is with us to examine
In these lie for us all that is certain, and all that is impor-.
tant.

What matter to us by what, by whom, for how long, from
whence, to what limits of space, through what extent of time,
the vast ethereal, in which our atom globe performs its revolutions, is peopled with sentient existence. How may we decide whether genii, or demigods, or beings unnamed and unconceived, live, and breathe, and exult in life through all the
bright worlds which stud our starlit heaven? Nay, or could
we decide, how should the knowledge profit us in this our removed, but, to us, all sufficient sphere! Were our human
attainments, indeed, co-extensive with human observation,
and our human wisdom all sufficient for our human exigences,
then might there be some apology for our borrowing the ka-
leidoscope of fancy, and gazing, through it, into the moon and
beyond the stars. Were all our human duties understood and
fulfilled, all the joys of earth developed, and its woes removed,
then might those speculations be more excusable, which now
steal our attention and our sympathies from the sphere we
occupy, and the fellow creatures, whose wants, interests, joys
and sorrows should be all our own.

But how far we are from this fulness of human knowledge
and human happiness, let nature with all her unexplored phenomena—let earth with all her wrongs and all her miseries—
let our own hearts with all their bitterness—our own minds
with all their prejudices, bear witness and attest. Oh, then,
let us, in this place at least, lay aside dreaming, and apply to
observing! Not that I would presumptuously dispute, or
uselessly reason, with the dreams of any fellow creature : I
would simply lead all to distinguish between their dreams and
their knowledge, to estimate the value of the one, and the
futility of the other, and to perceive that within the horizon of
human observation we may all inquire with profit, and in
fellowship; without that horizon only with danger of error,
and with certainty of differing.

Seeing, then, the useful discoveries to be made in the world
of nature as existing without us, and the world of the human
heart as existing within us, and seeing, also, the interminable
disputes fomented by inquiry abstracted by these, let us preserve our popular meetings in this place uncontaminated and
undistracted by religious discussions or opinionative dissensions.

L

I would apply this exhortation equally to the sceptic as to the believer, and the believer as to the sceptic. Are we believers? Let us believe as we may, but let us believe peacefully, in the depths of the heart, that our belief offend not that of our neighbour. Do we see with the eye of faith? Let us see what we may, and dream what we will, but let us dream at home. In our own closets be our worship, whether of god or gods, saints, angels, prophets, or blessed virgins; but here—here, in the hall of union, sacred to peace and to knowledge, let us study that book which all can read, and, reading, none dispute—the field of nature, and the tablet of the human mind. Or, on the other hand, have we learned to doubt the lessons of books, and the laws of men, let us beware in what spirit we set forth our scepticism, lest, haply, while discarding the dogmas, we retain the dogmatism, and lend even to truth, the tone of presumption, and the spirit of error.

It follows not, that in having lost some of our credulity, we must have lost our intolerance, nor that in correcting some of our opinions, we must have changed our feelings, and amended our habits. The effects of erroneous education, and the influence of unfavourable circumstances are, more or less, with us all. As believers, we have learned censoriousness with our creed of faith; as heretics or sceptics, we have learned intolerance from persecution. Judging or Judged, inflicting or enduring, our bosoms have been filled with bitterness from our youth up; our hearts estranged from each other, and our thoughts still bent rather on proving others wrong, than on seeking the right for ourselves. It is for this cause—it is for the frailties of temper, the errors of judgment, the harshness of feeling existing in us all, that I would deprecate in this place all discussions of speculative or abstract opinion. Were we all reasonable, gentle, indulgent, to discuss any or all subjects, real or imaginary, might be useful, or, at the least, amusing; but while we are all irrational, perverse, ill-natured, violent, prone to misinterpret, to offend in our manner, to irritate in our language, to wound and to be wounded, to give and to receive alarm, to judge ourselves in pride, and others with contempt—while we are as we are, and as all we see, or hear, or experience, in an ill-regulated state of society, combines to keep us, we are unfit to grapple with each other's thoughts—ill prepared to elicit truth by the shock of opinions in the subtle field of argument.

I mean not altogether to condemn religious discussions while the world is overrun with conflicting religious superstitions ; but, methinks, in our popular meetings, I would condemn them here. We must bear in mind, that we come together in this place as members of a family long divided and estranged by feuds and strifes; that we see in each other wanderers from every school of faith—it may be Jews, Christians, deists, materialists, with every variety of sect and class existing within the pale of each. Surely, then, prudence, if no higher virtue, demands that we set a watch upon our lips, lest, happly, we offend where it is our object to conciliate, and divide where we are assembled to unite.

Permit me here to reiterate an observation which I have already had frequent occasion to prefer, that the only sure way to correct erroneous opinions is to present facts to the mind. The more we know, the less, in the popular sense of the word, do we *believe*. The better we understand the phenomena of nature in the visible and tangible world without us, and in the mental, moral, and physical world within us, the more just and perspicuous must be all our ideas.

It is possible, indeed, to subvert, by process of reasoning, many human superstitions; and to confute by the *ad absur-dum* many books, maxims, and statutes honoured as wise, or worshipped as divine. But let us remember, that to expose errors is not necessarily to distinguish truths ; a train of deductive logic may suffice for the one, but dispassionate observation and accurate knowledge can alone suffice for the other.

I know that, up to this hour, the least safe and the least effectual method of disengaging the popular mind of error has been the one employed. This has been, perhaps, the necessary result of the system of religious teaching so long prevalent ; the nature of the evil suggesting that of the remedy, and the virulence of the clergy, struggling, at one and the same time, for the profits and tenets of their craft, provoking, perhaps, an excusable, but certainly an objectionable, hoslility on the part of their opponents. While the advocates of mental darkness found their strength in teaching religious opinions, the friends to mental enfranchisement might naturally be tempted to seek theirs in teaching the opposite. But, as I have already attempted to show, in my introductory discourses to the people of this city, opinions, whether true or false, are no proper subject for teaching at all. We have each of us to form our own, and we *must* each of us form our own,

L 2

if we would really understand *what our opinions are*—know their foundation, and perceive their practical consequences. All that a judicious instructor will attempt is to present to the mind, in suitable train and order, such evidence as is supplied by nature herself—in other words, to fertilize the intellect with knowledge, and to leave it to draw, on all subjects, its own free, fair, and unbiassed conclusions.

The practice, but too generally followed up to this hour, of promulgating laws, establishing creeds, laying down maxims, and *teaching opinions*, has tended to affect our species with a mental paralysis.

Accustomed to receive our knowledge, so called, from the *ipse dixit* of books, instead of seeking it ourselves in the bosom of nature and the occurences passing around us, and, again to receive our opinions from the nurse, the schoolmaster, or the priest, we but too often, nay, but too universally, live and die without exercising more of our faculties than our memory and our imagination—closing our eyes upon this beautiful world, and resigning our human existence, ignorant alike of the treasures so thickly strewed in the one, and the powers inherent in the other. So dead, or, rather, so unawakened within us, are the nobler faculties of observation and judgment, that, even if aroused for a moment to doubt the authorities before which we were trained in our infancy to bow our reason, we still shrink from the labour of being an authority to ourselves, and, at one and the same moment that we turn from the priest, have recourse to the philosopher—willing to see with his eyes, to hear with his ears, and to think with his thoughts, so that we may but escape the labour of exercising our own. Like the vain and impatient tyrant of antiquity, we must still ask of our instructor, not a royal road to the truths of geometry alone, but to all truths in matter or in mind. We would know all things without examining any thing, and, above all, little curious of the knowledge which is useful and attainable, we must ever crave that which neither concerns us nor has any existence for us.

Truly, if we consider the state of our own minds—our willingness, nay, our very anxiety to be bitted, and bridled, and led through any of error's labrynths, rather than to seek for ourselves the paths of truth—truly, I say, considering our own indolence and our own gullibility, we have small reason to exclaim against the presumption of priests or the dishonesty of teachers. Methinks we should rather bless their moderation

for cheating us so little in proportion to our credulity, and
riding as so gently if compared with our slavishness! The
marvel is, (permit me the freedom,) not that we should encounter much knavery, but that we should meet with some
honesty. The marvel is, that any should honour truth so
much and love man so well, as to attempt the enlightening of
ignorance or the correcting of error, without either tiring of
the task or betraying the cause.

Easy were that task and rapidly triumphant that cause,
could we understand that correct opinions may be found only
through knowledge, and that the task of the instructor is only
to show us facts, and thus to lead us to first principles. But,
so accustomed are we to be crammed with opinions and dictated to in belief, that the faithful guide who may refuse to
feed our diseased appetite may hardly win our ears, or command our sickly attention. Would he point to those interesting phenomena to which our eyes are now, as it were,
hermetically sealed, he is met by the question—*what god he
worships.* Is it explained to us that cause and effect are
words, either without meaning, or expressive simply of the
train of occurrences and succession of changes ever taking
place around or within us, we ask of our teacher, *if he believes
in a first cause.* Does a moralist instigate us to investigate
the numerous ills which afflict our existence, and, with a view
to the remedy of these, to study the phisiology of our own
bodies, the operations of our own minds, and then to distinguish what in human practice is in violation and what in
unison with the laws of our being, he is interrupted by inquiries as to his belief *in the distinct existence of a soul and its
future immortality in another world.* The disappointed instructor in vain interrupts the train of his observations to
explain, that, as his knowledge is necessarily bounded by the
horizon of his observation, so his instruction can extend no
farther than his knowledge; and that when he shall have
communicated all the facts gleaned in his studies, it will rest
with his pupils to draw such conclusions as those facts may
generate. Instead of appreciating the respect thus paid to
human truth and human liberty, his hearers, accustomed by
long habit to submit their reasons to whomsoever will take
the trouble to ride them, find perchance offence in that he
will not feed their curiosity by tampering with their credulity,
nor spare them the necessary labour of mastering the sciences,
and studying human life in conjunction with the human

frame, in order that they may think on all subjcts for themselves.

But let the friends of man be of good courage in a good
cause. Let them not faint with weariness under the heed-
lessness of folly, the obstinacy of error, nor the seeming ingrati-
tude of ignorance. Above all, let them not swerve from the
strait and clear path in which it must be their aim to lead the
erring and warring family of humankind. Let them be true
to themselves as children of science—true to their fellow
creatures as the simple expounders of nature, and by slow
degrees, the ears of men shall be won, and their minds com-
posed to reflection.

I am aware of the common persuasion that science regards
only what are called scientific men—which means, in plain
language, that *knowledge is only good to be made a trade of.*
It seems in the order of things, that the surgeon should
understand the structure of our frame, in order that he may
repair it if injured; that the physician should study its phisiology and pathology, in order to heal it if diseased. But it
strikes us not, that did we ourselves possess the same knowledge, we might oft prevent both the injury and the disease,
or apply, ourselves, the remedy. It seems natural that the
mechanician should study mechanics, the pharmacian chemistry, the lawyer law, the priest religion; not perceiving that,
while each part and parcel of human learning remains confined
to its ostensible professors, the public at large has no means of
estimating its real value, nor the possessor himself of understanding all its bearings and relations, distinguishing its truths,
or detecting its fallacies. Not seeing, also, that, in this
manner, every facility is afforded to the crafty and superficial
to palm upon society deficiency for skill, or error for truth.
Not seeing, moreover, that all the real sciences are so related
and conjoined, that no individual can thoroughly understand
any one without some general acquaintance with all. Not
perceiving, in fine, that it is in the absence of this general
acquaintance that false knowledge, pretended science, erroneous institutions, unwise expenditures, absurd customs, and
every species of fraud and folly obtain among men, and are
handed down from parent to child, like the heirlooms of
aristocracy in feudal Europe.

But I am aware, also, that the word science is asssociated
in the popular mind with mental fatigue, abstract study, and
scholastic application. True it is, that, according to the

method of instruction now usually followed, all these charges may be brought, with more or less truth, against every useful, no less than every ornamental acquirement. Yet, I think, those who have attended the opening classes already held in this building, under all the disadvantages of deficient accommodation and imperfect arrangement, will decline to admit, that the acquisition and imparting of knowledge is not necessarily the dry, abstruse, and uninteresting occupation that the perverted ingenuity of our ancestors had contrived to make it. I am tempted here to borrow the words of a teacher, whose lucid genius would reflect honour on the country which gave him birth, could genius belong to any country, which more truly belongs to the world. " Philosophy," says Alexander B. Johnson in his lectures on language, as delivered in Utica, New-York, "philosophy is not necessarily the frowning, sluggish divinity that her ministers have injudiciously represented. Her dress may be splendid, her decorations brilliant; the clearest light should always illuminate her throne, and disputation be banished from her presence."

Be it our object, then, to disenrobe philosophy of the cumbrous disguise with which human error hath veiled her features, and to present her in all her native loveliness—heightened, polished and enhanced by all the glow and the grace which judicious genius may know to impart; but never distorted by the whimsical and meretricious ornaments of depraved taste or perverted ingenuity. Be it our object to discover truths where alone they are to be found, in the bosom of nature ; and let us understand, that without a perception of these truths— that is, without a general view of the whole range of the sciences — we can neither judge ourselves nor our fellow creatures, possess any opinion, nor pursue any practice, in full certainty of its justice towards others and its utility to ourselves.

To obtain and impart this general view of the whole field of human knowledge, is the object of this institution. Whenever, therefore, this building shall be occupied by a teacher, nominated by the trustees as a popular instructor, it would appear to me desirable that this subject should be invariably one of explanation, not of disputation — one whose text shall be chosen within the pale of knowledge, not sought in the limbo of opinions.

Whenever this building shall not be occupied for the popular meetings under the direction of the trustees, it will be open for the use of any respectable teacher, be his subject what it may. Orthodoxy itself, if the day should ever come (which good sense and good feeling avert) that it should be driven forth as have been the advocates of truth, from house to house, until every door is shut against them—let orthodoxy itself here find a refuge, and win, if it can, the ears and hearts of men by the threats and denunciations of its gospel.

For objecting to religion, either as a topic of discussion or subject of instruction in our popular meetings, I would prefer two reasons : first, that religion appertains not to the table of human knowledge ; and secondly, that we see it every where give rise to interminable disputes and all varieties of bad feeling.

For objecting to party politics, I should prefer the same reasons. They have nothing to do with knowledge, and every thing to do with quarrelling.

Opinions apart from facts, and men apart from principles, may assist vanity to a field of display, ambition to one of power or profit, and passion to one of contention, but can never supply matter of interest to a people simply and honestly desirous of improvement, and aiming at union. We cannot enter the hall of science to learn nor to teach Christianity, nor Judaism, nor Islamism, nor paganism, nor deism, nor material- ism ; we can enter it only to study the world we live in, to study ourselves as inhabitants of that world, and to form our opinions in conformity with the results of our studies.

I have said—*to study ourselves.* Oh, my fellow-beings, what a study is here ! What a field of discovery—what a world unexplored is that of our own being ? What truths yet unperceived, what duties unexercised, what faculties un- improved, what delights unenjoyed, are in the nature— the neglected, the slandered, the perverted, the outraged nature of man ?

Let not bold inquiry apprehend that the field of human knowledge is confined in its horizon, and uninteresting in its details. While every path is rich with treasures and rich with novelty, there is one—and that the noblest and the fairest —on which the restless mind of man hath barely thrown a glance.

The master science—the centre path and fairest avenue in the field of knowledge, and from which and into which all others, if rightly followed, would be found to branch and con- verge—*the science of human life* remains to this hour in its

infancy. We have dived into the secrets of external nature—
we have pierced the blue ether and tracked the courses and
revolutions of its planets, its systems, its comets, and its universe of suns ; we have laid bare the bowels of the earth, disclosed their hidden treasures, and brought to light the past
phenomena of primeval worlds ; we have passed around our
globe and explored its realms and climates through the scorch-
ing tropics to the icy barrier of the poles ; we have torn the
lightening from the clouds, and jewels from the depths of the
ocean ; we have bowed the elements to our will, and, appro-
priating and guiding their strength, have achieved more than
the fabled exploits of demigods, or the miracles of prophets
and saints—we have, in truth, in ingenuity proved ourselves
magicians, in power all but gods ; yet is our knowledge only
ignorance, and our wisdom that of babes, seeing that while
exploring the universe we have left unexplored the human
heart, and while mastering the earth we have still to master
ourselves.

Oh ! let us not fear, that within the atmosphere of our own
world, in the powers and wants of our own nature, and in the
woes of human life, as originating in human error, that we may
not find a field of inquiry more than sufficient to fill our time,
enchain our thoughts, and call into action every latent faculty
and feeling of our nature.

Let, then, morals, or *the science of human life,* assume,
among a people boasting themselves free, (and free, rightly
interpreted, would mean *rational,*) the place of religion. Let
us, instead of speculating and disputing where we can discover nothing, observe and inquire where we can discover
every thing.

Surely it befits a people acknowledging political liberty, to
investigate the meaning of the word, and the power involved
in the principle. Surely it concerns a people claiming equal
rights to examine how they may exert those rights with a
view to equal benefit. What has been done towards this, let
the state of society attest. How far we have studied human
life as a science, let our human condition bear witness. How
far the people of this land have improved their republican institutions, or reduced to practice the declaration of '76, let the
state of society declare. We speak of equality, and we are
divided into classes; of self-goverment, and we fit not ourselves to govern. We hear of law and legislation, and the mass
of the people understand not the one, and take no interest in
the other. We complain of existing evils, and seek neither

their source nor their remedy; we see pauperism on the increase, and vice travelling in her footsteps, and we ask only for more jails and larger poorhouses.

Say, have we suggested here no subjects of interesting inquiry and profitable investigation? Should a self-governing people not understand the nature and object of government? Should they charter representatives to make statutes in the dark: and, leaving lawyers to interpret the laws which lawyers have made, rest satisfied to obey the reading of which we see not the justice? Should they permit taxation and encourage contributions, without directing the stream of their subtracted wealth into channels of national utility? Should they profess equal representation, and possess no equal instruction? Or, not possessing equal instruction, should they profess equal rights.

All these, and more questions, it behoves us to ask and answer. Every contradiction and deficiency in our institutions it concerns us to discover, and discovering, to supply or to remedy. Here may the good work begin. Here may we commence the work of reform by fitting ourselves to be reformers. Here, studying our common nature as human beings, our common interests as fellow citizens, may we present to a republican people a first example of republican union and republican inquiry. Here, too, let our efforts but be sustained, and we may present a first sample of that republican instruction whose dawn shall bring hope to the nation, and in whose fulness shall be salvation.

Far off may be the day of universal peace and universal knowledge; but every effort made, and every word spoken, approaches us to its dawn. And even now see we not omens of that dawn? Feel we not something stirring in the air? Hear we not, from time to time, some faint but spirit-stirring sounds prophetic of the light, and the life, and the animation which are to come? See we not ears opening? Perceive we not understandings awakening? Is not the spirit of inquiry abroad, and shall not the truths which would now startle the ear, ere long sink into the heart? All things may we hope for man, should our efforts in this place be successful. Let us water the seed we have planted, and from it shall spring a tree whose branches will shadow the land. Let us be true to the cause we have espoused, and it shall conquer the world. Let us preserve union and pursue truth, distinct from class or sect, or opinionative association, and yearly, monthly, daily shall we wax in strength, and our opponents grow fewer and weaker. There is no backsliding in knowledge. The human mind cannot unlearn facts, nor forget first principles. The reason, once cleared of prejudice by means of science, can never re-enter within the fogs of error. She will not experience seasons of darkness, doubts, and misgivings ; require the stirring calls of supernatural grace, or the frenzied fits and hysteria of miraculous revivals. Her operations are silent, peaceful, certain, ever enduring, ever gathering in light, in strength, in security. Let us, then, gather under her peaceful standard, and present a point of union to which gradually all of the present generation, not absolutely lost to reason and common sense, and, yet more especially, all the young and the ingenuous, may gather, until the nation, collected in her might, prepares, through enlightened legislature, for the training together as one family, all the children of the land in national or state institutions.

Then, in that day, shall we see equality ! Then, in that day, shall we possess liberty—beyond the fear of loss, beyond the possibility of assault ! Then shall we dwell in a free country ! Then shall a free and virtuous, a self governing and self-respecting people ; for then shall we be an enlightened people.

There is no halfway in these matters. There is no liberty for any until there is liberty for all. There is no surety for liberty but only in equality. And let us remember, that there is no equality but what has its seat in the mind and feeling. All—all is there —virtue, honour, truth, law, liberty and knowledge ! Build up these in the human breast, and we shall see the human beings walk uprightly.

Your institutions may declare equality of rights, but we shall never possess those rights until you have *national* schools. Your legislators may enact prohibitory laws and laws offensive and defensive, protective or invasive, it matters little which ; our liberties will never be secure, for they will never be understood, until you have *national* schools. Your spiritual teachers may preach damnation and salvation, henceforward through all the eternity of existence, and we shall never be wise nor happy, peaceful nor charitable, useful in our generation, nor useful through our descendants, to all generations, until ye open the flood-gates of knowledge, and let her pure waters fertilize all the land.

As preparatory, then, to greater measures, and prophetic of extensive reform, our meeting in this place, on this day and for our proposed object, may mark an era in the moral history of the republic. The greatest events have grown out of the smallest; the most important reforms have been generated by fewer individuals, than now fill these walls and affected too in countries less free to thought, to speech, and to action, than this favoured land. Here all is possible to truth if sustained by perseverance. In revolutionized America she has not to contend with the bayonet, nor to encounter the scaffold and the dungeon. The battle of blood is here happily fought, and the sword of freedom sheathed, as we trust, for ever. Yet great is the victory she hath yet to achieve. It is over the tyranny of ignorance, and the slavery of mind. Noble be her weapons, and spotless as her cause! let her seek them at the hand of knowledge, and wield them in the spirit of peace, of charity, and of love to man.

[The following odes, written by F. W. for the occasion, were sung: the first previous to the commencement of the address, the second at its close.]

ODE I.

Long have the nations slept: hark to that sound!
The sleep is ended, and the world awakes:
Man riseth in his strength and looks around,
While on his sight the dawn of reason breaks.

Lo! Knowledge draws the curtain from his mind;
Quells Fancy's visions, and his spirit tames,
Deep in his breast that law to seek and find,
Which kings would write in blood, and priests in flames.

Shout, Earth! the creature man, till now the foe
Of thee, and all who tread thy parent breast,
Henceforth shall learn himself and thee to know,
And in that knowledge shall be wise and blest.

ODE II.

Oh, sons of men! throw round your eyes
Upon the earth, the seas, the skies!
Say doth not all, to every sense,
Show beauty and magnificence?

See hill and vale with verdure spread !
Behold the mountain lift his head,
In stature, strength, and power sublime,
Unscathed by storm, untouched by time !

And see the flower which gems the sward !
List to the pipe of evening bird—
The streams, the winds, the balmy breeze
Making soft music with the trees.

And see the glories of the night !
The deep blue vault with stars of light,
The silver clouds, the odorous air—
All soft, and still, and sweet, and fair ?

And oh ! that hour of matin prime,
The cool, the fresh, the joyous time,
When. Sol, as if refreshed by sleep,
Springs blazing from the kindled deep.

Then mark how nature with delight
Exults and kindles at the sight ;
Earth, ocean, air—above, around,
All full of life, and stir, and sound !

Yes ! all unto the outward sense
Shows beauty and magnificence ;
All fair—unless that world we scan,
That *moral* world, as made by man

To all earth's blessings deaf and blind,
Lost to himself and to his kind,
With mad presumption, lo ! he tries
To pierce the ether of the skies.

His fancy wing'd to worlds unknown,
He scorns the treasures of his own ;
By fears of hell and hopes of heaven,
His noble mind to madness driven !

Oh ! first of all the tribes of earth,
Wake to a knowledge of thy worth !
Then mark the ills of human life,
And heal its woes, and quench its strife

Victim and tyrant thou, oh man !
Thy world, thyself, thy fellows scan,
Nor forward cast an anxious eye,
Who knows to live, shall know to die.

REPLY

TO THE

TRADUCERS OF THE FRENCH REFORMERS

OF THE YEAR 1789,

As given by Frances Wright, in the Park Theatre, New-York, January 31st, 1829, at the close of her discourse on Religion.

[Among the many artifices devised by the clergy of New-York, during the first and second delivery of these discourses, was the circulation of inflammatory playcards and pamphlets, in which the object of the lecturer was represented to be nothing short of a universal insurrection of the people against, and massacre of, themselves. The flying missiles of the tract house, were backed by the heavier artillery of the daily papers ; when, upon the night of the meeting held in Tammany Hall, in reprobation of the memorials presented to congress for the interruption of the Sunday mails, an article appeared in the Evening Post, which occasioned the following reply. It was first pronounced at the close of the third lecture, and repeated on the night of the fourth, for the reason explained by the lecturer.]

THE subject which has engaged our attention this evening, will permit me, without irrelevancy, to repeat the observations with which I concluded my discourse of Saturday. I am influenced to this repetition, by the knowledge, that many were prevented on that occasion from attendance, by the public duty which they were then summoned to fulfil, and the style and manner of whose fulfilment presents another evidence of the stirring spirit which is abroad, and the radical reform in opinion, as in practice, now in preparation for this brightest portion of the civilized world. I am tempted to this repetition also, by all the crowd of solemn and sacred recollections, which the circumstance that elicited my observations of Satuday had outraged in my bosom ; and which, allied as I have been in thought and feeling with the surviving veterans of the French revolution, and with the martyred and exiled partiots of Europe's latter years, who drank their inspiration from the heroes of '89, challenges in me, from outraged friendship, no less than from outraged truth, a reply as public and as bold as hath been the slander. With the view of rendering that reply more public, I shall here repeat it, and farther publish it in the columns of the Free Enquirer.

True it is, that the attack against human liberty, and its advocates, which challenged my notice, stands not singly and alone ; it forms only an item in the long tissue of falsehoods and misrepresentations with which the annals of human improvement have been sedulously darkened and confounded.

Let us listen to sermon, peruse religious tract, or religious essay, yea, or political journal under orthodoxy influence, or clerical dictation, what find we but exhortations to passive obedience ? laudatory apostrophes to thrones, dominations, and powers ? insidious reflections, or open denunciations against inquiry, under the name of infidelity ; against honest opinion, under the name of heresy; against self-respecting virtue, under the name of vice ; against resistance to oppression, under the name of sedition ; and against revolution, under the name of rebellion ? But I shall ask ye, for the moment, to look no farther than the editorial columns of the Evening Post, of Thursday last, in which, setting aside the momentary object, and consequent personal allusions of the writer, we find him openly advocating feudal despotism, and classing political revolutions among the crimes most inimical to man and odious to God.

This spiritual oracle presents the citizens of New-York with a quotation from the speeches of Edmund Burke, made *after that statesman had sold himself for place and pension to the throne he had once so boldly defied.* In these quotations we are presented with the foulest slanders against noble deeds and noble men ever pronounced by traitor or slave!

Know the citizens of New-York, who fathered the French revolution of '89, thus upheld in their daily journals to execration and opprobrium? The virtuous, the venerable, the venerated Lafayette. Know they the principles then proclaimed, and to which a Baillie, a La Rochefoucauld, a Condorcet, a Madame Roland, set the seal of their blood? They were the same signed by a Franklin, an Adams, a Jefferson, and all the worthies of '76. They were the same to which the people of this land stand pledged in life, property and honour. And while the fallen, the sold, the misguiding and misguided Burke, was thus confounding times and dates, blaspheming glorious names and more glorious eras, perverting words and perplexing principles, were the sages and heroes of '89, the virtuous men, and high-minded women, who had reared in Europe the standard of civil liberty and mental emancipation, expiring in sublime philosophy on the scaffolds of the *religious*—ay! of the *religious* Robespierre !

I have thus again condescended upon the pages of this journal, with a view to the exposure of the literary and religious fraud, now carried on under cover of the popular ignorance, through every vehicle of popular instruction. Not a fact but is misinterpreted—not a name but is slandered—not a system, not a principle, not a book, page, word, but is travested, tortured, perplexed, and belied, to serve the purposes of clerical ambition, and support a system of error and fraud, as inimical to the interest of the many, as it is abetting and flattering to the pretensions of the few.

And now, I will ask, how that very large portion of the community, who glean their only information respecting past or present events, from newspapers, magazines, tracts, and pamphlets, all more or less under the similar influence with the Evening Post, are to judge rightly respecting things or respecting men. I have now in my hand, a bill, or tract, I know not how the flying paper should be designated, which was distributed, among many others, to the citizens who attended the meeting at Tammany Hall, on Saturday evening. In this we find a similar confusion of times and circumstances, causes and effects, as that observed upon in the Evening Post. Here, again, all the horrors acted in France, subsequent to the bright dawn of the revolution, by an ignorant populace, excited to frenzy by the subtle emissaries of the British ministry, and by the hired incendiaries of a discomfitted court, aristocracy, and priesthood, are presented to the uninformed reader, as the work of philosophers and political reformers.

I shall hereafter take occasion to elucidate in the pages of the Free Enquirer, some of the leading events and characters of the French revolution; when it will be seen that the virtuous supporters of order, peace, brotherly union, and brotherly love, were the patriots and philosophers who, having raised the standard of equal liberty, died in its defence; while the ignorant and brutal Robespierre was signing their death-warrants in his chamber, and decreeing in his legislative hall, by act of assembly, *the existence of a God, and consecrating a day for his espcial worship.*

And how shall the people judge between what is and what is not, until knowledge shall be present to the mind? And how shall knowledge be present to the mind, so long as faith is made the only subject of instruction. Shall, then, the object for which we are met in this place, be defeated or deferred? Shall knowledge never own a shrine, nor truth a temple? Will a free people never pronounce the little words, LET US INQUIRE; the modest and national words, LET US LEARN?

ANALYTICAL TABLE OF CONTENTS.

Introductory Address to the Course, as Delivered for the Second Time in New-York. Observations on the violent spirit betrayed by the clergy and the press under their control. Persecution the reward of reformers in all ages. Determination of the lecturer to persevere in her under-taking. Appeal from the misrepresentations of designing individuals to the good sense of the audience, and pledge given by the lecturer to explain, in due order, her views on all subjects connected with the well-being of humankind.

LECTURE I.

On the Nature of Knowledge. Variety of opinions among men, throughout the world, and in our own country. Question started as to what constitutes truth. Conceived difficulty and real facility of its solution. Nature of evidence. True evidence to be sought in accurate know-ledge. Improvement the distinguishing principle in man. In it a surety presented for the excellence and happiness of the race. Desire of advancing in knowledge; universality and vagueness of the same. Erroneous ideas respecting the nature of knowledge. Inquiry into its real nature. Mode of its acquisition. Simplicity of all true ideas. Words the signs of things. How mistaken for the things themselves. Importance of taking aright the first step in knowledge. Confused state of the youthful mind under existing modes of instruction. Effects of college education up to the present time. Unassisted observation better than false learning. Minute examination into existing modes of instruction deferred. Chief position to be established in the present discourse. Acquaintance with an object, how obtained. Difference between knowledge and belief. Examples explanatory of the distinc-tion. Review of the field of knowledge. Divisions of the same. Be-lief how confounded with knowledge in the lessons of teachers. Effects of this on the mind of the scholar. Importance to the rising genera-tion of discovering and adopting a rational method of instruction. Effects to be anticipated from the same on the infant and adult mind. Importance to the present generation, of free and fearless inquiry. Erroneous conceptions respecting the nature of knowledge occasion the fear with which it is often regarded. Fearlessness and composure of mind necessary for its acquisition. These seldom possessed. Alarm occasioned by inquiry. Remarks on the place assumed by the lecturer

M

and the motives which influence her. General incapacity of public
teachers, and causes of the same. The peculiar dependence of the
clergy, and their consequent inability to probe the vices of the age.
Instance adduced from their conduct in the slave states, as contrasted
with their conduct in the free states. Their universal opposition to
science and all the practical reforms attendant upon its progress. Slavery of the press and all the learned professions. Importance to the
human race, that individuals independent of patronage and party,
should undertake the guidance of the human mind. Qualifications necessary in such individuals. Recapitulation of the topics embraced in
the discourse. Concluding remarks to the female part of the audience.
Peculiar influence exerted to prolong the ignorance of the female sex.
Appeal to the male sex to consider the indirect effects of this ignorance
on their own condition.

LECTURE II.

Of Free Inquiry. A just education possible only for the next generation ;
accurate and dispassionate investigation in the power of the present.
Selfishness betrayed by individuals in their pursuit of knowledge. Inconsistency of this selfishness with American institutions. Equal rights
of all to the equal development and exercise of the judgment. Equal
or greater importance of the same to youth than to age, and to women
than to men. Influence exercised by women. Mutual dependence of
the two sexes, and of all human beings one upon the other. The real
interests of all one and the same. Impossibility of discovering these
interests unless all be engaged in their investigation. Equality of instruction necessary to equality of rights. Absence of that equality, the
source of all the false influences which rule society in public and private. Misconceptions respecting the meaning of the word equality
and explanations on the same. Examinations into the nature of liberty.
How the same is violated. Instance adduced from the government of
children. Duties of the parent and rights of the child exhibited The human race more especially interested in the enfranchisement of the female
mind. Inconsistency of the arguments commonly presented against the
personal independence and intellectual cultivation of women. No sex
in knowledge, and no mystery in truth. Mystifications in science generated by false learning, professional dishonesty, and competition. To
simplify knowledge in all its branches and applications free inquiry
indispensable. Past and present effects of free inquiry on the condition
of man. Man always in a progressive state Remarkable epochs in
his progress. The greatest yet to come. Inquiry challenged—by
whom. Problem to be settled by inquiry at the present time. Summary of the topics embraced in the discourse.

LECTURE III.

the More Important Divisions and Essential Parts of Knowledge. First
great division. Relation in which we stand to all that surrounds us.
Identity of the simple elements of things ; their duration and varying
appearance, as decided by position. Order of nature's phenomena, and
our connection with the same. If rightly explained to the young mind,
advance in knowledge rapid and pleasant. How different at the present
time. Simplicity of the table of just knowledge. Actual impossibility
of developing the same without a reference to existing errors. Apology
for the necessity of employing unmeaning words, and discussing imma-
ginary subjects. Subdivisions of the two first divisions of knowledge.

Importance of those embraced under the first head. Enumeration of the subjects of leading importance found under the second. All easy of attainment. Why. Nevertheless rendered difficult. Difficulties lessened by the labours of enlightened individuals. Important step now made. Much knowledge necessary previous to an examination of our opinions. What knowledge in particular. Importance of acquiring the same. Order in which it should be acquired. Time for its acquisition ample. Time and money how wasted at present. Important subject for the exercise of free inquiry. Leisure hours and leisure day how employed; buildings, why raised, and teachers salaried. Apology to the audience for risking the wounding of their feelings. Reference to the influence of the clergy. Necessity of exposing their incapacity. Hypocrisy engendered by the habits of existing society. This more or less experienced by every one; in the highest degree by the clergy. Peculiarity of their situation. Instance of honesty in one of that body. Consequences of the same. Fault less in individuals than in their situation. Motives which induce the lecturer to probe the popular prejudices. Possibility of knowledge by faith questoned. Its impossibility exhibited, and its inutility under the supposition of its possibility. Propriety of hiring teachers to teach impossibilities questioned. Inapplicability of all spiritual lessons to human life and human beings. Lecturer deprecates the idea of questioning the opinions of her hearers or dictating others. Exhorts to examination and inquiry. Spiritual teachers warn against the same. Their counsels suspicious. Questions for them suggested to their hearers. Encouragement to examine without fear, and to exert each his own judgment. Claim of the clergy as moral teachers considered. Disproved. Appeal to their followers to exchange spiritual dreamers for experimental philosophers; churches for halls of science; to calculate expenses and examine effects of existing religious system; to compare value with cost, and strike balance. Importance of such examination. Twenty millions expended to make us foolish. If rightly expended, the effects on the population. Inefficacy of preaching against vice. Real cure for the same. This never supplied by the clergy. Their knowledge that of things unseen. Their virtue based on depravity. Theory unworthy of freemen. Baleful effects of the same. Vindication of human nature. Man's noble energies how evinced. Appeal to Americans to evince them farther. To improve their liberty by means of knowledge, and to seek knowledge in the world they occupy. Exhortations to the study of nature. To rely on the powers of the human understanding. To examine each for himself, and to question the infallibility both of books and teachers. Advantages of material science.—Truths exhibited when asserted. Examples. Prevalent notion that some truths exist apart from our physical sensations. Falsity of the notion exposed. Exhortation to weigh the words of the lecturer; to go to church and to weigh the words of the clergy. Warmth of the lecturer, and wherefore. Invitations to associate for the acquisition of sound knowledge, and to raise a popular edifice for popular assemblies. Proposal for a pattern school of industry for children, attached to a hall of science for adults. Advantages from the same, equal for the poor and the rich. Common nature, wants, and interests, of all human kind. Exhortations to unite in the courts of knowledge. To exchange declaimers for instructors, wise guides for ignorant threateners, and consistent science for inconsistent faiths. Summary of the topics embraced in the three first lectures, and subject of the next set forth.

LECTURE IV.

Of Religion. Its engrossing character. Lecturer's desire not to wound the feelings, or arouse the prejudices. Reasons for approaching the subject. Knowledge obtained by the senses. Erroneous modes of teaching science. Ancient Greeks false logicians, because ignorant of physical science. Grecian logic still retained. Aristotle. Pestalozzi. Enemies of human improvement more quick sighted than its friends. Rational education unfavourable to loyalty and credulity. Definition of knowledge. Is religion a science? Its cost. Are its truths apparent. Where shall it be classed. Knowledge not human of slippery foundation. What is religion. Revelation by special favour. Exhortation to leave things unseen for knowledge. Lecturer's creed. Turning churches into halls of science. Splitting of sects. Lecturer ignorant of unearthly phenomena. Jesus's mode of prayer recommended to the pious. Deprecation of intention to wound. Test of books and teachers.

LECTURE V.

Morals. Necessity of clearing the threshhold of knowledge. Religion excluded as unreal and furnishing no just rule of life. If there be a true religion, who has it? If religion deceive, what rule shall guide us? The rule of morals. Little progress in the science of morals since the early days of Greece and Rome. Modern morals based on religion. Definition of morals. A simple rule. Definition of religion. Religion and morals distinct. Religion never a source of virtue, even when the religionist is virtuous. Religion takes its spirit and character from the individual spirit and character of each of its professors. Virtue springing not in religion, but in the human heart. Of fear as a motive to virtue. A knowledge of true morals derived through our sensations. What produces morality? Test of moral precepts. Two great divisions of morals; separate yet blending. Usages of society, Not nature, to blame. Propriety not found in extremes. Connexion and importance of the sciences. Self interest alone might teach virtue; but selfish calculations superceded by cultivated sensibilities Negative virtue. Object of a just education to produce active virtue. Lamentable influences on the youthful mind. Orgrnization charged with evils which spring from ignorant instruction alone. Enlightened guides should replace dogmatical teachers. Simplicity of the science. Summary. Moral principle. Divisions of morals. Each branch must be developed as opportunity offers in connection and in order. Conclusion.

LECTURE VI.

Formation of Opinions. Importance of the subject, and consequences to be anticipated from a just understanding of the same. Persecution for opinion. Review of its dreadful effects. Examination of its cause. Meaning of the term opinion. Truth or error of opinions determined by the greater or less degree of our knowledge. Singular inconsistency in human feeling. Anger generated not against facts but the conclusions which they generate. Absurdity of this anger. What conduct would be rational in cases of difference of opinion. Only method by which to induce a change in opinion. Sacredness of mental liberty, how violated. Ignorance of the nature of an opinion, not the only cause of opinionative persecution. This unknown in countries without a priesthood. Instances therereof. Religion should be left alone. Knowledge, not opinions, should be taught. The people encourage the teaching of opinions at home and abroad. Honest opinions never culpable. Bitterness of sectarianism. Advantage of union. Persecution. Its nature and consequences. The clergy denounced as a body, though sometimes amiable as individuals. Secret influences more powerful than open force. The stage. The people's day of leisure. Spirit that persecuted Jesus, still abroad. Jesus would be ill received by modern religionists. Churches of faith and schools of knowledge. Lecturer of no sect. Signs of the times. A substitute for ancient errors required. Knowledge alone leads to just practice.

LECTURE VII.

Existing Evils, and their Remedy. Summary of the topics embraced in preceding lectures, and subject of the present. Ignorance the source of evils. The people the true reformers. Who are addressed? Distress. Imitation of Europe. Small progress in reform since 1776. Republican anomalies. Forms and principles. Practical freedom and equality Reality of evils. Philadelphia report. No effectual remedy found. Reform gradual. Difficulties in the way of popular effort to correct existing evils. Practical prejudices. Appeal to the rich. Parental anxieties universal. Their cure suggested, and the first measure towards the remedy of existing evils pointed out. Great measure of national education. Common schools inefficient. Plan of national institutions. Educational tax. Promise of further development. Exhortation to radical reform through the state legislatures.

ADDRESS I.

Celebration of Fourth of July, 1828. Reasonable to rejoice on the day. Fourth of July, 1776, a new era. Change, the distinctive attribute of American institutions. Change, the harbinger of improvement. Importance of constitutional provision of reform. One liberty. National advantages we possess. Much to be done. Patriotism only conditionally a virtue. Ancient patriotism. Misnamed patriotism. Selfish patriotism. Patriotism of a citizen of the world suitable for America. Mis chiefs of exclusive patriotism. Duties of Americans. Character of rational rejoicing.

ADDRESS II.

Celebration of Fourth of July, 1829. Reminiscences of the day. Martial pageantry out of character. Peaceful be its celebration. Lecturer's task to counsel, not to flatter America little known until she declared her independence. America now the refuge of liberty. Hopes entertained of her as a nation of self-governing citizens Her citizens responsible for national delinquences. Their responsibility how fulfilled. Reproof, Fate of America, fate of the world. National institutions. Elective franchise virtually forfeited. The press. Its temptations to venality. A promise kept. Two positions on which rest the fabric of American government. The people being governors, should be fitted

SUPPLEMENT

COURSE OF LECTURES,

CONTAINING

THE LAST FOUR LECTURES

DELIVERED IN

THE UNITED STATES.

BY FRANCES WRIGHT.

London:

JAMES WATSON, 18, COMMERCIAL PLACE,

CITY ROAD, FINSBURY.

(Adjoining the New Mechanics' Hall of Science.)

———

1834.

ADDRESS

ON THE

STATE OF THE PUBLIC MIND,

AND THE

MEASURES WHICH IT CALLS FOR.

[Delivered in New-York and Philadelphia, in the Autumn of 1829.]

THE present is an era of unparalleled interest to the moral observer, i. e. to him who considers all occurrences with a view to their influence on human society.

The principle of change is in all nature, but the principle of *improvement* is only (so far as observation has enabled us to ascertain) in the nature of man.

The scientific eye traces the convulsions of our earth's solid sphere back, through millions of untold generations, to eras lost in time, when animals of other form from those which now move on its surface, ranged from pole to pole, and (apparently in the absence of man, whose organic remains seem of more recent origin) fed on another vegetable kingdom, or preyed on each other as we now see their successors. Or let us observe what is passing around us in the field of existing nature : Each season brings its vicissitudes, each passing instant its changes—in the herb, in the flower, in the forest, in the mountain, in the jewel of the secret mine; in the vast bed of the ocean—dividing continents, engulfing or revealing islands, approaching or receding from its wonted boundaries, until the land-marks of other days are no more guides to the traveller or the mariner of these ; in all the forms of matter, whether gaseous, fluid, or solid, whether animate, or, to our perception, inanimate ; in every particle and unit atom that fills its place, and exercises its agency, through the endless succession of existence and duration of time. All, all is in motion, perpetual and eternal—in earth, in water, and in air; in the elements of our own bodies, and in the thoughts of our own minds. I said *in the thoughts of our own minds;* and here is that which converts the world of difform and rugged nature into one of enlightened culture. Here is that which can impart new order and method to the phenomena of matter, and convert change without design, into progressive improvement.

Let us mark the primeval forest, where man's footsteps have never strayed. Tangled and impervious to all but the panther and beast of prey, the jungle, the brake, and the stagnant swamp load the rich earth with rank vegetation, and the air with vapour pestilential to the higher grades of animal life. Then first comes the human hunter, and opens a passage with venturous courage; clears, in the season of drought, the cumbered earth with fire reducing to stubble the undergrowth thicket, and thus calling into being the more delicate herbage, and preparing the spring pasture, and the open glade, for the deer and the peaceful herd. Next comes the husbandman, to break the rich glebe, and throw the first seeds of a more plentiful and peaceful industry.

I have seen the father of waters—the deep, and rapid, and unbordered Mississippi, sweeping down the wreck of mountains, plains, forests, and acres of fruitful soil; and, as I have traced its career of destruction, I have seen the art of man suddenly arresting its violence, raising a barrier to its accumulated waters, and bordering its now mastered and innocuous deluge with the richest productions of human cultivation. And what we may trace in progress in our own western regions, we perceive to have taken place throughout the habited globe. It is man alone, of all the beings we behold, that hath faculties to distinguish the alterable phenomena of nature, and power to attempt reform where he distinguishes defect.

You will remark, that I have here preferred no comment on the moral depravity which, up to this hour, has mingled with his intellectual ingenuity, and made of his work such a tangled web of good and ill, that we are alternately tempted to bless and to curse those powers which, in developing the treasures of earth, have so often perverted their uses, and. while ornamenting its bosom, have stained those very ornaments with blood.

STATE OF PUBLIC MIND.

Before adverting to the errors of man, I wished to observe with you his powers. I was desirous that we should distinguish how, to his agency, all physical improvement is attributable. He finds earth a wilderness; he makes it a garden. He finds it peopled with tigers, bears, panthers, wolves, and poisonous reptiles ; and, through his influence, these give place to milder tribes, until we find the sheep and the tamed cattle browzing under his protection in velvet lawns, and the birds of song gathering their food amid fields of nutritive grain planted by his industry. We perceive, through his means, a similar melioration to take place in the earth's atmosphere and climates. Where is care and judicious cultivation extend, winter recedes, and its rigors diminish ; fogs and miasmata disappear, and the drained morass, now a smiling champaign, yields its rich produce, under a pure sky, to tribes of intelligent beings. We see, too, races of animals improving in beauty and in instinct : the dog appear with quicker scent and livelier sagacity ; the horse with finer proportions, nobler stature, and redoubled speed. We see the fruits of earth change under his hand. The golden grain swell in size, and increase in weight and nutriment : the apple, the peach the grape, supercede the crude berries of the forest ; and all the vegetable kingdom—tree and plant, and fruit and flower, glow with new beauties, of hue, and fragrance, and luscious juices.

We see, then, man introduces order and design, beauty and utility, where before simple phenomena were discoverable only. Wherever he appears we see intelligence preside over matter, and the changes and occurrences of nature, guided in their course, move in order, as on a plan of progressive improvement.

Mighty, indeed, are the powers of the human animal. Through earth, through air, though ocean, his influence extends. The stamp of genius is impressed on the whole surface of the globe. Land and sea, vale and mountain, the howling wilderness of earth's civilized frontier, the scorched desert of simoom-swept Africa, the storm-besieged coast and boundless fields of ocean's restless waters, the glaciers of the poles. the iced peaks of Alps and towering Andes—all nature's deep recesses, most stupendous features, and to hidden phenomena, bear witness to his restless activity, to his dauntless daring, to his aspiring curiosity—to his conquering perseverance.

We may be bold to say, that wherever man hath pierced, and whatever he hath essayed, (not absolutely in contradiction with those unvarying phenomena of matter to which he has given, albeit inaccurately, the name of laws,)—wherever he hath been, and whatever he hath essayed with steady purpose, there, and in that, he has been conqueror. He hath been conqueror—I say, for good or for evil. Wherever he hath closely observed, accurately calculated, boldly designed and obstinately persevered, he hath triumphed—triumphed over every obstacle, executed every project, attained every ambition.

I speak now with reference to the human race in the aggregate, and of their *united*, as well as calculated exertions ; albeit, even with individuals, steadiness of purpose will usually vanquish difficulties, and he who strains perseveringly at any object, may anticipate, with probable certainty, its attainment. But, wherever nations, or bodies of men, have applied their united and sustained energies, observation, and calculation, to any undertaking, good or evil, scarcely with. an exception, we shall find them to have succeeded. Have they sought military conquest, and bent all their institutions to form a race of warriors ? They have carried their ambition. Have they applied to the ornamental arts ? Look to the architecture and sculpture of Athens, the paintings of modern Italy, and all the brilliant, though, oftentimes, unless magnificence of ancient and modern empires. Have they addressed themselves to science ? to commerce ? to manufactures ? Mark the rapid discoveries in every branch of knowledge ; the fleets which cover the ocean, the wonderful inventions in mechanics, and applications of machinery. Have they sought spiritual dominion ? Note the rise of the priesthood of every nation, from the Bramin, Hierophant, and Levite, of India, Egypt, and Judea, to the apostles, fathers, bishops, popes, jesuits, and many coloured priests of christendom. These last, in monarchies, have proved stronger than kings ; in aristocracies, than knights and nobles; in republics, than the people. And to what has been, or yet is, attributable this ascendancy, but to that perseverance and undeviating steadiness of purpose which supports, to this hour, and even in this land, a power and an influence at war with the spirit of the age, and the genius of the nation?

True it is, as all histories and observation attest, that a

strong moral purpose, whether conceived for evil or for good, will,, for the most part, prove superior to mere physical odds, and omnipotent over mere physical opposition. In this, the little band at Thermopylæ, whose watchword was their country, withstood the hosts of the Persian. In this, the children of Romulous, and robbers of the Palatine, overwhelmed from their little mountain the tribes of Etruria, and, persevering in the spirit of their founder, conquered the world. In this, the peasantry of Switzerland humbled the power of Austria and the pride of Burgundy. In this, the feeble provinces of Holland, having chosen for their emblem a ship unfurnished and unequipped yet struggling with the waves, braved the supremacy of Spain, the legions of Duke Alva, and the united powers of catholic Europe. And, in the same fixed purpose of the mind, the thirteen weak and infant colonies of these now magnified and multiplied independent states, threw down the gauntlet to the parliament of Britain, and, planting in their soil the simple banner of the rights of man, vanquished the armies of tyranny, and brake the sceptre of kings.

If thus, then, the empire of man be co-extensive with this globe and with time—if his influence can effect even nature's phenomena ; if his volitions may be calculated so as to ensure their object, and thus, for evil or for good, his fixed resolve can prove omnipotent, how urgent that such resolve should be for good—always for good—always for the advantage of his race —for the promotion of his vital interests, for the improvement of the world he occupies, and for the just cultivation of all those faculties of his own compound being, in whose wire or unwise exercise is involved all virtue or all vice, all happiness or all misery !

Seeing, then, how great the powers of man, and seeing what those powers have affected, we may all conceive how immense must have been his progress had he applied them with uniform wisdom. To say this in regret of the past would be idle, but to reflect upon it with a view to the future, must be all important. If the powers of man have been perverted to evil, or wasted upon trifles, this has been the necessary result of imperfect knowledge and insufficient experience.

Know we cannot, and it were idle to *imagine*, the train of circumstances which, by first starting the human mind upon wrong principles, led it to fabricate that complicated system of errors which falsely passes among us by the name of *civilized society*. It matters not, I say, to imagine how this came pass ;

we see that *it is*. Yes! we now begin to suspect that we are
in a wrong road; that we have followed out the false principles started by our ancestors, in ages of savage ignorance,
until we can pursue them no farther with any hope of good
result. The suspicion is now afloat that fear and violence, in
all the forms we have applied them—by the sword, by the
rack, by the ascendancy of brute force, by spiritual tribunals,
and all the phantasmagoria of superstition; by the nets and
traps, tricks and quibbles, false pretences, artful circumven-
tions, absurd contradictions, demoralizing oaths, debasing
penalties, and solemn cruelties of law—the suspicion is afloat,
I say, that all these inventions upon which man has expended
his ingenuity, neither have affected, nor can ever effect, the
purpose we must suppose to have been intended.

The suspicion is afloat, that religon, as publicly taught in
this land, at a cost exceeding twenty millions per annum, is
a chimera; that the clerical hierarchy, and clerical craft,
which have been elevated upon this chimera, are the two
deadliest evils which ever cursed society; that our system of
law is powerless for the object it ostensibly has in view, *the
just regulation of the conduct of men one towards the other*,
and rather omnipotent to effect the reverse of that intent,
namely, to effect the perversion of the human understanding,
the corruption of the moral feelings, and the utter destruction
of all the social relations of the great human family; and,
finally, that government, as executed to this hour, is inadequate to secure what it proposes, *the happy existence of the
governed*. I say, that the suspicion is afloat, that something
is wrong in the whole fabric of civil polity, and that hourly
this suspicion is strengthening into conviction.

All, more or less, can read the signs of the times; though
some may read them with hope, and some with fear. The
most dull can perceive that a moral excitement, new in its
nature, and rapid in its progress, pervades the world. In
either hemisphere old superstitions and old pretensions sound
the alarm. The priest trembles for his craft, the rich man for
his hoard, the politician for his influence. Among the great of
the earth the cry is up of "sedition! rebellion! danger to the
state!" From the sanctuary the shouts are heard of "heresy!
infidelity! danger to the church and its treasury?" From the
people—ay! from the people, arise the hum and stir of
awakening intelligence, inquiry, and preparation.

Every passing event announces the dawn of a new era—

proclaims a new epoch in the history of man, foretels for all the civilized world, and first for this nation, as first in the ranks of civil liberty—foretels a REVOLUTION.

Yes ! a revolution. Does any ear startle at the sound ? Some there are, some unhappily there must be. But not the righteous patriot shall it affright ; not the friend of man ; not they, who, in the inner mind, have wed their country's noble " declaration," and whose hearts yearn after the tenure and the exercise of those equal rights their fathers first boldly claimed for man.

I have used, my friends, a word of mighty import, and one that, in every land save this, would be of threatening import. In hapless Europe *revolution* is still destined to wear the scarlet robes of blood. The people, in that hemisphere, have yet to win what you possess—political freedom. The sword is there in the hand of oppression, and they who would correct abuses have a royal army to vanquish, and a royal exchequer to drain.

Not so with America. The field here is won ; the battle fought—unless, indeed, the spirit of her youth is departed, and she should tamely yield in her prime the vantage ground she seized in her infancy.

In the crisis now in preparation for this country, three terminations present themselves as possible ; and, between these, the people may now choose. A short period hence, and the selection may be no more theirs. The change to which I point, and which every reflecting observer must perceive to be impending, will not be the simple effect of a progress in opinion ; were it so we might consider it with interest wholly divested of anxiety ; but it must also be impelled by the force of circumstances. What these circumstances are we shall pass rapidly in review.

First ; the novel and excessive impetus given to commercial and manufactural enterprise by the improvements in machinery, in navigation. roads, canals, &c., and, yet more, by the principle of competition carried out until it results in the ruin of all small capitalists, and in the oppression of the whole labouring class of the community.

Secondly : the banking system, an evil which I rejoice to see is now beginning to attract the popular attention. Let the people pursue the clue they have seized, and it may lead them farther than they suspect. It may lead them to their legislative halls, and oftimes explained the measures there carried ;

to their election polls, and explain the influence there exercised;
to their canals, railroads, and all the scheme of internal
improvement, *as now conducted* to the advantage of speculators and capitalists, real or pretended, and to the ruin
of the honest labourer, and farther depression of the wages of
industry. It will lead them from their eastern to their western
borders, to new towns without inhabitants, new houses without tenants, new ships without cargoes, new stores without
customers, new churches without congregations, and new jails,
bridewells, poorhouses, and hospitals, full of paupers, debtors,
swindlers, felons, dying wretches, and outcasts. Yes! it will
lead them through the whole labyrinth of speculation, false
calculation, overtrading, false trust, and deceiving credit,
where more families have found ruin, and more honesty hath
made shipwreck in these United States, than in all the countries of the earth, perhaps, taken together. Let the people,
then, follow out the whole system of bank chartering, paper
money, as now in use, and stock-jobbing of all descriptions,
and they may soon detect one of the deepest sources of industrial oppression and national demoralization.

Next, but closely connected with the evils already enumerated, comes your professional aristocracy, compounded of
priests, lawyers and college-graduated aspirants to the trade
of law making, charter signing license granting, Sabbath protecting, and I know not what interferences with the rights
and interests of the many, for the vain exalting, and false ad-
vantaging of the few.

And, lastly, as the root of all these many abuses, we find a
false system of education stolen from aristocratic Europe, and
which, under favour of the popular ignorance on the one hand,
and the craft of false learning on the other, places the public
mind under the dominion of priests, the legislatures at the
mercy of lawyers, the industrious classes at the mercy of speculators, and, generally, all honest men and simple women at
the mercy of rogues.

Such are some of the many circumstances which combine to
hasten a crisis that every reflecting observer may perceive to
be impending ; and which, if left to work out their own consequences, must bring about a change in public affairs by the
worst means.

I observed, that the revolution now in preparation for this
country, may assume one of three possible forms. First :
things may be allowed to follow on in the course they have taken up to this hour, and to move uninterrupted and unimpeded

in the accelerated ratio which events, like falling bodies, acquire in progress, and which the circumstances we have enumerated, and many others, combine to urge forward with additional velocity. I say, things may be allowed to move forward as they are moving, with no resistance presented on the part of the people, and every momentum applied by the privileged classes.

Under this supposition, the crisis must be consummated by the destruction of American liberty, and with *American* liberty, that of the world.

Then must we witness the final degradation of industry, the extinction of all moral principle, the enslavement of the mass of the population, (even as is now the case in Great Britain,) and in lieu of a nation of self-respecting, self-governing freemen, we shall see a crafty priesthood, and a monied aristocracy, ruling a herd of obsequious dependants, trembling fanactics, and sorrow-stricken paupers.

This fearful termination, however, I hold to be highly improbable, I will say all but impossible. How great soever may have been the popular supineness, we may observe, at this time symptoms of a general awakening; and even, were it possible, which it is not, to close again the eyes which have once caught a ray of the light of truth, still is there such saving power in the institutions of the land, that, in the last extremity, they alone would suffice to rouse the children of the men of '76, and save from capture this last strong hold of human liberty.

No! let Presbyterian ambition ring her peal; it shall be answered by the larum of freedom! Let superstition spread her mists, and thick clouds of darkness; they shall be dispersed by the sun of knowledge. Let false pretension and false wealth, spring their mind under the citadel of the state; the people, though they slumber, yet shall they awake, detect the ambush, and defeat the treachery. Let priestcraft devise his nets, multiply his emmissaries, pour his wily lesson into female ears—let him " eat the fat, and drink the sweet," and make heavy the strong box of his treasury—let him bribe, and threaten, and flatter, and slander, and persecute, all *in the name of the Lord ;* and, under the false colours of truth, where there is only error; humility, where there is only pride; and peace, where there is deadliest war—let priestcraft so strive, with poisoned arrow and dagger aimed in darkness, against the true interests of man, the true dignity of woman,

N

and the weal of the human race—let priestcraft, I say, so strive, unarmed truth shall baffle his wiles, and break his sword of flesh with the sword of the mind.

No! my fears picture not the worst of all catastrophes, the final triumph of spiritual oppression and monied corruption, in this last haven of liberty and hope of the world. No! the cause of the people *must* triumph. But how? Here is the only question; and here is the only anxiety which ever clouds my hopes, or alarms my confidence.

The second form which the approaching revolution may wear, even in this land is more than possible; and nothing, indeed, but timely measures, planned with wisdom, and carried with perseverance, can avert it. This second mode supposes some farther supineness on the part of the people, while existing evils and abuses increase and accumulate, until, the cup of popular calamity being filled, the last drop shall make it flow over. The American population, then, not coerced as in Europe by standing armies, and all the convenient machinery of despotism, shall suddenly take their wrongs into their own hands, and rush, without deliberation, and without knowledge, to their remedy.

Alas for the unsullied robe of American liberty, should this be so. Alas for that unsppotted shrine which the hands of sages reared, and which the foot of wisdom should alone approach. Oh, not thus—not thus be the victory won. May the means be pure as the end. May the cause which brings us here this night, be secured without one act to raise a blush, one step to wish retracted, one deed to wish undone!

The third mode of revolution, then, be ours; that mode which is alone worthy of a people who have assumed equal liberty for their motto, and declared their *expressed will* the law of the land. Let the industrious class, and all honest men of all classes, unite for a gradual, but radical reform, in all the objects, and all the measures of government; and let this be done through, and by the means supplied in their constitutional code: namely—*through their legislatures.*

But, will it be said, this is sooner recommended than effected? Yes; and better that it should be so. Were the people to carry the citadel while unprepared to use wisely the advantage, better that it were not in their hands. Power without knowledge is like an unbroke horse, it runs fast, indeed, but misses the goal.

First, then, the people must bear in mind, that to be

successful they must be united; to be united they must be of one mind; to be of one mind they must distinguish the first best measure to be carried; and, having distinguished that best measure, must set hand to hand, heart to heart, and vote to vote, for its adoption and execution.

I have already delivered it as my opinion, that this measure will be found in a plan of equal, universal, and republican education, and explained how and why I consider it as alone commensurate with the two great objects we have in view— the relief of the present generation, and the improvement of the next.

First: the relief of the present generation. So long as the industrious classes remained burdened with the charge of their families—with their food, clothing, education, and fitting out in life, it is impossible for them to be relieved of their burdens. And, so long as virtuous parents of any and all classes, shall see for their children no surer protection than that supplied by their own uncertain existence, it is impossible for all, or any, to know peace of mind.

Second: the improvement of the next generation. It will be my object hereafter to show in developing the principles of law and government, (to which I pledged myself at the close of my discourse on the nature of moral science,) it will be my object, I say, hereafter to show, that, with a few exceptions, the whole of government, private and public, national and domestic, will be found, when properly understood, to resolve itself into education. At present I shall only reiterate a remark often presented to my hearers, that a rational education is the only road to knowledge, virtue, and happiness; a republican education the only road to equality; and a national education, (by which I understand an education conducted at the expense, and under the protection of the people, acting through their fairly chosen and properly instucted representatives,) the only safeguard of youth, and the only bulwark of a free constitution. ·

Some fears have been expressed lest the measure now proposed should be perverted by the restless spirit of orthodoxy, and the all-meddling ambition of priestcraft, to a source of evil instead of good; lest, in fine, it should be associated with the Sunday School Union, Bible Society, and Tract House. A little consideration will, I think, expose the groundlessness of these apprehensions. In the first place, it will be observed, that the measure will be national, and not sectarian; political, and not religious? proposed by the people's voice for the people's good? canvassed in broad daylight, carried in broad daylight, and paid for in broad daylight. Priests have never worked save in the dark; priestcraft can only thrive by means of secret associations. Orthodoxy owes all its strength to the disunion of the people, and to the habit of silent and sectarian congregationing in churches, in lieu of popular assembling in popular halls. The organization of popular assemblies must form a necessary part of the reform now contemplated. Before the measure of republican state schools can be carried, the popular union must be cemented by means of popular meetings. A people uniting for any purpose are no longer sectarian; and, when no longer sectarian, they can, in this country, be no longer priest-ridden. Let the fate of the Sabbath mail petitions foreshow the issue of all priestly or sectarian interference with a question really popular. Let such a measure as that in contemplation be brought forward by the people, and let orthodoxy intermeddle if it dare.

But the safety of the measure will appear more clearly when we shall have developed the *mode* in which, as I conceive, it can alone be carried; and the model of which we must seek in the opening page of your national history.

When the American people, galled with the yoke of British servitude, resolved to pass the circumstances of their condition in review, they convened a general assembly of delegates from all the then colonies; and thus unity of design was effected throughout a population feeble, scattered, and, up to that hour, unaccustomed to consider each other as fellow citizens. Now, without calculating upon a spirit of enthusiasm approaching to that of 1774, which existing circumstances suffice not to engender, I believe it more easy now than it was then to fix lastingly the attention of the people upon some measure of general utility.

This nation is fairly tired out with religious quarrelling and religious taxation, and favourably disposed to receive any better substitute. It is also warmly attached to its political institutions, and prone to estimate justly any measure calculated to fix them deeper in the heart, and to enhance their practical excellence. I may remark, in evidence of this, that it has not happened to me once to touch upon the subject of popular union as attainable, and attainable only, through the means of a uniform plan of education, without eliciting a spontaneous sentiment of approval.

I have now made the experiment from Missouri to Massachusetts, along the line of our eastern cities, and in the towns of the interior. I have addressed, not small assemblages, but masses of the population, and I have invariably found the popular sentiment on the side of knowledge *versus* faith, and union *versus* sectarian divisions. I think, then, the public mind ripe for the measure, or rather for the discussion of the measure, which is all that, in the first place, should be proposed.

To facilitate, then, first its discussion, and then its execution, I would suggest the propriety of organizing in each city, town, and district of influence, popular associations, for the simple object of discovering and promoting the true interests of the American people, distinct from all class, all sect, all party, and all speculative opinions. That, the better to impart energy and unity of plan to the whole, a central point be chosen, say Philadelphia, that city appearing the best prepared to take the lead; and that, by means of standing committees, a correspondence between that centre and all parts of the country be opened.

In this manner the attention of the American nation may rapidly be awakened, the spirit of popular union fostered, useful inquiry set afloat, the plots of orthodoxy and priestcraft exposed and defeated, pledges interchanged for carrying, at the elections, friends to human liberty, or, rather, *men pledged to the support of upright measures* ; and, first and chief, to the carrying the one great measure of a system of equal universal republican education.

I would not propose, however, that this great measure should be entrusted to any man, or set of men, without the revisal and distinct approval of the people. Let individuals be appointed to draft, or to cause to be drafted, a bill setting forth the plan in all necessary detail, and let the same be submitted to the people through their committees of correspondence. After due consideration, and general publication throughout the country, let that be made the turning point of the elections—until, in one legislature, no matter which, it be presented, and presented again and again, until, being carried, the first stone of that temple be laid in which we may find hope, and the rising generation prosperity.

In presenting this sketch of the plan of procedure, which, after deep and earnest reflection, presents itself to my mind as best calculated to ensure purity and unity of measures in the great national reform so greatly requisite, and, by all good minds, so ardently desired, I would not be understood as counselling hasty measures. Though all reform be possible in a country blessed with a government purely representative in principle, the progress of reform must always keep pace with the public mind. Faster it cannot advance, and faster wisdom would not desire it. Revolutions that are effected in a day are ever deceptive. They involve a change of men rather than of measures ; of names and forms rather than of principles. The revolution we have to effect is mental and moral, and must be reached through the means of instructional improvement.

But, as I had occasion to observe on a former occasion, to remould the national character through the rising generation, we must begin by informing ourselves as to the best means for effecting the alteration. We must inquire ; we must examine ; we must deliberate ; and we must inquire, examine, and deliberate together. While split into sects, and parties, and classes, the strength of the American people must continue paralyzed, and their noble institutions next to useless. Without union there is no strength without union there is no progress, without union there can be no republic.

To unite, then, but to unite on true principles, be our motto : to move steadily in the right direction, *not to move fast,* be our object. Doubt we what are true principles? The pen of the immortal Jefferson hath proclaimed them. In this noble instrument, *(unrolling the declaration of independence,)* signed with a nation's sanction, sealed with a nation's blood, shall we find them.

The equal rights of all, as set forth in this instrument, the common interests of all, as discoverable by inquiry, be it the law of our hearts to respect the labour of our lives to establish.

In applying ourselves to this good work of honest citizenship, let us question no man's faith ; let us wound if possible, no man's prejudices ; let us ask the sacrifice of no man's honest opinion. But, neither, on the other hand, let us gainsay a truth in order to conciliate folly, nor immolate a principle with a view to expediency. Let us not court the rich man, humour the fanatic, nor favour or disfavour the sceptic. Let us win the battle, if slowly, yet surely, under the shield of unarmed truth, in the strength of a righteous cause. Thus let us associate ; not as Jews, not as Christians, not as Deists, not as believers, not as sceptics, not as poor, not as rich, not as artizans, not as merchants, not as lawyers, but as human beings, as fellow creatures, as American citizens, pledged to protect each other's rights—to advance each other's happiness.

Not to build up a sect, then, let us associate, but to lead all sects to this altar of union (*holding up the declaration of independence*) which they have forsaken—this shrine of human liberty—this law of a common country which they have forgotten.

So let us unite, my fellow citizens! and, strong in the same principle which achieved this nation's independence, shall we heal the wounds of the land, remedy its evils, stifle its dissentions, until we gather as one family, into the courts of knowledge, of virtue, of happiness, and of equality.

ADDRESS,

CONTAINING A

REVIEW OF THE TIMES,

[As delivered in the Hall of Science, New-York, on Sunday, May 9, 1830.]

THE six months I have been absent from this city, have not been sterile in events. They have exhibited a change in the public mind, such as ere long must produce a change in the public measures. They have witnessed in this metropolis the breaking up of parties, the alarm of politicians, the anathemas of bigots, the noise of demagogues, and the awakening, and the gathering, and the uniting of the people. Throughout this state, they have sufficed to quicken a spirit in unison with that of its metropolis ; throughout the union, they have kindled thoughts and started inquiries which never again shall sleep.

It needs not the gift of prophecy, nor even the skill of experienced wisdom, to see in the stir and preparation of the present hour, a future big with important changes in the condition of man and the policy of nations. The time is arrived, when even the dull and the cold-hearted must admit the conviction, that all is not quite as it was, nor promises to remain as it is. Even the spiritual enthusiast rouses himself occasionally from his day-dreams, to look, with wondering eyes, upon the face of a world, which, till now, might, with some reason, seem unworthy of regard.

When I recal the state of the public mind in this city, last January was a twelvemonth, and compare it with what now exists, I almost seem to dream in my memory of the past, or in my perception of the present. Then noisy polemics and ambitious churchmen engaged the people's ears, and crushed the people's spirit. Then troops of speculators bought and sold the people's voices, and the state's honours, unchallenged and unheeded. Then corruption struck down its roots into the soil, stifling the tree of liberty planted by a noble generation, and they who should have tended, and fenced, and watered the lovely sapling, stood silent by and watched its ruin. Then truly had the days foretold by Jefferson arrived: " The rulers had become corrupt, and the people careless. Their faculties all absorbed in making money, every shackle that had not been knocked off at the revolution had grown heavier and heavier, until the nation's rights had to revive or expire in a convulsion."*   *Now*—Yes ! already may we venture to trace the contrast of the picture—*Now,* the people, awaking from their lethargy, prepare to search out the land.   They call their servants to account ; scrutinize the laws of their enacting, the follies devised by their ignorance, and the corruptions countenanced by their venality.   *Now*, weary of vain speculations touching unknown worlds and inconceivable existences, they call their thoughts from the clouds, and prepare to confine them to the earth.   *Now*, convicted to their own reason of having misspent their time and misdirected their faculties, they turn from the expounders of dreams and readers of prophecies, to study the realities of human life, to find the scource of its evils, and divise the remedy of its wrongs.

It is not to say that the great work of reform is acheived. It is not to say that it is fairly commenced.   It is not to say that in the work, when commenced, there shall not be found many difficulties, nor that in the course of its prosecution there shall not arise many lets and hinderances.   We need but to bear in mind, that they who have to effect the reform are themselves corrupted—that the people have drank deep of the poison mixed by their rulers, and forgotten, even as their rulers have forgotten, the great principles on which their fathers laid the foundation-stones of their greatness.   It needs but to bear in mind, that the change which the people have to effect is *in themselves,* and the difficulties of the work will be all apparent.

But, immense as these difficulties are, the people of these states are equal to the surmounting them.   Their whole history evinces that energy which the spirit of liberty only inspires, and which, in every extremity, will suffice for their salvation.

Hitherto that energy hath been variously exerted, sometimes for good, sometimes for evil ; but, whenever or however exerted, it has been successful.   In colonization it conquered nature herself—the wilderness and the savage ; in revolution, it prevailed over armies and discipline, and ancient custom

---

* See Notes on Virginia, end of Query xvii.

and prejudice sanctioned by time.   In the struggle which de
cideded the character of the government, it silenced the
doubts of timid patriots, and confounded the intrigues of crafty
traitors ; it set the seal of democracy on the national institutions, and gave into the hand which penned the charter of
American freedom, the helm of the state.   In the mad conflict
of European ambition, when the haughty insolence of Britain,
and the blind fury of a Napoleon, equally menaced the existence of the young Republic, threatening to sweep her flag from
the universal seas, and her name from the list of nations ; then
again was the energy of a free people displayed, and the liberties of man secured in those of America.

Yes ! this distinctive characteristic of a free people shines
forth in every epoch of American history.   We see it in 1607,
prevailing in the swampy wilds of Virginia ; again, on the
rocky shores of New-England.   We find it ever awake and
struggling through all the colonial history, until it rose to its
height in 1776.   We find it alive in 1789 ; we behold it burning with new vigour in 1801, and see it crowned with victory
in 1815.

Here we see the energy inherent in the national character,
inspiring noblest resolves, preferring and defending true principles and wise institutions, resisting oppression, distinguishing
false counsel, rejecting blind rulers, and uniting, round the
altar of a common country, conflicting parties, private enemies,
and political disputants.   Thus has the energy of the American people, when wisely directed, sufficed for their protection
and advancement.   Would we judge also how it has sufficed
when ill directed for their ruin ? let us mark their career in
trade, their thirst of gain, their mad pursuit of every absurd
and mischievous system, practice, and contrivance, until human
ingenuity has reached the *ne plus ultra* of extravagance.   Look
to the religious mania, which has made the land groan beneath
the weight of churches, and the more onerous burden of priests,
turning alike our merchants and mechanics into speculators in
pews and conventicles, and splitting every city, village, and
almost every family, into sects and parties, until it would be
hard to contrive more distinctions without devising a creed,
building a temple, and ordaining a priest for each individual !
Look to the banking system, restricted throughout the greater
part of continental Europe to the simple purposes of discount,
deposit, transfer, and exchange, in England, and in these
states to far greater excess, its operations have been extended
to *false coining*, until here, with the enterprise peculiar to

the people, it has converted trade into gambling, covered commerce with disgrace and industry with ruin, brought into just discredit the reputation of Americans abroad, all but annihilated confidence between man and man at home, exonerated fraud from dishonour, and hurried the whole population into habits of extravagance and practices abhorrent to honesty.

We may look indeed where we will—consider every principle started in this country, every experiment tried and system attempted, and we shall find that, whether right or wrong, wise or foolish, the restless enterprise and persevering energy, generated by the political institutions, have carried and carry the people to the utmost verge of what is practicable. Once started in any road, they stop not until they find no farther thoroughfare ; and what in other countries might take a century to effect, is here but the work of a few years. Thus was this continent invaded and usurped by the first colonists ; thus multiplied and grew their population ; thus flourished and strengthened their liberties ; thus burst they into a nation before Europe was generally aware of their existence ; thus reared they the beautiful edifice of American government ; and thus, with equal rapidity, have the same people suffered the pollution of that edifice, and rushed ahead in the paths of error and corruption.

But we see—but we know—by experience we know, that the American people can reform with the same—nay ! with better energy than they pervert. Here, even in the nation's evil, we find the surety of its good. By the rapidity of its career in vice, we may calculate the ratio of its advance in virtue, when once it shall be started in the right road, and its energy shall be stimulated by rational motives and worthy objects.

Had I not, from study of its history. and its character, thus judged concerning it, I had not raised my voice to challenge its errors, nor to kindle its enthusiasm. But, confident that with the American people was the power to amend every evil and rectify every error, when distinguished as such; and that with them also was the means to amend and to rectify the same constitutionally and wisely, I addressed myself fearlessly to their understandings, neither doubting to waken them from indifference, nor apprehensive of urging them to rashness.

The means employed were surely peaceful, and peaceful has been, and the promises to be, the result. Vainly would the

wrath of disconcerted politicians, aided by the ambitious zealot, who fights ever his own battle under plea of fighting his
God's—vainly would dishonest intriguers deceive the people
as to the nature of the principles advocated and the measures
suggested ; vainly would they confound these with the ravings
of visionary theorists, or the propositions of inexperienced enthusiasts ; vainly would they appeal to fanatical prejudice by
shouting infidelity, or to worldly interests by prophesying confiscation and robbery. The American people (praise be to their
political institutions !) have within them a store of good sense,
ever equal to the discrimination of truth from falsehood, reason from declamation. Equal also to the distinguishing honest
counsel from crafty manœuvering, courage from rashness,
and peaceful, wise, and practical reform, from violent, premature, and convulsory changes. No ! the American people
are not to be deceived when once truth hath met their ears.
It *has* met their ears ; and already throughout the vast extent
of this continent, the popular mind is, more or less, alive to the
true nature of the reform contemplated by the great mass of
the free electors of this city, and I may add, of this state.
More yet will I add—the American people generally throughout the union, are ripe for a similar reform, are prepared in
mind to recognize it as indispensable for the practical development of those equal rights consecrated in their political institutions ; to recognize it as involving the sum of human
liberty, of human happiness, and of national greatness; as
capable, in its progress and result, of remedying the moral and
physical evils which now afflict the community ; of casting in
a new and pure mould the American character, and of imparting to the whole civilized world an impulse as novel as it must
be virtuous.

In the course I judged it useful to pursue, for the purpose
of quickening the popular energy and directing it into
wholesome channels, I distinguished, not without pain, the
indispensable necessity of assualting many established interests
and powerful influences, and thus, while my object was
simply the good of all, of rousing the hostility of many.
Foremost among these interests and influences, indispensable
to assail and expose, stood those of a craft which has never
existed in any country without sapping the liberties and
poisoning the mortality of the people. In the clergy, every
lover of freedom, in every country, has seen freedom's worst
enemy. No honest patriot, whatever his faith, whatever his

religious zeal, ever loved or trusted, *as a body*, the servants of the temple. Their interests are one, and the people's are another; no faithful guardian, therefore, of the public weal, could ever view without distrust the movements of the tribe of Levi. Without distrust they never *have* viewed them. To look no farther than this Republic and its history. Who among the fathers of the national liberties and independence, but have left us pledges, more or less direct or indirect, private or public, according to the greater or less boldness of their individual characters, or the temper of the times and nature of the circumstances in which they stood—who among the founders of this nation's greatness, betrayed no doubts, no bequeathed, no warnings touching the character of the clercial functions? Washington!—too wise and prudent to agitate a question prematurely, or to risk the conversion of doubtful friends into open foes at a period when enemies were many and friends but few—Washington! ever cautiously silent or evasive through life, firmly refused in death the aid and services of men who would fain have engraven upon his tomb, "Washington, the Christian apostle!" instead of " Washington, the patriot hero!"

This trait would suffice us for all that regards the public character of Washington touching the matter of religion. This trait, as showing him opposed to the profession and office of the clergy, would supply every information respecting the religious views of that great man, which could be of any real importance to his fellow citizens to possess; for, will not all exclaim, " what matters the faith, or the want of faith, of an honest man and a faithful citizen!" Who but the wildest fanatic will dissent from this? Yet who, possessing common sense, and cherishing human peace and human liberty, but must also own that he were unfit to be a ruler in a young Republic, who viewed not with jealous eyes the priestly calling. That Washington thus viewed it, the manner of his death declared. For the rest, in silence might we leave *his* opinions whose practice was pure, did not incendiary tongues ever labour to confound scepticism and heresy with vice and disorder, and essay to prop up error by coupling it with sacred names:—if also it were not important to meet boldly the ungenerous prejudice so artfully inculcated by designing teachers, that all good men must believe after a certain fashion, and that all who do not so believe are bad men. For these reasons, and for these reasons only, is it important that we now hold, upon the authority of Jefferson, what was always surmised by the more intelligent portion of the public, and asserted privately by the surviving confidential intimates of the father of his country. *Washington was not a Christian*—that is: he believed not in the priest's God, nor in the divine authority of the priest's book.

My friends! I could ask pardon of common sense—almost of human liberty itself, that principle before which all sectarian names, and thoughts, and feelings, disappear. I could ask pardon of liberty and reason for this allusion to the private opinions of even so public a character and great a citizen as he I have named. If I have adverted to them, it has been in the same spirit which must have guided the pen of the noble dead when he left the words for posterity— ·· Washington was no believer in the Christian system." I quote the statement as Jefferson bequeathed it, to disarm prejudice of its poison, calumny of its sting, and to lead Americans to pause ere they echo, after designing men, the the opprobrious term of "infidel" against any among the dead or the living.

Well may the strong equally with the weak have hesitated, up to this hour, to make a clear statement of their dissent from opinions generally received by an ill informed generation, and fiercely protected by an interested priesthood! Well might a Washington ever publicly evade an open declaration of his sceptism. Well might John Adams breathe, only in secret correspondence to a friend and philosopher, ·· the result of fifty or sixty years of religious reading, is in the four words, *be just and good ;*" and " if by *religion* we are to undersrand *sectarian dogmas,* in which no two are agreed, this would be the best of all possible worlds were there no religion in it:" thus marking that distinction so important to human happiness, and so studiously confounded by pulpit teachers, between faith and practice, religion and virtue. Well even might the high and fearless minded Jefferson prefer to speak from the grave those truths which, if uttered too boldly when living, would have drawn around his age clamour and insult worse than were visited on his prime. Well might the fathers of American liberty, who faced without fear the wrath of kings, hesitate to kindle the vengeance of priests. Well might the lion-hearted leaders in a political revolution, who feared not to stake, with an unarmed people, life, property, and honour, against the trained legions, equipped fleets, and full coffers of a mighty empire, shrink from a conflict with the fanaticism of their fellow citizens; and, if they hazarded censure of the ruling madness of the hour, utter it only in parables and dark sayings, even as we read that Jesus did before them. No! let not the people marvel, that so few have been found boldly to meet and to wrestle with errors which every false influence and every idle craft were interested in protecting. True it is, that all the great intellects of every generation have discarded the particular superstition of that generation; and equally true it is, that their heresy has, for the most part, been known only to the initiated like themselves, while the subtle scribes and pharisees of the day, trusting to their silence and the people's creduilty, have belied the principles, and taken in vain the names of patriots and philosophers, making the reputations of wise and good men the props of their craft and the vouchers for their impositions. Thus has it been in every age, and every nation of the world, where religion has been made a craft, and where the interests of priests have been allied with the worship of the popular deities. But thus has it most grossly beeu in this free country, where the priesthood, being despoiled of direct power, had only to reign by influence. And truly they *have* reigned by an influence the most extraordinary—an influence, not only established and sustained by every art and artifice possible to human ingenuity, but consecrated by every sacred name that fraudulent pens and tongues could steal from history or wrest from philosophy, to palm upon the ignorance of mankind for orthodox believers in a superstition they disclaimed, and obedient sons of a church they suspected. Would not the American people do better to seek the opinions of their great men in their own works and those of their confidential cotemporaries, than in the trash of the tract house and the libels of the pulpit? Would they not do well to understand, before they take alarm at the senseless cry of " infidel," that Washington, that Jefferson, that Franklin, that John Adams, that Ethan Allen, that Horatio Gates, and all the nobler host of worthies, who secured this country's independence, were all, according to the priestly acceptation of a meaningless word, *infidels*—that is, all disbelieved the compound Jewish and Christian system, and looked upon its mysteries and its miracles as upon nursery tales.

I could say more—but I will not quote the living. Few

are there, even now, when truth hath boldly broken the silence of ages—few are there even now, among the rich, the talented, or influential, who will openly reveal their secret thoughts, or lift in public the veil of hypocrisy which it is still safest to wear, and which the people are not entitled to challenge, until they evince respect for honesty, and frown to silence every scoffer at the sacred rights of conscience, free thought, and free speech.

Let me not this night be misunderstood—*misinterpreted* I will not say, for that were a vain request. Mean spirits and false tongues are as yet many among us. But let misrepresentation lead us, each and all, to receive nothing upon trust; and, instead of enemies, we may see in our slanderers our best friends.

Let me not this night be misunderstood by one ingenuous mind. If I see no merit in faith, neither see I merit in its absence. I perceive no use, and much mischief, in the distinctive epithets of Believer, Sceptic, Christian, Infidel, and I know not how many more beside. Such terms are not acknowledged by reason, and tend to produce violations both of human peace and human liberty. In opinions there are but the true and the false; those founded upon fact, and those not founded upon fact. To hold a false opinion is no crime, though it may prove a misfortune; to possess a true one is no virtue, though it must be an advantage. We have more or less knowledge—a more extended or more restricted acquaintance with the phenomena of nature and the phenomena of our own bodies; in consequence, our conecption of things is more or less correct, our judgment more or less exercised, and our opinions more or less consistent with truth.

Not then to establish nor to pull down opinions have I laboured. My object has been to find a test for all opinions; I have encouraged my fellow creatures to seek it in the nature of things as present to their senses, and in their own nature as discoverable by observation. Have they, upon examination, found all existing phenomena in contradiction with existing superstitions?—and are they transformed into *infidels* because they prefer fact to faith, the living truths of nature to the assertions of men who earn their livelihood by the tale they are telling? Does infidel, then, mean one conversant with realities, and by infidelity are we to understand knowledge? If such be the meaning of the terms, I, for one, will hold them in honour; and the warmest wish of my heart shall be, to see all my fellow creatures infidels, and the whole earth flooded with infidelity.

But here has not been all my sin. I encouraged my fellow creatures not only to test opinions by facts, but the practices of society by their utility, and the existing condition of human beings by the national declaration, *all men are free and equal.* The cry of infidel then rose yet louder. How shall we translate it now? Does infidel mean also a consistent republican, a friend to the human race, an advocate of the equal rights of all? Then am I indeed doubly an infidel, and an infidel in common with the fathers of this nation, and with all the worthy among their sons.

But greater yet, my fellow citizens, has been my sin. I have ventured to suggest the means by which consistent republicanism might be developed in practice, human happiness secured, and the equal rights of all established in very deed, beyond the power of time or circumstance to subvert or to assail. I appealed to the citizen and to the parent. I pleaded for the young, the helpless, the friendless, and the poor. I pleaded the cause of all—rich and poor—one with another. I essayed to show that equal liberty, to be more than an empty word, must exist in the mind, in the feelings, in the habits, and in the condition of a people ; that thus to exist, it must be planted in infancy, and nourished in youth ; that thus to be planted and nourished, the nation itself must assume the guardianship of the rising generation, and, curtailing all other expenses, waving, if necessary, all minor reforms and improvements, apply all its energies to the raising up of a new race in habits of equal industry, in possession of equal advantages, and in the cultivation of those feelings of companionship and fellow-citizenship, with which we should in truth be civilized beings, without which we are but savages.

Here, then, was the climax of my heresies. To this all my other offences had been but preparatory and introductory, and compared to this it would seem they had all been venial. To enlighten the present generation was indeed atheism ; but to educate rationally and equally the next, was robbery and murder ! My friends, if the meaning of words is to be thus inverted, we must make a new dictionary, and go to school over again.

I observed, that in pursuing the course which had presented itself to my mind as the most useful, and consequently

O

the best to pursue, I had found myself under the necessity
of openly confronting the interests of the priesthood ;—a body
of men that no individual, not absolutely bent on self-mar-
tyrdom, would wish to have for enemies ; but which no
honest reformer ever had, or ever can have, for friends.   I
could have wished this otherwise.   It is far from agreeable
to rouse a nest of hornets ; but, unless some had been willing
to risk their sting, it was clear they would suck for ever the
people's honey ; and, worse, with their continued buzzing
so confuse the people's ears and understandings, that common
sense and practical suggestions could have no chance for a
hearing.

To awaken the people's attention, therefore, to the affairs
of earth, it was necessary first to draw their thoughts from
the clouds.   It was necessary to engage them in a calm examination of the nature of truth, and by leading them to seek
and to find *what is*, to prepare them quietly to discard *what
is not*.   Now, during this process of preliminary inquiry,
I meddled neither with the faiths nor the forms of the popular
superstition.   I neither discussed the Trinity nor the Unity ;
I called not in question the existence of a devil, nor questioned the possibility of our thoughts and feelings, or (to use
the term familiarly applied to them) *our souls* existing hereafter in some unknown world apart from our thinking and
feeling organs.   I discussed none of these topics, I criti-
cised neither Bible nor catechism, objected to no translations,
quarrelled with no readings, challenged no discussion, but
ventured the remarks—that theology was very expensive,
its disputes very injurious, and its teachers very intermed-
dling, and encouraged the public to examine, whether its
utility was equal to its cost ; whether its quarrels added to
the comfort of society ; whether its doctrines were consistent
with human experience ; whether its teachers were what
they professed to be—meek and lowly in heart, despisers
of the goods of earth, and layers up only of spiritual treasures
in a spiritual Jerusalem, and whether training up human beings wisely in youth, would not produce a better state of
society, than scolding them once a week when full grown,
and roasting them eternally when dead ?   These questions
were plain and simple, and the clergy, apprehensive apparently that the answer would be unfavourable to their
calling, declared, that to have heard them was immorality,
but that to answer them would be atheism, which last term

they explained to signify the infraction of all the laws of
the decalogue, and of the states and the United States into
the bargain.

The cry, and the noise, and the running to and fro in
the land were great. Every advantage seemed on the side
of the clergy. They had all the pulpits, and in those days,
all the press of the country ; they were backed too by
all the wealth, and all the sinister interests of a corrupt
generation. But the American people have a large store
of curiosity, and, as was observed before, of good sense.
" So much noise," they said, " argues little reason. To
ask ourselves a few questions can be no sin. To weigh the
cost and utility of our religious system can do no harm, and
to examine the state of our earthly condition, may do some
good." The clergy saw their error ; they said no more
in public, withdrew themselves into the inner sanctuaries
of drawing-room scandal, and, by frightening women for
their reputations, sought to win back men against their will
and their reason. But all would not do; questions had been
asked, and the people had answered them ; useful inquiry
had been started, and wholesome, peaceful, and constitutional measures suggested. The people of this city raised the
standard of reform, and their fellow citizens throughout the
union gave signals of approval. The alarm that followed,
my hearers witnessed. The discomfited politician stood
now with the alarmed priest. What cry could *he* raise ?
Democracy ? He dared not. Democracy is no crime in America. Sedition ? That too sounds better in London than
New-York. What could he cry ? He begged his watch-word
of the priest, and cried—for there was nothing else to cry—
infidelity.

My friends, seeing that in the sense in which this word
has been employed against the free electors of this city, and
against all who aided in awakening their attention to the
necessity of bringing republican education to the aid of republican government—seeing that the same word was
sounded against him who stamped on this country the character of a republic and a democracy, who set forth in the
name of the American nation the equal rights of human
kind, and who, at all times and under all circumstances, encouraged and vindicated the free exercise of the rights he
had proclaimed ; seeing that against him—the noble, gene-

rous, enlightened, consistent patriot and statesman, Thomas
Jefferson—the same cry of infidelity was raised, that is now
raised against honest reformers at the present time; let us
receive the intended insult both as an honourable compliment
and as a good omen—as a compliment to the soundness
of our principles, and as an omen of our success. Let none,
then, be alarmed at a word which, in the mouths of office-
hunters, signifies *political honesty,* and in the mouths of
priests signifies *common sense.* Let it be remembered, that
the cry of infidelity preceded the administration of Jefferson
and that, if doubters in miraculous revelations and biblical
theology, are to be styled infidels, they can only wear the
name in common with all the wisest and boldest patriots
of America's revolution. Let the mass of the people, then,
defeat their enemies by practically evincing that good sense
which distinguishes them as a nation. Let them baffle intrigues and disarm intriguers, by firmly adhering to the
constitutional principle, of effecting wholesome changes
peacefully through their legislatures, and that, not by hastily subverting the existing *forms* of society, however unwise
or unjust, but by preparing a change in the *very soul* of
society—in its thoughts, in its feelings, in its habits, in its
motives, in its social economy, in its moral character, in its
every day practice, and, above all, by distinguishing that
this change in our race can alone be affected by surrounding
youth with all the moral, intellectual, and physical advantages which experience can suggest, observation discover,
the wealth of the state provide, and the protection of the
state secure. And, while pursuing this righteous object,
and seeking out the means for its attainment, may every
honest citizen unite in repressing all discussions calculated
to lead astray the popular attention, to divide the popular
sentiment, or, yet worse, to rouse the popular passions.

At the present moment, when the noblest cause is in progress which ever roused the energies of man, we cannot
mingle too much caution with our courage. In all seasons
of unusual excitement, some are always found with more
zeal than discretion, more wit than wisdom, or more ambition than honesty. That such should rise up in these stirring
days, is little surprising; but, happily we may add, that
such should rise up *in this country* is little alarming. I, for
one, have all confidence in the American people—in their

good sense, and in their political experience. I fear no violence even from their enthusiasm. I think I may say, I fear no *rashness.*

True it is, that closet theorists and imprudent schemers have arisen, to lead astray the inexperienced, to alarm the timid, and to give a pretext to wily enemies. Better had it been, to leave to another generation the discussion of topics, for which passion, prejudice, false habits and selfishness, have ill prepared the present. Better had it been to take a first step, upon the safety, necessity and constitutionality of which all honest citizens are agreed, without straining our sight and whetting our curiosity to examine the ground far a-head of what we shall be called to traverse. But when questions have been prematurely started, and incorrectly treated by inexperienced, imprudent or ambitious individuals, it may be well calmly to meet them. As the most familiar objects, when imperfectly distinguished, have passed for hobgoblins, and frightened a whole village, so may the simplest subject, when falsely presented to the mind, or imperfectly distinguished, pass for some great moral monstrosity, and frighten a whole nation. Of late mingling with the old farcical cry of infidelity, has been heard the more novel and alarming cry of *agrarianism.* This last indeed would seem all but to have drowned the other. We have seen, I think, this evening, the emptiness of the word infidelity, and the groundlessness of the alarm it once excited. I believe a little investigation would expose the equal groundlessness of the alarm excited by the word agrarianism.

I am satisfied, that we of the present generation, have nothing to do with the question, *How shall the property be equalized?* We are neither wise enough nor honest enough, *practically,* to answer it; and as for answers in theory, the world has had too much of them. Still there are some principles at the root of this question, that it might be useful at the present season to investigate. I shall take occasion to do so in a future discourse, when it will be also my endeavour to discuss several subjects of weighty importance.

ADDRESS TO YOUNG MECHANICS.

Delivered at a Meeting in the Hall of Science, New-York, June 13, 1830.

————

IN addressing myself this evening to the young mechanics of our city, I would not be understood as considering their interests distinct from those of other classes of the community.

The interests of the whole human family, in nature and in reason, are ever present to my mind as one and the same. But the ill directed efforts of successive generations have placed us in an artificial state of society. The bond of union originating in the common instincts, wants, and desires of all our species, has been severed instead of strengthened by miscalculating ingenuity or fortuitous circumstances. Occupants of the same earth, citizens of the same country, creatures of the same form and nature, we are partitioned off into classes, and arrayed against each other, in despite even of our own will, by the habits of our youth, and the contrasted and conflicting interests of our after years. In such a state of things, they who are desirous of aiding in the cementing the shattered fractions of society into one whole, have to select first the largest and the soundest fraction—they have to address themselves to the more numerous, as well to the more moral of the classes, which, happily, is also that whose immediate interests are most in unison with those real and natural interests which it is desirable that all should be induced to distinguish and consult.

If therefore I have addressed myself, at all times, more especially to the industrious classes, it has been for two reasons —First; that they comprise the only large mass among the heterogeneous fragments of society; and, secondly, that their interests at the time being are more nearly approached to the great natural interests of man, and incline, therefore, more immediately to wholesome reforms and general union.

While addressing myself however, to this largest and soundest body in the state, it has been my endeavour to excite it to action rather than to opposition; and, if ever my words have provoked a feeling of hostility in man towards man, or in class towards class, I have sinned against my intention, which has been ever, singly and purely, so far as I can read my own heart, to arm men collectively against abuses, and to fraternize their feelings towards each other.

In calling you together at the present time, my young friends, it is not therefore with the view of addressing your peculiar interests as a class, but your interests as citizens, and my only motives for selecting you from your fellow citizens are—that your habits of industry must enlist you on the side of reform, and that your age admits of such cultivation of talent and improvement of feeling as may fit you to become effective reformers.

To the title of WORKING MEN as the distinctive epithet of reformers, I object. All men and all women ought to be *workers*, but, at the present time, when operative and intellectual labour is unhappily separated, the title sounds unfairly exclusive, and, our object being union, exclusion, even in sound, should be avoided. As a man is not necessarily honest because he labours with his hands, so neither is he necessarily *dis*honest because he knows only to labour with his head. In both cases there has been error in education, and there is error in habit, but the fault is in the arrangements of society, not in individuals; and in all our efforts to amend those defective arrangements for the next generation, we should bear in mind that we of the present are all more or less imperfect beings; always *half* trained, and almost always *ill* trained. Indulgence, therefore, on the part of one class towards another, is imperiously called for; every expression calculated to excite jealousy should be carefully shunned, and every watchword of the hour should insinuate union, and breathe of national fellowship, liberality, and harmony.

But while I object to the title of WORKING MEN, as distinctive of reformers, and, yet more, to that of a " working man's *party*," as distinctive of the great national cause of reform. I do look to the industrious classes, generally and especially, though by no means *exclusively*, for the salvation of the country, and expect the youth of those classes to supply to sound reason and sound measures their most ardent, and also their most skilful champions.

Whatever may be the *conceived advantages* of college education, it is but rarely that a bold intellect or a sound judgment issues from the walls of privileged, and but too often useless and superannuated learning; while, on the other hand, what are the *real disadvantages* of the neglected child of labour, he is saved from the conceit of pedantry, and the jargon of sophistry, and thus remains free to profit by whatever lessons experience may bring, and to distinguish simple truth whenever it may meet his ears.

I have made human kind my study, from my youth up; the American community I have considered with most especial attention; and I can truly say that, wherever the same are not absolutely pressed down by labour and want, I have invariably found, not only the best feelings, but the soundest sense among the operative classes of society. I am satisfied, and that by extensive observation, that, with few exceptions, the whole sterling talent of the American community lies (latent indeed, and requiring the stimulus of circumstance for its development,) among that large body who draw their subsistence from the labour of their hands.

The intellectual and moral inefficiencies of our professional classes is but too apparent in our governmental arrangements, and, generally, in all our institutions civil and religious. Legislation, in their hands has been turned from its true intent, and applied to the perplexing, instead of the simplifying of all human affairs. Industry has been sacrificed to trade; honest trade, or the fair exchange of commodities, to speculation; statutes have been multiplied; justice embarrassed; onerous, expensive, tedious, and incomprehensible systems of law and theology, encouraged, to give false occupation to individuals and bodies of men, at expense of the peace, and the reason, and the labour of the mass; and erroneous and imperfect education given to all—to the few in what are called colleges, and to the many in common schools, charity Sunday schools, or no schools at all, whereby aristocratical distinctions are entailed upon the community—some raised unwisely to submit, and others unwisely to govern.

That this is a fair statement will, I think, be admitted by all who inspect, closely and impartially, the frame of existing society; and, I think, such will be disposed also to admit that, so far as reform may be practicable during existing generations, it is more likely to be effectually promoted by the classes who *directly suffer*, than by those who *immediately live* by the errors and abuses it is proposed to rectify.

We do indeed know that honest men may be found among dishonest professions; and, when found, as the lustre of their integrity is greatest, so ought it to be most respected and rewarded. But, generally speaking, the people must look to their own ranks for their own servants, and to prepare themselves for that service, is at once their interest and duty.

It was in the view of aiding the people in such preparation that this building was purchased, and that the teachers herein have laboured. I must observe that the exertions of the friends of popular improvement have been made under every disadvantage. They have had to meditate at odd moments and over hours, snatched from regular avocations, wholesome recreation, or necessary rest, those lessons which a course of regular and undisturbed study should supply. Suitable apparatus and all other conveniences have also been wanting —without funds, and without leisure, they have brought nothing save zeal and perseverance to their voluntary task; and if, under such circumstances, advantage has accrued to the public, we can but distinguish how easy would be the full communication of all useful truth, were but half the pains, and one twentieth of the treasure expended for its development, that is now applied to the propagation of error.

Hitherto the current expenses of this building have been chiefly defrayed by the receipts taken at my lectures. I announced, a short while since, my desire to resign the personal responsibility I had hitherto borne, upon which a subscription was opened for filling up the sum of 600 dollars, to meet the main expenses for the current year. The receipts of this evening will, it is thought, close the accounts of the past season.

In resigning the responsibility, of course I resign all share in the management of this Hall; and the trustess, hitherto appointed by myself, will withdraw to be succeeded by such as shall be elected by the subscribers. If the sum required be made up this evening, it is proposed to nominate the new trustees, and to consider how, in the frequent deficiency of suitable lecturers, the building may be occupied to the greatest possible advantage.

In conversing on this subject with some of our subscribers, I have understood it to be the general impression that public debates would tend, more than any other exercise, to the development of the popular mind, and the eliciting of popular talent. Such is decidedly my own individual opinion; and if, at the first opening of this Hall, I entertained and expower of influencing the public measures, it is your bounden pressed some apprehensions of an exercise I now venture to advocate, it was simply because I doubted our then moral fitness to engage in the sifting out of each other's errors. I feared lest, gathered as we were, from all the various sects and schools of religion and philosophy, we should rather dispute than reason, and judged that before we ventured to try the strength of our wit, we had better make sure of that of our temper. We have now had a twelvemonth's practice and experience; we know something more of each other, and, I believe, of ourselves. The popular mind, awakened to practical inquiry, begins to distinguish the importance of reciprocating indulgence for every variety of human opinion. Faith, of whatever colour, or no faith at all, claims, and is likely soon to be allowed, equal liberty of expression. Free inquiry can encounter orthodoxy with tolerable good humour, and even orthodoxy herself, begins to understand that the air and light of heaven are not her exclusive possessions; and that, after all, there is room enough, and to spare, in this world for those who doubt as for those who believe. But it is, above all, the sounder and more practical views that are now rapidly spreading through the community, which will enable men of all creeds, or no creeds, to meet on common ground; to discuss topics of real importance with a sincere desire of eliciting truth, and even, occasionally, to sport with their speculative fancies without seeing a pit of sulphur opening at their feet, or feeling disposed to pitch thereinto an obstinate opponent.

To you, my young friends, more especially, I conceive the proposed exercise will prove of the highest utility. I have already stated why I regard you as destined to supply the best props to the reformed political edifice of your country. But it is not rashly, nor presumptuously, that you should reach forth your hand to steady that sacred structure. No unrighteous ambition—no petty vanity—no thirst of worldly gain, or worldly influence should lead you to lift your eyes to that—*in principle* the most honourable, *in fact*, alas! but too often the most dishonoured—THE STATE's SERVICE.

As members of the human family, it is your bounden interest and duty to make human nature your study, with a view to the detection of all the causes of existing evil, and, equally, to the discovery of all the sources of possible good. As citizens of a free state, holding not only the right but the interest and duty, to investigate—*first*, the principles laid down by the organizers of this republic; to weigh those principles in your reason and to test them by those acknowledged by your own inner minds. *Secondly :* To study the political institutions established as in conformity with those principles, and to judge how far that conformity has been preserved. *Thirdly :* To consider the statutes enacted, and the laws and practices countenanced and upheld by those legislative bodies, charged (under the guidance and restriction of those principles and institutions) with the administration of the *res publicæ,* or common interests of the whole community. It is, in fine, your bounden interest and duty to make both *man* and *men* your serious study ; or, in other words, to consider attentively society as it now exists, and society as it ought to exist.

Connected with these great moral and constitutional exercises of the mind, (which each and all may follow out in private, with the aid of the more liberal publications of the day,) the careful exercise of the faculty of speech will be found, not merely to promote your public usefulness, but your own individual improvement. A ready command of language assists even the process of thought itself, and is absolutely indispensable to render our thoughts useful to others.

True it is, that no art has been more abused than that of oratory. It has been employed to disguise the hideousness of error, instead of to enhance the loveliness of truth. It has been turned to the confounding the human mind with sophistry, instead of enlightening it by reason. It has been pressed, even openly, into the service of injustice, falsehood, hypocrisy, superstition, and corruption ; and when, in degraded and falling Athens, Demosthenes gave successively, for the three requisites of an orator, "manner," "manner," "manner," he satirized not only the ignorance of his own age and nation, but that of all others.

We know full well how lamentably up to the present day, the truth of the ancient satire has been preserved. The bar and the pulpit, and, alas ! the senate, of modern times, have equally substituted sound for sense, and art for argument, with the rhetoricians, pleaders, and soothsayers of antiquity ; albeit, and here there is cause for thankfulness, our sophists have more generally succeeded in imitating the false matter, than the winning manner of Grecian eloquence ; even as our modern mythology has preserved the delusions and immoralities of the ancient, despoiled of its grace, its passion, and its poetry.

But, as even the abuses of speech bear evidence to its power, so does it regard us as rational creatures to wrest that power from evil, and turn it to our good. And oh! far, far other is the music of the voice, and the elegance of the period, when truth speaks in the harmony, and the love of human kind inspires the fervour of the language. Nor, indeed, is this any longer the age, still less is this the country, in which sound will pass current for sense, as it did with our forefathers. Whosoever in these days, would be listened to, *must* address himself to the reason; but in so doing he will be most injudicious who neglects the conciliation of the feelings, or even who despises the pleasing of the ear. A harsh and ungoverned voice, a forced and imperfect articulation, unseemly expressions, unsightly gestures, tedious repetitions, a hurried, a violent, or, worse than all, a studied and affected delivery, (betraying that the speaker is more occupied with himself than his hearers,) might suffice to stop the ears of an audience to the wisdom of a Franklin, supposing it possible for wisdom so to sin against good taste and propriety.

But all these and other defects will soon disappear wherever there exist two requisites—an ardent desire of improving ourselves, combined with that of rendering service to others. We read that the greatest orator of antiquity was, in the opening of his career, *a stammerer;* and I myself once saw an eloquent pulpit enthusiast move, by his tones and energy, a whole audience to tears, who, one year previous, I had known afflicted with a stutter so excessive as to impede not merely his utterance of a phrase, but even of a word.

The art of good public speaking is rare at the present time, only because it is neglected by the mass, who have considered it to be no business of theirs, and studied by individuals and bodies of men who have considered it the business of their peculiar professions—which professions have required not its use, but its perversion.

Now it will appear evident, upon reflection, that public speaking ought to be the peculiar study of all Americans, even as public affairs ought to be their peculiar business. I know not, therefore, how the leisure evenings of the week could be more beneficially employed by the citizens than in public debating, and to that purpose it has been proposed to devote this building, on all the first evenings of the week, unless a suitable lecturer should be obtained and preferred.

Under the impression that this proposal, as made at a

former meeting, may be acceded to now or hereafter by the body of the subscribers, I feel tempted to venture a few more observations respecting the frame of mind which, not only here, but elsewhere, and through life, it is the duty of every member of the human family to engage in argument. To preserve the order of a meeting, strict regulations and good moderators may suffice, but to impart to it a tone of harmony, there must be the spirit of moderation reigning in each breast. There must be a love of truth, and a desire to prove ourselves worthy disciples, as well as skilful advocates, of truth, before we can come prepared to convince or to be convinced.

It is a high compliment made to the more liberal in opinion, that their enemies are ever extreme to mark what they do amiss. If the orthodox christian sentence his brother to public scorn in this world, and perdition in another, his wrath is styled holy zeal, and counted to him for righteousness ; but if the sceptic in things unseen and unearthly, forget the equanimity befitting all human beings, but which, alas! too much at present conspires to disturb, no epithet is accouuted too harsh by which to stigmatize his self-forgetfulness. Let us not complain, my young friends, of this severity. Let us rather learn to be equally severe with ourselves. Let us take the gibe whenever it is merited, but let it be our ambition to merit it as seldom as possible. Youth is accounted hasty, and is so, for it is inexperienced. Yet do I believe it far more capable of self-correction and self-government, at the present time, than maturer age. To the young, then, do I look for most zeal in the cause of reform, and most tenderness of its houour. From them do I venture to hope the readiest compliance with every useful regulation, and the readiest censure of every departure from propriety, of every rudeness, self-forgetfulness, and unseemly personality. Nor is it only in this building I feel encouraged to see in them the jealous guardians of the honour of free inquiry and practical reform. In the walks of life, I trust, their bearing will be such as to win respect for the principles they advocate ; and, on every occasion, when their opinion may be called for, or their influence may be exercised, may it be found, not only on the side of honesty, but also on that of good manners, forbearance, and moderation. With such reliance on the good sense and good temper of the frequenters of this Hall, I leave them for the season.

PARTING ADDRESS.

[As delivered in the Bowery Theatre, to the People of New-York, in June, 1830.]

(The Declaration of Independence lies open beside the speaker, who will be understood as frequently appealing to the same.)

THINGS move fast in a new world. The human mind, once launched, shoots like a ray of the living sun in a free country. One short year of preparation, and the people of this city are already in action. What say I—of this city? The nation stirs through all its commonwealths; and suggestions, which but yesterday passed for the dreams of enthusiasm, promise ere long to assume the shape and substance of realities.

And it was time for America to give evidence to the world of her advancement in civilization. It was time for her to exercise the high privileges she possessed over the rest of the nations. She owed it to herself, and she owed it to the human race, to exhibit once more in healthy action, that moral energy she displayed in her revolution, and which her free institutions should have nurtured and purified, not quelled and perverted.

After a sleep of many years, this nation awakes to a knowledge of its powers, and a consciousness of its responsibility. The present will count as an epoch, not in the annals of this country alone, but in those of human civilization. Reform once started here, it will make the tour of the globe, and Americans, who have been hitherto known in the ports of trade as gamblers and speculators, will be the heralds of knowledge and virtue to all the people of the earth.

Such is the high destiny this nation was called to fill, when, in its Areopagus of sages, the equal rights of human kind were proclaimed to a startled world. I turn, fellow citizens! to the instrument of your independence, and I see that you stand sponsors for the human race; I look around on the face of the land, and I see the pledge about to be remembered and fulfilled.

And more than *I* have read in the signs of the times this augury. More than *I* have distinguished that the ear of the popular minds is open, and its eye bent on the searching out of all hidden things. Yes! we are told in these days by enemies no less than friends, that " the design exists to subvert the present order of things." Such is the cry raised by every short-sighted office-holder and office-hunter, and echoed by every knave throughout the corrupt ranks of society. But woe to the evil-minded! the kindling patriot and the righteous reformer echo back to the panders of corruption, the cry of their own raising. It is returned to their ear, not in the note of alarm, but in that of exultation. " The present order of things" is weighed in the balance of public opinion and found wanting, and the free people of this city, and this commonwealth, have sworn to subvert it. And who are they that would challenge the pledge? You shall find them in our pulpits of sloth and of slander, in our colleges of exclusion, in our banks of dishonesty, in our law courts of extortion, in our legislatures of special pleading, in all and every of those anti-American institutions invented or perverted to favour the pretensions of the few, and to crush down the rights of the many.

Yes! I for one will admit the charge, and admit it in the name of a daily increasing mass of reflecting citizens. " The design *does* exist to subvert the present order of things." But how? Here is the question whose answer is fraught with alarm, or with peace and security. Let our priests and our missionaries, our stock-jobbers and place-hunters, our ringleaders of faction, and their worthy tools, the hirelings of a venal press—let those solve the question, by what means and to what end the present order of things is to be changed, and they will answer, with the fool in his folly, *by the preaching of infidels to the massacre of christians, and the confiscation of their houses and furniture.* But let us ask the peaceful citizen, how he anticipates a change in the face of society, and he will say, *by the substitution of practical inquiry for spiritual dreamings, which shall lead to the gradual detection and correction of abuses, and to the adoption of such measures for the training of youth as shall absolve future generations from the errors of the present.*

In the simple answer of the peaceful citizen, what is there
to apprehend? Nothing for the honest man, every thing for
the knave. I say every thing for the knave.—I mean every
thing according to the false calculations induced by habits of
dishonest speculation.

It is not that wholesome reform would in reality be injurious
to any. One man's loss ought not in reason to be another's
gain: would not, *in fact*, be another's gain, if men were only
trained in similar habits, and with similar feelings. This they
are not; and, because they are not, are their interests ever
at variance, and their mental sight but too often blinded to
those true and natural interests which point to other motives
of action, and to a more just organization of society.

Yet however obvious the evils in our present motives and
practice—in our present systems of trade and of law, in the
multitude of false employments, and in the excessive competition which so frequently threatens with ruin all employments,
the honest as the dishonest.—However obvious these evils,
and however opposed to the *true* interests of all classes and
all individuals, it were idle to expect all classes and individuals
to co-operate in their correction. Convince the reason, and
habit would run counter still. The gambler, how often soever
the game may run against him, will still haunt the board
which tempts with one chance of gain against a thousand
chances of ruin. The speculator, rather than seek a moderate
and unfluctuating profit, will risk bankruptcy and starvation
in sight of a bare possibility of seizing upon uncertain wealth.
The vain man, blinded by a false education to real honour and
dignity, will prefer an uneasy conscience and mean dependence,
to honest, but, unhappily, despised labour; and even genius
will ambition paltry distinctions, the trappings and profits of
office, rather than the high consciousness of advancing the
public weal.

How salutary then soever reform may be, many will there
be found to oppose it. Corruptions of old growth are dear to
those who have grown old with them; and, as all reformers
have seen, so see we at the present hour, that the misguided
partizans of error will cling to the false, anti-social, and anti-
American fabric, raised on the noble foundation laid by the
fathers of this people, until it crumble to dust before the magic
influence of a more enlightened public opinion, and give place,
in a new generation, to an edifice truly American, the pillars
of which shall rest on republican education, and its walls shall

embrace a nation of freemen, equal in knowledge, in rights, in duties, and in condition.

Such is the change "in the present order of things," the reformers of the present day have dared to anticipate; the people of this city and commonwealth have sworn to effect, and the American nation will be found ready to imitate. No other than a change thus peaceful has been proposed; no other than a change thus gradual could be feasible, and no less than a change thus radical can effect the practical development of American principles.

Upwards of half a century these principles have claimed the love of this people and the admiration of the world. Upwards of half a century has "Liberty and Equality" been the motto of this nation. Upwards of half a century has this motto existed in words, these principles in theory; and now that the people have resolved the practical development of the same, we hear them, at this hour, in this city, denounced as visionary, impeached as iniquitous, and their advocates and vindicators blasphemed as incendiaries and infidels!

Is it come to this? Has treason gone so far in this land, for EQUALITY to be denounced as a dream of enthusiasts, an innovation of foreigners, and a doctrine of Marats and Robespierres? Fathers of this nation! well are ye asleep in your graves! By the sword of Washington, by the wisdom of Franklin, by the honest democracy of Jefferson, it is time for Americans to arouse, and to vindicate the words of this charter!

Fellow citizens! the season is arrived when what is here set forth as abstract truth, must be referred to with a view to practice. The equal rights of human beings are here proclaimed self-evident to reason, inherent in the nature of things, and inalienable in justice. Life, liberty, and the pursuit of happiness, stand particularized among the equal, inherent, and inalienable rights held in virtue of our existence.

Wisely did the framers of this instrument declare these truths self-evident: for he to whose intellect and moral feelings they speak not at once, convincingly, unanswerably, has been perverted by sophistry and corrupted by false habits and example beyond the reach of argument or the persuasion of eloquence. These moral truths speak to the mind, as physical truths to the eye. They speak alike to the child, the savage, and the sage; the blind and heartless advocates of the past and "present order of things," as existing in what is unblush

P

ingly termed *civilized society*, can alone resist their force, or question their universality.

The truths here set forth as self-evident—for which the blood of patriots has been shed, and to which the honour of the dead and the living has been pledged or is pledged—these truths self-evident involve all that the sage ever pictured, or the philanthropist desired　In the equal rights of all to life, liberty, and happiness, lies the sum of human good. Let us pause, fellow citizens! on the words, and see what is required for their fulfilment.

Life. Respected as it is in this land, compared to all other lands beside, our laws still sanction homicide—enforcing the decree of an ignorant and cruel superstition, " blood for blood."

Liberty. Fresh and ever gathering in strength as she dwells under the shadow of this charter, how trammelled as yet are her young limbs and her glorious mind! Still bigotry challenges her thoughts, and prejudice her actions. Still sex, and sect, and class, and colour, furnish pretences, for limiting her range, and violating her purity !

Happiness! Alas! where is it on the face of the earth? Who pursues that whose pursuit is here guaranteed to all? Every one or none. Every one, if we listen to the vague assertions of men ; none, if we look to their actions. Happiness enters not even into human calculation. Man has placed his time, and his labour, and the fruits of his labour, and his pleasures, and his affections, yea! even his honour and his liberty, at the mercy of gold. From youth to age he sees but money ; and, in pursuing it, pursues the shadow of a shade.

Yet, to secure these our equal rights, we read that " government is instituted among men." Is it so ? What has government done up to this hour towards securing the equal rights and equal happiness of our race ? You will say it has done much in these United States.

Fellow citizens! Permit me the remark, and reflect ere you pronounce it erroneous. Government, even in this land, blessed above all others—government, even here, has favoured unless by what it has done, than by what it has *not* done. In the declaration of rights, which limits its powers, find we the source of all the good we possess over other nations. Restrained behind the bulwark of prohibitory constitutional decrees, government here has established no throne, installed no aristocracy, armed no church dominant and militant, erected no hereditary power, sanctioned no hereditary honours, instituted no secret tribunals, effected no arbitrary arrests, imagined no constructive treason, ejected no exiles and aliens, revenged no assaults of the tongue, or even libels of the pen —or, if ever it attempted aught or any of such transatlantic violations of this charter of a new world, Jefferson s were found to sound the alarm, and a nation to stir at the call.*

Thanks, then, to the restrictive constitutional provisions which sprang out of this charter, American government has steered clear of violence. Time is it also, that it should steer clear of corruption, and apply itself actively to the purpose for which we here read it to have been instituted—the development and protection of the equal rights, together with the promotion of the equal happiness, of each member of the human family.

I may not now investigate the object, end, and duties of government in detail. Circumstances will not at the present time permit to me this labour, nor are we, moreover, advanced to that stage of action, when from the truths discoverable in the investigation, it could be useful to deduce all their practical consequences. Our object at all times should be, not merely to develope truth, but to develope it with method and in order. This necessary precaution has been ever too much lost sight of by reformers, who, in consequence, hurrying forward in argument ahead of the popular judgment, impel to measures before their motives are duly weighed, and their results duly calculated—thus producing change rather than reform, advancing only afterwards to retrograde, and, by creating confusion, giving opportunity to the evil-minded to excite disorder and even to provoke to violence.

I observed in a former discourse, that numerous are the topics which a prudent people (and such I conceive the American people to be) will leave to an era more advanced, and a generation more wise than the present. To prepare for that better era, and to model that wiser generation, is *our* duty; and a worthier, a nobler, a more sublime, never fell, nor ever will fall, to the lot of any. To speculate beyond what we can execute is folly; in these days it is worse—it is madness. So much lies within our reach—so much chal-

* The American people will remember the eventful era of 1801. It was then the character of their government was decided.

lenges our attention—so many lets and hinderances have to
be removed from our path before we can make one effective
step in advance, that for us, my fellow citizens! to be
dreaming about all the probable or possible governmental
regulations, or modes of social life which may hereafter be
adopted by our race, were but to lower our understandings
to the level of spiritual enthusiasts, who, while walking on
the earth, have their imaginations in the stars.

I would not, however, be understood to mean, that, while
limiting our progress, coolly and firmly, to one step at a time,
we should not examine in what course and to what final goal
that step is to lead. I would not counsel that in bringing our
united power to bear upon one measure, we should not consider well the general result we intend that measure to produce. I am not for walking myself, nor for having others
walk, in the dark. This would be well were we treading
the path of error; but, on entering that of truth, we must
have an open eye, and an awakened mind. If prudence
require that we move slowly therein, dignity and good sense
demand that we move fearlessly. To move thus we must see
the road before us, and distinguish the final object it is our
ambition to attain.

What is then that object, my friends? What is the purpose of our souls? When we speak of reform, what hope
we to produce? *The universal improvement of our human
condition.* When we bend our minds and efforts to the great
measure of a republican system of education, what do we
intend to effect? *The equalization of our human condition;*
the annihilation of all arbitrary distinctions; the substitution
of the simple character of human beings for that of all others
—the honourable title of American citizen, for that of all the
silly and mischievous epithets introduced by sectarian superstition and anti-social prejudice, to the confounding of our
understandings, the corrupting of our feelings, the depraving
of our habits, and the subversion of our noble institutions.

I said that our object was at once the *equalization* and the
universal improvement of our common condition. It is
necessary to bear this two-fold specification in view, as otherwise, it may convey alarm to many, and false impressions
to all.

Under the existing arrangements of society—the misapplication of human labour, devoted by more than one half to
what is useless or mischievous, and rewarded, not only

unequally and arbitrarily, but in a ratio inverse to its utility—the misapplication also of machinery acting, at the time present, nor to the relief but to the oppression of the human labourer—the false operation of money, as now in use, laying ever at the mercy of the holder of specie or its paper representative, the real wealth of society—namely, *the productions of human industry*.—Under such and other existing circumstances, to speak of equalizing the general condition excites vague apprehensions on the part of the more favoured classes, that benefit is intended to the mass, at expense of injury to individuals.

True it is that we might here demand, where, under " the present order of things," however panegyrised by the dishonest or unreflecting, where is there a class *truly favoured?* where even an individual who feels himself securely happy, and placed beyond the reach of worldly disaster or reverses? But we are not reduced to any begging of the question. Let men construe as they will the advantages or disadvantages of their peculiar class, profession, or position, I would say to all, that poor indeed were the reform which should *lower any*, that only can be reform which should *raise all*.

I do not speak here of worldly fortunes, such as Rothchild's or Gerard's. I do not consider any individual as intrinsically happier for a wealth beyond human ingenuity to employ, nor have my observations regard to any such extreme, and fortunately in this country, rare cases. Undoubtedly the social regulations of a wise generation would render impossible the accumulation of inordinate wealth, not indeed by *prohibitory statutes*, but by the abrogation of all unequal privileges, the absence of all false stimuli, and, above all, by the spread of sound knowledge, the universality of just habits, and the consequent moderation of human desires, and greater moral elevation of human ambition.

But if I do imagine that an improved state of society would present us with no inordinate fortunes, I feel equally satisfied, that it must present us with universal ease, comfort, and security. The equalization of human condition, as ambitioned by philanthropy, or, say but common sense, cannot surely presuppose the disturbing the happy, but the comforting the wretched; not the depriving any of real advantages, but the extending and securing every possible advantage to all.

But how is this to be effected? will be hastily asked.

Certainly not by wresting violently the possessions of some to bestow them upon others, or to divide them among all. Certainly not by upsetting the frame of society which surrounds us, and hastily patching up another out of its ruins. Certainly not by lessening any of the securities, already too few and too weak, by which property is held at this hour, and individual rights and enjoyments, even such as we see them, are secured. The universal improvement of our condition, can only be effected by creating new and more certain securities than any up to this hour known among men. The greatest evil now existing in society is the want of security—the uncertainty to which the tenure of all property, and the fluctuations to which the value of all property is subjected. Could any community, or any portion of a community, not afflicted with confluent madness, propose for object the increase of the very evils which make our curse at the present hour? Could any people, accustomed even to the forms of law, not to speak of justice, be brought to plan and execute the subversion of the very principles it is most for their common interest to respect, the outrage of the very feelings it is most for their honour, and their peace, and their welfare, to cultivate? Individuals, biassed by peculiar circumstances, or excited by a false education, or secluded habits, to speculate rather than to reason, or to reason in the absence of sufficient observation, may indeed shape in their fancy, motives of action at war with all the principles of the human mind, and a state of things as opposed to reason as what we see around us with novelty superadded to render the proposed substitute more insupportable. Certainly individuals may be found, and ever have been found, to advance unwise propositions, and to support the same by unsound arguments. But what then? have we not as good a right to reject as others to make them? What necessity is there for our adopting, either in our individual or national capacity, the proposals of any one, even should the proposals be wise, let alone their being foolish? Or what probability is there of our adopting collectively what is hostile to the habits and feelings of all individually? Truly the alarmists of the present day must themselves perceive something very attractive in the proposal for a national auction of all the lands of the state, and all the goods and chattels of its citizens, to apprehend its adoption by the people of the New-York commonwealth. Or is it only that they consider the understandings of America's citizens unequal to the distinguishing truth from error, the just from the unjust, the useful from the mischievous? Verily it is not they who cover our city walls, and disturb our public meetings with the senseless cries of "infidelity and agrarianism," whom we shall authorize to take the measure of the popular intellect, albeit they have had some opportunity of estimating the popular forbearance!

But no! neither the one nor the other suspicion has originated these shouts of Babel among the scouts and whippers-in of corruption. They well know the zeal and righteous purpose which their plots and cries are impotently devised to hide and to drown; and well they know too, that the people of this city and commonwealth see to distinguish and prefer wise measures from foolish, and are bent upon distinguishing and preferring honest servants from rogues. No! our intriguers, political or spiritual, are not blind to the true dangers of the hour. They know that the danger is to hypocrisy not to virtue, to party not to patriotism, to fraud not to industry, to speculation not to property. They know what is threatened by the quickening spirit of a reviving people—even the party jobbing, intrigue, and corruption, which have made of this city a by-word in the land, and sent, through the foul conduit of the foulest press which ever libelled a nation in the eyes of the world, the rank steam of political iniquity, forth to the ports of distant empires, blasting the fair fame of a free people where most, for the honour of liberty and the weal of the human race, it should shine resplendent, even in the courts of kingly pride and garrisons of military power.

No! the partizans of corruption are neither ignorant themselves nor deem their fellow citizens ignorant of the true object of reformers at this hour, although I deem they have nourished the hope of frightening them into a temporary disclaiming of their object, through fear of seeing it confounded with the crude schemes and ill digested arguments of Thomas Skidmore in the columns of the Courier and Inquirer. But let them despair of their hope. Our object is not too righteous, but, in this land, too *constitutional*, to require concealment or apology. Our object, however harsh it may sound in the ear of the spoiled child of fashion or pretension, (alas! that such should be found within the pale of this democracy,) will ever be dear to a heart truly American, whether it beat in the breast of a rich man or a poor. Our object, however reviled by false ambition, odious to knavery, offensive to vanity, or misconceived of by error, will ever be recognised by the great mass of this people as consistent with their national institutions, and as requisite for the practical development of the truths set forth in their declaration of independence. No! we shall not be driven to deny, nor seduced to qualify, the object, to which, as to the ultimate goal of reform, we, as Americans, are constitutionally pledged to aspire. That object—that ultimate goal is, as I have said, *practical equality, or, the universal and equal improvement of the condition of all, until, by the gradual change in the views and habits of men, and the change consequent upon the same, in the whole social arrangements of the body politic, the American people shall present, in another generation, but one class, and, as it were but one family—each independent in his and her own thoughts, actions, rights, person, and possessions, and all cooperating, according to their individual taste and ability, to the promotion of the common weal.*

Taking this comprehensive view of all that is embraced in our *ultimate* object, every intelligent mind will distinguish that it is not attainable in this generation, and that all we can do, (though this *all* is immense,) is to exercise our own minds, and school our own feelings, in and by its contemplation, to correct such abuses as more immediately tend to exalt, at the present time, individuals or bodies of men at the expense of the mass of the community and, first and last, and above all, to prepare the way for the entire fulfilment of what I conceive to constitute the one great constitutional duty of Americans —namely, the equal promotion of the happiness of all, by laying the foundation of a plan of education in unison with nature, with reason, with justice, and with THIS INSTRUMENT.

Such then is our ultimate object, and let us boldly declare it; such are the means—gradual and constitutional, but sure and radical, by which we propose that object to be obtained. Such is our ultimate object, and let those who challenge it forego the name, even as they have foresworn the feelings of Americans. Such are the means we stand ready to adopt, and let those who blaspheme them forego the title even as they have foresworn the principles of honest men. Here—in our design or in the mode laid down for effecting that design, there is nothing to conceal, and nothing to *concede* or to *extenuate.* I will take on me to speak, in this matter, in the name of my fellow citizens—constitutional is our object, righteous our means, and *determined our resolve.* We have no fear, no doubt, no hesitation, and no concealment. Why should we have ? thought here is free, speech is free, and all action free, which has in view our own benefit, combined with the benefit of our fellow man.

Behold, we have every advantage with us, which, as honest citizens, or as reasonable beings, we could ambition—a righteous object, a constitutional object, and an object feasible without violence to any, and with certain benefit to all. In Europe, the reformer, how expanded soever his mind, or generous his heart, may indeed hesitate to express the fulness of his desire. *Liberty and equality* there, is a cry whose very thought is treason, and its utterance death ; but here, treason lies only in its challenge. How then should there be a point at issue with American reformers ? All true and honest citizens *must,* upon reflection, have the same object—for, behold ! it is engraven on their national escutcheon— it is engraven in never dying letters, in this HOLY BIBLE of their country's faith, their country's hope, their country's love. To commence the practical illustration of the truths proclaimed to the world by the fathers of this nation's liberties, is what we ask at this day —no more could human philanthropy desire, no less could American patriotism demand.

For myself, I feel proud to declare, that no less perfect and entire is the democracy of my views and principles, than what by this charter is demanded of an American citizen ; and, had I felt it otherwise, I had not claimed the noble title. I would see the righteous declaration here penned by Jefferson, signed by sages, sealed with the blood of the fathers of this nation, and solemnly sworn to by their sons on each anniversary of its birth.—I would—what shall I say ? *see* its realization ? That cannot be. But see such measures adopted as shall secure its realization for posterity, to the fullest extent ever conceived or conceivable by the human mind. Yes! my democracy has no reservations ; my yearnings for the liberty of man acknowledge no exceptions, no prejudices, no predilections. Equal rights, equal privileges, equal enjoyments—I would see them shared by every man, by every woman, by every nation, by every race on the face of the globe. But, as I distinguish that equal rights must originate in equal condition, so do I also distinguish that equal condition must originate in equal knowledge, and that sound knowledge ; in similar habits, and those good habits ; in brotherly sympathies, and those fostered from

youth under a system of RATIONAL AND NATIONAL REPUBLI-
CAN EDUCATION.

I have now broadly stated the ultimate object of reformers
at this hour. I have admitted it to be the gradual but
effectual attainment of equality in rights, privileges, and
opportunities, for the pursuit of happiness. They who assert such equality to exist at the present time, are blind
to all facts, or wantonly trifle with words ; and they who
imagine such equality attainable by any other process than
that of a just and similar training of the thoughts, feelings,
and habits of human beings, in youth, distinguish not the
nature of existing errors, nor have a conception of what is
requisite for their reform. As they who would fell a tree
must strike at the root, so they who would rectify the practice of men, must dive to the springs of action, which are in
the mind. True it is—most lamentably true, that change
may be impelled, even as it may be prevented, by compul-
sion ; but reform, that is, *wise and lasting change,* can only
be wrought by conviction. Theorists may dream dreams,
tyrants may issue edicts, legislators may enact statutes,
but wise education alone, by awakening just views, and
forming just habits, can produce a rational and really republican state of society.

What may be the measures adopted by a generation nurtured as equals under the wings of their country, it is not
for us to say ; but of this I am persuaded—that no measure
will by them be adopted, but with the common consent of
all. The feelings even of the minority on any question will
then be consulted, and co-operation rather waited for than
enforced. New motives of action will then originate in the
human breast, new circumstances will gently arise in and
around those young nurseries of freedom, such as lofty minds
and pure hearts can picture, but which to speak of now
would be but to theorize.

Yet, while declining myself, and recommending to others
to refrain from idly recounting our dreams of earthly futurity, as certain to occasion dispute as those so long encouraged respecting the futurity of a heaven, I would fain enter
my protest against all challenge of the liberties of those who
choose to forestall time and circumstance, to advance false
arguments, to propose wild measures, or even to harangue,
if such could be found, in favour of crime and confusion.

Under the blessed institutions of this country, and favoured by that habit of reflection and spirit of forbearance which they have generated, we need never apprehend evil from boundless liberty of speech and of the press. Let all who will, speculate, and publish their speculations. Let all who choose, advocate rash measures, or wrong measures, or prudent measures, or wise. This is no country for error to make proselytes when Truth is in the field ; nor is this a country where challenge can be given to human rights in any case, without shaking the pillars of its constitution. The whole fabric of American government is based upon confidence in human reason—that is, in the capacity of man to distinguish between what is for his good and what for his evil, when both are fairly presented to his mind.

In full confidence in this his capacity have I spoken ; and, though I have dared much, and of course, something encountered from the wrath of incensed parties and misguided individuals, I feel at this hour my confidence strengthened, not only in the truth, but in the final triumph of the principles, of which I have been a zealous, and, I feel, an honest advocate. The task then, thus far, has not been thankless, if it has been arduous ; and, though in its execution I should have offended many, perhaps even they may live to render justice to my intentions, or, what were far better, if truth be on my side, to approach more nearly to my views. This only will I say, that I have assailed what I believe abuses ; that I have advocated equal rights in place of unequal privileges, appealed to fact from faith, to reason from credulity, to justice from law, to virtue from prejudice, to the ever during principles of the inner mind from the changing and fleeting forms of ceremony and superstition, and, bear witness, fellow citizens ! from the unconstitutional and anti republican divisions of sect, class, and party, as existing around us, to this sacred charter of the common rights of equal freemen and American citizens. Oft have I appealed to this charter, and never without reverence ; nor without reverence this night I claim it for the text book of all my heresies, the authority for all my suggestions, and the warrant for all my confidence. On this —the first sure anchor of moral truth—the only inspired scripture, written for human kind, and destined to be acknowledged by all nations—on *this* may the reformer build his hopes as on the rock of ages, on *this* have I builded mine, on *this* must all Americans build theirs.

And now, my fellow citizens! after two years of public exertion in a work I have believed righteous, and called for by the accumulated corruptions and errors which had gathered in and around our social edifice, I feel warned, for a season, to retire. The people are now awake to their own interests. They have taken the cause of reform into their own hands ; and the same boldness which, when they slumbered, I was encouraged to assume, would now appear to me as presumptuous as it has, perhaps at all times, appeared to others. But this is not all. The unwarrantable use made of my name by the abettors of old abuses, during and since the period of the last elections, would alone determine me to remove this poor pretext for party cries and appeals to old prejudices. It is not enough for the people of this city to know that they are rallied around principles and not individuals ; the same must be known to the nations at large and, as soon as may be to the world. So long as I alone was concerned, the noise of priest and politician was alike indifferent to me, but I wish not my name to be made a scarecrow to the timid, or a stumbling-block to the innocently prejudiced, at a season when all should unite round the altar of their country, with its name only in their mouths, and its love in their hearts. For these motives, which I trust my fellow citizens will appreciate, I shall take the present season for attention to some more private interests of my own, and shortly leave this city and the country for a few months, not to return, until after the decision of the autumnal elections.

THE END.

Watson, Printer, 18, Commercial Place, City Road.

BIOGRAPHY,

NOTES,

AND

POLITICAL LETTERS

OF

FRANCES WRIGHT D'ARUSMONT.

FROM THE FIRST BRITISH EDITION.

No. 1.

Containing the Biography and Notes.

NEW-YORK:
PUBLISHED BY JOHN WINDT,
99 READE STREET.
1844.

PREFATORY NOTE,

FROM THE AMERICAN PUBLISHER.

———

THE circumstances which led to the recent publication of this Memoir in Great Britain, together with that of the Political Letters appended to it, will be found explained in the British publisher's note, at the end of the Biography.

The present number, comprising the Biography and Notes, is all that we have as yet received from the British publisher. The second number, containing the Political Letters, was in the press when the first number was forwarded. As soon as the second shall be received, it will be published in the same style as the present.

BIOGRAPHY AND NOTES

OF

FRANCES WRIGHT D'ARUSMONT.

MADAME D'ARUSMONT, better known as Frances Wright, was born in Miln's Buildings, Nethergate, Dundee, on the 6th of September, 1795. Her father's family, which originally came from the Northern Highlands, appears on the Dundee records, as extensive holders of city property as far back as the year 1500. The father of Frances Wright was the only son of a wealthy Dundee merchant. He, as afterward his daughter, was left an orphan at an early age, and was consigned, by his father's will, to the guardianship of a friend and townsman, who proved his fidelity and sense by securing to his ward every educational advantage within his power to procure.

After passing his boyhood in the best academies of Perth and Edinburgh, he followed up his studies in the University of Dublin, and then devoted two years to travelling. At this early age he was the correspondent of Adam Smith, Dr. Cullen, and other distinguished men of science and letters, both in England and Scotland. Scarcely had he reached his majority than he was incorporated into many of the literary and scientific associations of the two kingdoms. The British Museum in London was indebted to his active antiquarian researches, and to his donations in rare and valuable coins and medals. He had a favorite scheme of elucidating and rectifying history by means of medalurgy. He had himself an exten-

sive and valuable collection of ancient and modern coins.
He also devised and cast some pieces of uncommon beauty,
and made a peculiar study of the chemical admixture of
metals best suited to the purpose. He was regarded and
consulted as authority, in all connected with these matters, by Dr. Pinkerton, Mr. Planta, keeper of the medals
in the British Museum, and others.   Nor was he less
conversant with the principles of law and government,
nor less devoted to their study.   The following extract is
made from a MS. in his handwriting, recently found by his
daughter among the family papers. It shows a somewhat
singular coincidence in views between a father and daughter, separated by death when the first had not reached the
age of twenty-nine, and when the latter was in infancy.
The coincidence is the more remarkable, from the fact
that the daughter was raised in an opposite quarter of the
island, and removed from all acquaintance with her Scotch
relatives.

    " The spirit of law and the tenor of the conduct of gov-
ernments, in order to be well-adapted to the mutable and
ever-varying state of human affairs, ought constantly to
change according to existing circumstances and the temper of the age."*

    It appears from the same papers, that he took a lively
and deeply sympathizing interest in the great events and
the greater principles which agitated Europe during the
French Revolution.   He was instrumental in spreading
through his own city and neighborhood, popular translations
of French treatises, political and philosophical.   He circulated, also, the works of Thomas Paine ; and, as having
promoted a cheap publication of his *Rights of Man*, became
an object of governmental *espionage* in, 1794.   His high
standing as a scholar and a gentleman, and the prudence
and measure which he knew how to throw into his mode
of doing everything, saved, however, himself and family
from any positive annoyance.   It was probably at this
period that he changed the motto of somewhat singularly

    * See and compare the address delivered on the 4th of July, 1828.
—*Frances Wright's Popular Lectures.*

qualified loyality on his family crest, " *Pro rege sœpe,*"*
for the more philosophic motto, " *Patria cara carior liber-
tas,*"† a motto which his daughter seems instinctively to
have adopted.

The most confidential friend of Frances Wright's father was his own maternal uncle, the liberal, amiable,
talented, and extensively known and respected, James
Mylne, professor of moral philosophy in the University
of Glasgow. With this her paternal grand-uncle, Miss
Wright became acquainted, during her visit to Scotland,
at the age of eighteen. A mutually warm affection was
the result of their first meeting ; and, though necessarily
separated by the active pursuits of the one party, and the
steady professional occupation of the other, the feeling of
confidential friendship then conceived knew no interruption
until the death of the venerable professor some years since.

The mother of Frances Wright, issued on the father's
side, from the Campbells of Inverary, and the Stewarts
of Loch Awe, Scotland ; and, by the mother's, from the
lettered aristocracy of England. Her mother's father
was a general officer in the British service. The gifted
Mrs. Montague was her mother's grand-aunt, who is understood to have bestowed on her niece and god-daughter
the kindness of a mother, together with those graceful
accomplishments, and that intellectual cultivation, for
which she was as much distinguished as for uncommon
beauty and angelic goodness. Baron Rokeby, (Friend
Robinson,) Primate of all Ireland, and the most liberal
prelate who ever swayed the Protestant ascendency in
that island, was her mother's uncle. Her mother's
brother was the well-known, and much beloved General
William Campbell ; who, deeply versed in the Oriental
languages, highly accomplished as a man and a soldier,
was the companion of Malcolm in his embassy to Persia,
rose rapidly to command in India, and was killed at the
close of the last battle which he won.

Frances Wright was one of three children, who lost

* For the king sometimes.
† Our country is dear, liberty dearer.

both father and mother in infancy. She was herself two
years and a half old. At the wish of her maternal grandfather, General Duncan Campbell, she was taken to
England, and raised, as a ward of Chancery, under the
guardianship of a maternal aunt. Her brother passed
his boyhood under the charge of his grand-uncle, Professor Mylne. A youth of uncommon promise, he was
unfortunately sent, at the age of fifteen, to India, as a
Cadet in the East India Company's service, and killed on
the passage out in an encounter with a French vessel.*

* A brother of Frances Wright's maternal grandfather, (the General Duncan Campbell above mentioned,) by name Archibald Campbell, came to the United States, and lived and died in the city of
Baltimore, Maryland, in wealth and high standing. This gentleman
left two daughters, one of whom married Commodore Ridgeway, of
the U. S. Navy; the other remains single. The circumstance of
the existence in her adopted country of two first cousins of her mother, became known to Miss Wright before her return to the United
States, in 1824. Passing through Baltimore, she inquired for their
residence and was on the point of visiting them. Her foot was on
the very door-steps of their house, when she was arrested by considerations of prudence and delicacy, which the reader may see to
interpret from some observations presented at the close of this memoir. At the period adverted to, she was already deeply engaged
in researches on the slave question, and entertained a suspicion that
she might sooner or later feel herself called upon to act a somewhat
singular part in her adopted country. They who feel conscious that
their motives of action are different from those of the world they
live in, should keep themselves, as far as possible, aloof from all ties
likely either to embarrass their own proceedings or the feelings of
others. This rule Frances Wright has ever done her best to keep
in view.

All the relatives of the subject of this memoir would appear to have
been singularly thrown into opposing political parties, or led by con-
trasting views or circumstances of descent or destiny, to follow out
their career in distant countries, under differing standards of government. Three brothers, of the unfortunate name of Stewart, uncles of
the same General Duncan Campbell, who lived and died a meritorious officer in the British service, and whose brother transferred his
fealty to the United States, embarked the lives and fortunes of their
house in the Jacobite adventure of 1745. By a singular caprice of
fortune, the only daughter of this devoted house, was married to the
confidential agent of John, Duke of Argyle, who managed the correspondence, and executed, for the most part in person, the dangerous mission of exchanging dispatches and verbal communications
between the astute leader of the Scotch whig party and the cabinet

Frances Wright's infant sister remained some years at nurse in the neighborhood of her native town, and was then taken by her kind foster-mother to her maternal relatives in London. She passed her life with her sister, and died in Paris, in 1831.

To the circumstances of her early life, to the heart solitude of orphanship, to the absence of all sympathy with the views and characters of those among whom her childhood was thrown, to the presence of a sister who looked to her for guidance, and leaned upon her for support, Madame d'Arusmont is disposed to attribute the chosen severity of her early studies and prematurity of her views.

Surrounded at all times by rare and extensive libraries, and commanding whatever masters she desired, she applied herself by turns to various branches of science, and to the study of ancient and modern letters and the arts. She was, at an early age, surprised at the inability of masters to answer her questions, which usually turned

of London. It was during an absence of this kind that his wife received, through a faithful clansman, the news of the battle which had decided the fortunes of Prince Edward, and of her own paternal house. One brother lay dead on the field; another was in flight with a price on his head; the third lay dying of his wounds in a cavern on the side of Ben Nevis. She was far advanced in pregnancy, but started on the instant with the messenger of her clan to the aid of her kindred. Her most direct and secret route—the greater part of which has been traversed on foot, by the subject of this memoir—led, by a distance of thirty-five miles, over the highest mountains, and through the most savage passes of the western highlands. She reached the hiding place of her dying brother, received his last breath, aided the escape of the survivor to Canada, (where it is believed his descendants still are,) gave birth in the cavern to an infant, and returned with it, through a thousand dangers, to her husband's home.

This episode may not be without interest for those capable of distinguishing in the energies and devotion of woman—when these shall be duly developed, and turned to account for the weal of collective humanity—the fertile source of the virtue, greatness, and happiness of future generations. It is thought also that this long and rather gossiping note, may be found not incuriously to elicit how all the various and conflicting political convulsions of Europe have invariably tended to throw into the New World, the most daringspirits and noblest energies of the Old.—*Note to the first American edition.*

1*

upon the nature, origin, and object of the subject submitted to her attention. Being checked on one occasion
by a deep and shrewd mathematician and physician, who
observed that her question was dangerous, she replied—
"Can Truth be dangerous ?" "It is thought so," was the
answer. She learned on the occasion two things: the
one, that Truth had still to be found; the other, that men
were afraid of it.

The same conclusion was ever more and more pressed
upon her mind, when, in her solitary studies, she remarked the discrepancy of views and opinions existing in
books; and again, in society, when she listened to those
accounted authority in learning, letters, or morals. If no
two are agreed, no *one* has discovered Truth; and, if so,
Truth has still to be found. But where?

Such was the process of research and reflection which
led to that general tone of mind which dictated, in her
nineteenth year, the little unfinished treatise of "Epicurus," published under the name of "A Few Days in
Athens." In evidence of the extent to which she had, at
that early period, pushed inquiry, it may be stated that
she had even then penned the substance of the three chapters which precede the speech of Epicurus on religion.
And, in evidence, also, of the conscientiousness which has
ever guided her, from the earliest period, in giving publi-
city to any of her ideas, it may be also stated, that she
withheld those chapters at that time, not only from publication, but from every eye. Her motives for withholding
these from the first London edition of the work, and
which afterwards decided her to effect the suppression
of the work itself until circumstances should permit to
her its thorough revision, appear in one of the letters
recently addressed to the *Star*, which letters are now
subjoined to this Biography.

But the attention of her early years was not altogether
confined to the study and the speculations of the closet.
Her sympathies were powerfully drawn toward the sufferings of humanity, and thus her curiosity was vividly
excited to discover their causes. She was perhaps fifteen
when this question was suggested to her mind, upon wit-

nessing the painful labor of the aged among the English
peasantry ; and, again, when she saw that peasantry
ejected, under various pretexts, from the estates of the
wealthy proprietors of the soil among whom she moved :
" Has man, then, no home upon the earth ; and are age
and infirmity entitled to no care or consideration ? }'

Upon one occasion, peculiarly distressing to her feelings, her soliloquy was to the effect that some strange
secret—some extraordinary vice, lay at the foundation of
the whole of human practice. What should she devote
her whole energies to its discovery ? At the close, she
pronounced to herself a solemn oath, to wear ever in her
heart the cause of the poor and the helpless ; and to aid
in all that she could in redressing the grievous wrongs
which seemed to prevail in society. She not unfrequently recalls the engagement then taken, and feels that she
has done her best to fulfil it.

It was while engrossed, perplexed, and often depressed
with silent and unsuccessful efforts to arrive at a satisfactory view of truth in anything ; to unravel the complica-
tions and evident contradictions existing alike in the
opinions and practice of men—it was while thus occupied,
that she first accidentally opened, as appears in her preface to the American edition of her Volume of Popular
Lectures—the page of America's national history, as
portrayed by the Italian Bocca. From that moment she
awoke, as it were, to a new existence. Life was full of
promise ; the world a theatre of interesting observation
and useful exertion. There existed a country consecrated to freedom, and in which man might awake to the full
knowledge and full exercise of his powers. To see that
country was now, at the age of sixteen, her fixed but secret
determination ; for not to a living being did she communicate the intention until the moment of its execution, six
years afterward. Some circumstances, connected with
the first yearnings of her young enthusiasm toward a
country, whose history had kindled a new life of hope in
her soul, might amuse the reader.

She had absolutely devoured the Italian historian, and
was in the full tide of ecstacy, when a sudden apprehen-

sion seized her. Was the whole a romance? What had
become of the country and the nation? She never heard
of either. A panic terror seized upon her. She flew to
examine every atlas in the library. The first was not of
recent date, and showed no trace of *United States*. She
opened, with trembling hands, another and another. At
length she saw *United States* marked along the Atlantic
littoral of North America. Still, after all, was the story
she had read a true one? She now sought carefully
among the more modern authors in the library, and found
Belsham's History of George III. Its perusal quieted
her apprehensions. Her heroes were true men, and her
land of promise had a local habitation and a name.)

It could not be many weeks afterward, that, on visiting
a British Admiral in whose house she was familiar, she
found the veteran, who had retired blind and infirm from
the service, but full of zeal for it and his country, in a state
of great agitation. To her inquiries, he replied, that she
came like his good angel, to throw oil upon the troubled
waters; and that much he had need of consolation, for
those wicked rebels were at their old work again. "What
rebels, my dear sir?" "Ah, my child! those impudent
rebels of our American colonies. It's an old story of
which you know nothing, and the less every body knows
the better; but they are picking up our ships again,
all over the ocean;" and then came such a storm of
passion, and honest vexation, from the worthy veteran,
that her curiosity was silenced by her sympathy, and
she passed some hours in diverting his attention from a
subject which she burned to investigate.

From that day forward, while all around her were
engrossed by the news of the day, touching the alternate
reverses of the French and the Allied Powers, her thoughts
dwelt with unceasing interest, frequent alarm, and unsatisfied curiosity, on the fate and history of the young
nation upon whose short but gallant war of defence, the
papers of the day scarcely vouchsafed an intelligible
notice, and the sound of whose name never greeted her
ears nor passed her lips.

It was not until the visit of Frances Wright to Scot-

land, at the age of eighteen, that she found it possible
to procure the peculiar information which she coveted,
and which had regard more especially ;—First, to the
early colonial history and character of the primitive set-
tlers; and, Second, to the then actual condition and
point of progress of the American population. Under
the last of these heads she could obtain little information ; but, after some search, she was enabled, in connection with the first, to obtain the most varied and
ample records in the library of the University of Glasgow. Upon explaining the nature of the documents she
wished to procure to the librarian, Professor Muirhead,
he led her to a remote and little frequented compartment
of the gallery ; and, pointing around it, filled as it was
with volumes and pamphlets from floor to ceiling, observed that she would find there all that had ever appeared in print respecting the American colonies, adding that,
if she was curious in the same, she might select and
study the records at her leisure, as they were seldom
consulted. She turned the opportunity so far to account
as to familiarize herself with the character of the American nation in its origin and infancy ; and thus to prepare
her mind for its more accurate inspection at the present.

Frances Wright passed three years in Scotland, during
which period she employed her summers in visiting its
Highlands and Lowlands ; and her winters in closet study.
She then returned to England ; and, in 1818, after having
arranged her pecuniary affairs, and those of her sister
she embarked from Liverpool for New-York.

Her real motives for this voyage were disguised from
all but one gifted female friend, and from Professor
Mylne. The former, who had accompanied her husband
to the United States, in his flight from persecution, in
1794, and returned to Europe upon the death of her
husband, two years afterward, supplied the few letters she
was willing to take. The latter, to whom she only communicated her intended voyage at the very moment of
its execution, and after her passage, with that of her
sister, was secured in the New-York packet ship, Amity,
came to meet her in Liverpool, and saw her embark with

2

her young companion for a distant country in which she knew not a living creature.

To the gentle reproach made by her uncle, on account of her singular reserve on the subject of a voyage so startling to all her friends and painful to him, her reply was to the effect that, had not her determination been the result of the most mature reflection, and had it not also been irrevocably fixed, she should long since not merely have given him her confidence, but asked his counsel. As it was, she put it to his good sense, whether she had not acted wisely by rendering all discussion impossible; and given the best proof in her power of her high opinion of his liberality and elevation of mind, by confiding to him the real object of a voyage which she conceived few, if any but himself, could appreciate. With respect to the preference she gave to America over Italy and Greece, which he had recommended to her attention as more in unison with her early studies, she asked in reply, if a young country inhabited by freemen, was not more worthy to attract curiosity than countries in ruin, inhabited by slaves? "The sight of Italy, dear uncle, prostrated under the leaden sceptre of Austria, would break my heart." The generous and enlightened friend to whom she spoke received her explanations with sympathetic kindness, observing that she was the child of her father, and must have inherited her views and principles in the blood

Such are the circumstances which preceded and induced the first visit of Frances Wright to the United States, and decided her to adopt them as her country. This was at a period when they appeared, as it were, blotted from the recollection of Europe; or known to it only as a field of mercantile speculation, or as an asylum for the political exiles of its continent. The chivalrous tale of that opening revolution, which a Franklin had represented at the bar of the British parliament and at the court of feudal France, had died away in the European mind, drowned and effaced by the cannon of a thousand battles, the agitation of a thousand schemes of ambition, and the unreal honors of a thousand pageants and victories. The nature of her impressions, as received during a first glance at the cherished country of her young en, thusiasm, appear in the volume published on her return to England in 1820.

Her visit to America had been made entirely for her own instruction, and with no immediate view to that of others. The eager inquiries addressed to her from all quarters on her return, and the general and absolute ignorance betrayed by the character of these questions touching the past history and present condition of the country she had hastily and imperfectly inspected, led her to prepare for the press the volume of letters which, at the time, excited no small attention from the thinking portion of the European public. Their appearance changed the tone, and somewhat corrected the views, of leading British periodicals, while they revived, on the European continent, old reminiscences of the country of Franklin and Washington, and a new ardor in the cause of religious and political liberty.

This work, published in London under the name of "Views of Society and Manners in America," and translated without her agency into most of the continental languages, necessarily brought her into relation with the prominent reformers of Europe. Her natural taste for retirement, and strong dislike for all fashionable, or other society unsuited to her views and feelings, has led her, as a general rule, to shrink from letters of introduction. She delivered three only on her first visit to the Unit t States ; not one in France, and doubts if she has made use of six, unless in the way of business, in the course of her life. Experience taught her, in very childhood, how little was to be learned in drawing-rooms, and inspired her with a disgust for frivolous reading, conversation, and occupation. But more especial has ever been her disgust for every kind of quackery and pretension, literary, scientific, and, more than all, political and philanthropic. The all but universal and ever increasing leaning of the age in that direction, has driven her into all but seclusion, from which she has issued only, but always, when

impelled by the hope of achieving any real good to the
cause of human liberty and improvement.

Frances Wright made her first visit to Paris in the spring
of 1821. At this period commenced her intimacy with
General Lafayette, from whom a pressing invitation had
previously sought her in England, as the author of a work
necessarily possessing for him a peculiar interest. The
heart affection which that venerable soldier of liberty retained, to the last moment of existence, for all connected
with the American Republic, was in this case the bond of
a friendship of no ordinary character. Miss Wright possessed his most intimate private and political confidence,
interrupted only by their separation at the period of the
General's return to France, from his triumphal tour through
the United States. That tour Miss Wright witnessed with
peculiar interest, and marked it as the opening epoch of a
political revival in the American nation, which, from the
close of the revolutionary war until that period, (with the
exception, indeed, of the second struggle for independence
between 1812 and 1815,) had been engrossed by the indispensable preliminaries of greatness, namely ; the growth
of population, the conquest of the soil from savage nature,
the extension of commercial relations, and of the influences consequent thereupon, and the creation of all industries
indispensable to comfortable human existence, and without
which no nation (during the prolonged reign of powerful
and rapacious governments, organized alike for hidden
fraud and open robbery) can be readily independent of
foreign influences and foreign domination

Frances Wright's residence in France was prolonged
until 1824, and it is worthy of remark that during that
period, though necessarily known to possess the general
confidence of the revolutionary leaders throughout Europe,
she was never in any way molested under the Bourbon
Government of the elder branch. This was attributable,
no doubt, to her unvarying prudence in writing and speaking, and to her habit of looking to principles rather than to
men ; a habit which has preserved her through life from
party spirit or opiniative violence, and that, even when

most exposed to violence from others. Her short residence in America, previous to her visit to France, had also supplied her with valuable opportunities for judging men, apart from their opinions, and even from those acts, however violent, to which opinion alone impels. Opinions she had perceived to be more frequently the consequence of early impressions acting upon peculiarites of temperament, than of any consistent reasoning from substantiated premises. It was thus that while herself republican in all her views, hopes, and affections, she had learned in the United States to appreciate the private virtues and intellectual endowments of many leading French royalists and Bonapartists. Among these, she held in more especial esteem Monsieur and Madame de Neuville and General Bernard. With the former, who returned from M. de Neuville's diplomatic mission to Washington aboutthe time of her arrival in Paris, her personal relations were naturally renewed, and although these as naturally relaxed during the frenzied reactions of the restoration, she continued, from time to time, and at hours when she was not likely to encounter political characters, or to find M. de Neuville himself, her visits of respectful affection to his lady, with whose sincere and unobtrusive Christian catholicism and devoted loyalty no harsh bigotry or political violence ever blended. In connection with this subject, the following anecdote may possess some interest for the reader, and may tend to illustrate Frances Wright's feeling with regard to it.

She had witnessed, during three consecutive days, from the tribunes of the French Chamber of Deputies, those scenes of parliamentary violence which closed with the expulsion, by an armed soldiery, of the upright and fearless Manuel from the representative body. It happened on that evening, that she was in the saloon of the witty and accomplished Count Segur. A knot of political characters, and all prominent members of the opposition, gradually assembled. The event of the day was the natural topic of discussion, and the leading legitimates received, as naturally, their share of censure and vituperation. " *Ce Hyde de Neuville! c'est un homme de sang ; un vert* *table tigre contre revolutionaire."** Miss Wright, who had been conversing apart with Madame de Segur, here rose, and, advancing toward the circle of politicans, observed that she was doubtless about to surprise them, but that she had known M. de Neuville personally and intimately, and that she must give her testimony to his possessing a very different character—*" Forcené comme nous l'avons vu Messieurs, je le connais pour un homme doué d'une compassion sans bornes et de la candeur d'un enfant."†* However astonished, the party could not but admit the testimony of one whose political principles were so well known, and the tone of the conversation changed to philosophical reflections on human inconsistency.

But if at all times indulgent toward intellectual or even moral aberrations, having their source in opiniative error or in the passion of prejudice, Frances Wright has ever felt, and seldom disguised, an unconquerable repugnance for characters but too common in every party—men who make their opinions ladders to their ambition and cloaks to their dishonesty. Hypocrites are not found only in the suite of theology, nor knaves in that of aristocracy. She has known men as poor in honor, and as bankrupt in rectitude among skeptics as among believers, and among democrats as among their opponents. The moment that a party arises, partisans may, and more frequently do, attach to it their selfish interests than their honor; and—trustingthe defence or the concealment of their vice to the spirit of party, or the generosity of those they have injured—not unfrequently pass themselves off for paragons of virtue and martyrs of principle. In an age of peculiar demoralization, as always must be an age of transit from one order of practice to another, it is well to soften with pity our contempt for human meanness and profligacy; yet still, they who respect themselves, will ever shun an association with the dishonest or the dishon-

---

* This Hyde de Neuville is a man of blood—a very tiger of counter revolution.

† Furious as we have seen him, gentlemen, I know him to possess the compassion of a woman, and the candor of a child.

orable ; or if, unhappily, they have been deceived in the estimation of individual character, will break, without possibility of return, from all private intimacy with those whom they have distinctly recognized to be base in their nature. Were the criterion followed, of looking to the moral elevation of men rather than to their opinions, it would be possible to select from all parties, as from all sects, a chosen band of reform leaders. These are times when prejudice can hardly fail to give way, but when principles are very difficult to acquire. An honest royalist, or an honorable aristocrat may, and will become, in the propitious hour, an honest patriot and an honorable promoter of reform. And, in like manner, a sincere Christian, in suitable circumstances, may and will become an ardent inquirer after truth, and a devout disciple of knowledge ; but a dishonest and dishonorable man, whatever be his belief or unbelief, his political notions or associates, must, sooner or later, disgrace every cause, and the very form of humanity which he wears.

Having followed, with painful interest, the course of ill-conducted, and therefore necessarily unsuccessful, efforts at revolution, until the close of the horrible French campaign, and martyrdom of Riego in Spain, Frances Wright returned to the United States in 1824. The observations made upon men and events during that disturbed epoch, had somewhat modified and greatly matured her views. Though familiar with all the movements of the revolutionary party, and deeply interested in the fate of leading individuals, she had but seldom anticipated success to efforts of which the object appeared to her ill-defined, and those who pursued it far from agreed among themselves. The general want of political knowledge and political experience, the frequent vanity and frivolity of individuals, the confidence placed in more than suspicious characters, the absurd drawing-room intrigues and fashionable conspirators, contrasted strangely and painfully, though sometimes almost ludicrously, with the serious character of a struggle in which human lives, and those often of the young and the chivalrous, were the stakes of the game.

Her mind now fixed, singly and unalterably, on the United States, as on the country in which human progress was rendered at once safe and certain, by the nature of its institutions, and the condition and character of its people.

The essential difference between the American institutions and those of all other countries, has been frequently elucidated by the subject of this memoir. It appears in her first " Views of America," and is fully illustrated in such of her published discourses as are known in Europe. Perfect in their *theory*, of which the principle is *change, according to, and in unison with, the progress of the sovereign popular mind*, and perfect also in *that provision of their political framework* which facilitates, at all times, *the moulding of the constitutional code of practice, so as to keep pace with that progress*, the duration and continuous growth of the American empire appear placed above the shock of accident, even by the very nature of man, and by the nature of things as influenced by human power.

The essential difference between the character of the American population, and that of all other countries, she distinguished to be this: Its moral and intellectual, no less than its physical force—in other words, *its soul* no less than *its body*—is found in the fields of agriculture. On the European continent, the laborer of the soil is still, in form, manner, and mind, a peasant. His sight and his thoughts extend no farther, as the saying is, than the steeple of his village church. Nor can the military service be said, even in France, the most advanced continental nation, to effect any wholesome exception to the rule. A soldier is but another form of the slave; and the phrase is proverbial, that one who has passed the four best years of his youthful prime in the ranks of the army, is ever afterward good for nothing.

The independent landed proprietors of France, as multiplied by the revolutionary law of inheritance, might indeed, and would—if all the wise and beneficent provisions made by the National Convention for generalizing instruction had been allowed to take effect—have constituted the powerful nucleus of a free and independent nation. Those provisions annihilated by the astuté despot Napoleon—who, of the whole magnificent instructional system devised and launched previous to his accession to power, at the head of a victorious army, preserved the *Polytechnic alone,** as the nursery of military captains— those provisions annihilated, the whole agricultural force became, in the summities of its intelligence. a military force, and, in its labor, a brute force.

During, as since the period of the empire, every successive government has applied itself systematically to vanquish the intelligence of the agricultural force by corruption ; and, where that may have been impracticable, by persecution ; and, where it may have been raised beyond the reach of direct annoyance, to drive it from the field of public utility into the inactive walks of private life. But there has existed another, and a yet more powerful bar to the saving influence of the more intelligent land power in revolutionary France—*the annihilation of the provincial sectionment of the country.* By this means the supreme administration of all local affairs is carried up to a national centralization, in an overgrown capital, drowned in luxury, effeminacy, and vice, of which the best theories are but visionary dreamings, and of which the absolute control is now vested in cannon-crowned *bastiles, forts,* and *bastions !*†

The condition of things in Great Britain differs, in important particulars, from that in France, though certainly without being better. Under this head enough will be found in the letters which follow this Biography.

* Napoleon *preserved*, and did not *create*, the Polytechnic School, as has been the impudent assertion of his panegyrists.

† This is not to say that, at the point of time when France, insurgent against the feudal power, both of the nobility and the Church, sought protection in centralization against provincial influences, that such policy was erroneous. The error has been in prolonging that policy beyond the emergency which generated it. Feodality in France is a buried corpse, which even the *majorats* of Napoleon could not galvanize, nor the frenzied efforts of the restoration resuscitate. The land power of France is no longer a tyrant, but a victim—and a victim tied, bound, taxed, and tormented to please an army of rapacious placemen, stock-jobbers, and speculators.

3*

Fully alive to the essential differences existing between the points of progress attained by the most advanced nations of Europe, and that occupied by the American Republic, Frances Wright now returned to the latter, better able, indeed, to distinguish the defects and inconsistencies which she suspected to exist in her adopted country, but yet with increased confidence in the promise of its futurity.

Her attention, in the first instance, was more immediately attracted to the consideration of negro slavery, as existing in the Southern States. She was satisfied that the subject, to be understood, demanded serious study and an intimate familiarity with all its bearings. The knowledge she possessed of the country in its past history, led her to distinguish, at least, as much to admire as to anathematize in the conduct of the master race toward the subject African; and, reasoning from these premises, she inclined to expect that, if the complex difficulties which surrounded the subject could be satisfactorily met, the will to act justly would not be wanting. The historical facts which were present to her mind, and which encouraged her to push enquiry with the hope of its turning to practical account, were as follows:

1. The negro was originally carried to colonial North America *forcibly* by the ships of the mother country, contrary to the feelings, and in despite of the resistance of he colonists, and of the reiterated and solemn protestations of their legislative assemblies.

2. After a course of uninterrupted opposition to the slave-trade on the part of the colonies, we find the violent prosecution of the slave-trade, as countenanced and enforced by Great Britain, among the wrongs enumerated by colonial Virginia, in that solemn protest addressed to the British Parliament which opened the Revolution. And, moreover, the same appears in the declaration of political rights of Virginia independent, and, yet farther, was inserted in the preamble of the constitution of that State.

3. The same was farther inserted among the list of grievances enumerated as authorizing rupture from metropolitan dominion in the original draft of the revolution-

ary Act of Independence, as drawn by the illustrious committee, Franklin, Jefferson, and Adams ; and subsequently effaced from considerations of general policy, easy to appreciate under the circumstances.

4. The slave-trade was immediately abolished by the United States independent.

5. The slave-trade was afterward assimilated to piracy, and punished with death by a law of the United States.

6. Slavery was abolished in all the American States, in which the number of slaves was not sufficient to render an act of enfranchisement menacing to the major interests of public order, industry, and the general welfare of the country.

7. This abolition was full and entire from a certain date specified, and was passed without any question of indemnity to the masters. But the act so rendered, be it observed, was not an act of spoliation, made by a government distinct in interests, or removed by distance, from the population ; but an act of conceived (if not altogether of real) propriety and wisdom, on the part of governments making part of the population. Both the population and governments of the northern States had the good sense to distinguish that, under the circumstances of their position, the public welfare would be better promoted by recourse to free labor, while the absence of sufficient experience prevented them from distinguishing the disadvantages, more especially to the enslaved race, of sudden emancipation : disadvantages everywhere, and at all times, immense.

8. According to the laws of negro enfranchisement, passed in the northern States, a prohibition existed to enfranchise any slave, past a certain age, without the free consent of such slave, or without his master being bound to furnish him with the means of subsistence. Under the protection of this clause, many gray-headed negro servitors, of both sexes, remained with their masters at the period of Frances Wright's return to the United States, in 1824.

Such were the facts which inspired her confidence in the national character, and encouraged her to bring the whole ardor of her disposition to the practical study of a question, of which she at once distinguished that the gravity was the least appreciated by those who treated it the most magisterially. From the very outset, she had but little sympathy with professed abolitionists; among whom she usually found much zeal with little knowledge; and, not unfrequently, more party violence than enlarged philanthropy. Hatred of the planter seemed oftentimes to be a stronger feeling than interest in the slave; a mode of envisaging the question more especially peculiar to foreigners and adopted citizens. These, accustomed in Europe to carry all things with struggle and violence, and to believe that their own view of every subject is precisely the right one, are apt to take little pains to investigate the views of others; and satisfied, upon arrival in the country, that they know both how everything is, and how everything ought to be, are but too frequently more impatient to teach than to learn.

As the spirit which actuated her was the very opposite of this, Frances Wright sought information everywhere, and more especially at its source, in the southern States themselves. She was satisfied that, to embrace all the difficulties—industrial, political, individual, local, states, and federal—with which the question was surrounded, she . must consider it more especially on the very soil of slavery, and in the interests of the two populations there brought into juxta position. She procured in Washington extracts from the registers of all the laws of the slave states, bearing directly upon the labor and the government of the negro. She travelled through the greater part of the Union, visited familiarly the planters, and consulted them on her object and her views; seeking the aid of their experience, and discussing with them the dangers for the country, the disadvantage to the master race, the pernicious example to youth, the monstrous anomaly in the institutions presented by a state of things which associated labor—the source of all that is good and great in man—with social degradation, political nullity, and brutal ignorance. On the other hand, she readily admitted the impossibility, even the absurdity, the dan-

ger to American institutions—alone fitted to guide and to
regulate bodies politic, endowed with intelligence, and
habituated to the exercise of sovereign power—the common ruin, in short, for the two races, of an act of simple
enfranchisement similar to that which had been passed
in the northern States. She knew from observation the
evil effects produced by the mere governmental abolition
of an evil which has its seat in the mind, the habits, and
through hereditary influences, in the very physical organization of a race. She had distinguished, at an early
age, that human enfranchisement—which is but another
name for civilization—is, in its beginnings, a slow, gradual, and complex operation ; and that, to insure its certain advancement, it must be made to move forward simultaneously in the soul of the internal man, and in the
external influences which surround him. It has been
this conviction, which has ever more and more guided her
efforts and moulded her views, as it has become ever
more and more rooted and reasoned in her mind by observation, experiment and reflection.

It was during the course of these preliminary inquiries
that she visited the German colony, which had founded,
and which then occupied, the village of Harmonie, on
the river Wabash, Indiana ; the same afterward purchased by Mr. Owen, and of which the name was then
altered into New-Harmony. Upon inspecting all the de-
partments of industry, and more especially the agricultural, which formed necessarily the large base of the
growing wealth and prosperity of the property, she was
forcibly struck—not merely with the advantages of united
and organized labor, which may be seen at any time in a
cotton-mill, or in any other public work or institution
whatsoever—but with their peculiar appropriateness to
the object which, at the time, engrossed her attention.
Nor was there, indeed, much difference in the point of
intellectual advancement between the mass of the German
laborers, there submitted to the spiritual and temporal
control of astute leaders, and that of the southern negro.
The same and a yet more startling and degrading prostration of the moral and intellectual being, she subse-

quently witnessed in the Shaker establishments, of which
some four or five then existed throughout the United
States.   In all, Christian fanaticism and subjection were
the means employed to stultify the intelligence, and hold
the physical man submitted to the will of others.   As
will be imagined, the physical man thus depressed, performs his daily task without any of the inspirations of genius.
In consequence, these communities, (so called) in which
labor—easy, indeed, after the first clearing of the soil,
and other rude works of preparation, have been effected
—is the regular and unvarying occupation of the mass,
broken only by psalm-singing and other tedious, and
sometimes ludicrous ceremonies.   In consequences these
communities present nothing striking beyond well-culti-
vated farms and gardens, and well-conducted manufac-
tories.   No great or beautiful works of art ; no libraries ;
no laboratories, or scientific workshops, devoted to aid the
progress of invention and the sublime conquest of matter
by mind ; and no men and women, beaming with intelligence and that joy of the soul, the necessary result of
worldly independence, justly earned by exertions justly
requited ; and no rising generations trained to excellence
by the spur of emulation, and promising to start ahead of
their predecessors, and to be themselves vanquished in their
turn by successors profiting by their example and experience, and by the ever-accumulating knowledge and
capital of society !   And yet such should be the result of
united labor, or it fails in its object.   If it centuples not
the power of the individual, both for the enfranchisement
of the individual, and for the greatest possible welfare,
wealth, and grandeur of the body politic, it does no more
than what has been ever, more or less, done to this hour.
No tyranny has ever been blind to the advantages of
united and organized labor ; but liberty, enlightened by
knowledge, can alone resort to it fearlessly and powerfully, because beneficially, to man.   Poor, indeed, is the
benefit which feeds the body without nourishing the mind.
The military despot may feed his soldiers, at once liberally and economically, from a common kitchen, and
lodge them comfortably in clean and airy apartments ;

yet what free man would not prefer a crust, a draught from the spring, and a rude shelter from the weather, than such accommodations. purchased by the sacrifice of all individual nobility and independence.

Admiring the order, method, and facile result of labor as organized, although on the whole, very imperfectly, in the German society, Frances Wright procured much valuable information from its directors. Among these, she found a man of singularly enlarged and philanthropic views. and communicated to him freely her sense of what was deficient in the colony. She found him alive to its perception, and greatly desirous of seeing new moral principles of action infused into the population, and a more just mode of administration substituted for the spiritual government of its directors. He promised that, failing his success to effectuate a reform in his own society, he would join her in the undertaking she contemplated. in the southern States. Frances Wright visited a second time, in the same season. this German colony, and witnessed its departure when Mr. Owen took possession of the estate. She afterward twice visited her German acquaintances in their new settlement of Economie, below Pittsburgh, on the Ohio ; and saw, as it were. a new village— with its fields. orchards, gardens, vineyards, flouring-mills, manufactures—rise out of the earth beneath the hands of some eight hundred trained laborers. A startling circumstance occurred previous to her last visit to Economie. This was the sudden and ill-explained death of the distinguished Becker. The frightful apprehensions which circumstances generated. but which she did her best to stifle in her mind, she afterward found to have been very generally entertained both in and out of the society. He had attempted to induce an alteration in the tenure deeds of the property in favor of the mass, and to extend to the same, the rights of administration. The circumstances of the case. and the various surmises which they generated. inspired Frances Wright with additional distrust and abhorrence of all associations not founded upon the broadest principles of justice. and of which the bond of association, the tenure of land and capital, and the mode of direction, were not made clear to all concerned. It is self-evident, indeed, that wherever this is not the case, the whole must end in a trick of swindling, or a game of children.

It is distinctly from the inspection of the German colony of Harmonie, and afterward of Economie, that Frances Wright dates a first conception of the mode in which might be effected the gradual abolition of negro slavery in the southern States ; and, equally, the gradual reformation of civilized society. The more closely and widely she had considered the first of these questions, the more closely she distinguished its connection with the second, until she soon perceived that the positive enslavement of the laborer is but another, and a more primitive, form of that universally existing curse of the earth—the enslavement of labor. A necessity in the earlier stages of civilization, it becomes ever more and more discordant with the nature of man, and the nature of things, as mutually improved and improving with the advance of knowledge, productive art, and mechanical power. In the course of its progress toward annihilation, as followed until this hour in the Old World, the evil has undergone various modifications ; while in the southern section of the American United States, it has remained in *statu quo*. This has proceeded from three causes. First, the character of the American institutions. Second, the difference of race existing between the subject and the master population. Third, the immensity of distance in the point of advancement between the two races thrown into juxtaposition without possibility of moral and intellectual contact.

Neither the red savage nor the negro slave can be converted into American citizens, by acts of legislation ; and this not because the one is black, nor the other red,'but because *the one is a savage, and the other a slave*. As civilization, at this hour, is an impossibility for the Indian, so is political sovereignty at this hour an impossibility for the African. The former, when unhappily immersed in white civilization, as he was while resident in the bosom of the American States, became, and could only become, degraded, imitating the vices, without acquiring the in-

dustry, of the white population ; and so the latter, if le-.
gally installed in citizenship, would degrade the institutions to the level of his own moral and mental state, long
before the institutions could elevate him to their own
standard. In both cases, the circumstances of color and
feature increase, though they do not constitute, the diffi.
culty, which has until now barred the progress of either
race, while placed in juxta-position with one, their superior in knowledge, and therefore necessarily the sovereign
disposer of their destinies.

It was evident to Frances Wright, that to effectuate the
emancipation of the negro with safety to the material interests of the country, and with mutual advantage to himself and to the master race, he must be made to go through
a real moral, intellectual, and industrial apprenticeship.
This apprenticeship would evidently have to embrace the
improvement of negro labor, and the gradual preparation
of the negro himself to direct it, to estimate its value, and,
in general, to administer his own affairs. From the first
generation litle comparatively could be expected, but the
enabling them to clear the expenses of purchase and outfit by executing the first rude labor of a settlement on the
southern frontier ; to familiarize them with the order and
method of organization ; to keep their own accounts ; to
encourage them to the earning of their enfranchisement
and removal to a free colony, on the African coast or
elsewhere ; and, generally, to improve their habits, and
inspire them with ambition for the further improvement
of their children. The children, brought up distinct from
their parents in schools of agriculture and industry,
might evidently be expected to effect more. The clearing of the forest and first breaking up of the soil effected,
their labor would present the advancement of agriculture,
the general sanification and improvement of the country
—by the draining of swamps, opening of roads, clearing
of navigable streams, and other works difficult for the
white race in a southern latitude. In the rising, and,
better, in all successive generations, the advancement of
the negro race itself in the scale of being might be presented, and its preparation for independence and civiliza-

tion secured by its acquisition of all the useful arts, and
of a familiarity with mechanical power—that mighty
humanizer of man, and conqueror of nature and the elements.

It will be understood that, to prepare for the realization
of a perspective so vast, an individual could only propose
to furnish a limited experiment, capable of supplying to
the bodies politic of the Southern States, some first data
upon which to ground a general plan of procedure. That
plan, when once undertaken by the States themselves,
would necessarily insure to the southern section of the
Republic, a futurity of ever-increasing power and grandeur. The African race, trained and civilized by its
American guardian, and leaving behind it a country prepared for facile cultivation by the white race, would necessarily supply to tropical climates, colonists fitted by
organization no less than experience, to vanquish their
dangers and sanify the richest, though now the most deleterious, regions of the globe. The boundless regions open
to colonization—round the Mexican gulf, through the
Panama isthmus, into the tropical belt, where now flooded by the Amazons and Oronoco—may employ the African during the generations of his training, when the
southern section of the United States may have no further
demand for his labor. And in that extensive region of
the globe, it may be the proud destiny of the trained African, and of the Indian—won by a more benign civilization than that which now tames man but to degrade him
—it may be the destiny of these two races—the one redeemed from servitude and the other from ferocity—to
found an empire of wealth, beauty, and freedom, where
now stretches, through degrees of latitude and longitude,
the deleterious swamp, peopled by the savage, the reptile,
and the beast of prey.

It will be understood also, that, in the general view
embraced by Frances Wright, one-half had reference to
the master race. If the slave was to be prepared for independence and civilization, the master had equally to be
prepared for that highest order of independence and civilization, when man is to exchange dominion over his fel-

low man for dominion over nature ; when the power of inert matter, rendered instinct with life by human genius, shall replace the weak energies and abject servitude of the human laborer ; and when political science, breaking for ever the rod of tyranny, shall weigh in the balance of justice all human interests, and surround the individual, from birth to death, with guidance, protection, and care.

It is not necessary to enter into details touching the first labors of an agricultural establishment in the bosom of the forest. Having remarked the fatal dependence of the planter, at that period, on upper-country supplies for all articles of food, and his so frequently ruinous reliance on the high price of a staple produce, the object of Miss Wright was rather a good farm than a cotton plantation. The position she selected, therefore, was on the edge of the cotton region, in the thirty-fifth degree of latitude, and bordering upon a then Indian country. She purchased here two thousand acres of good and pleasant woodland, traversed by a clear and lovely stream, communicating, thirteen miles below, with the Mississippi, at the old Indian trading station of the Chickasaw Bluffs.* She then purchased several negro families, comprising, at the outset, fifteen able hands. She found, in her new occupation, intense and ever increasing interest, but of which it would be too long here to present the details : suffice it, under this head, to say that the worst was accomplished, when, seized by severe and reiterated sickness, she was forced to make a voyage to Europe for the recovery of her health, which, entirely prostrated at that period, was never afterward such as to permit to her free exposure to the sun, and bodily and mental activity through all seasons and all hours. During her absence, too, an intriguing individual had disorganized everything on the estate, and effected the removal of persons of confidence. Increased, instead of diminished, exertions were now called for, until she could find an intelligent superin-

* This appropriate name is now changed for the rather absurd one of Memphis. This rising city occupies the most beautiful and commanding position in the whole southwestern quarter of the United States.

tendent of the farming operations. It should be added here, that all her serious difficulties proceeded from her white assistants, and not from the blacks. The habits of dependence implanted in this race, by the servitude of ages, renders them readily obedient, and easily attached to their owner, so that he learn to unite kindness with unflinching firmness.

The American character, as being peculiarly fitted for command—presenting an admirable admixture of energy, composure, patience, and rigid adherence to the rule laid down, until altered upon a conviction of its inefficiency or error—must be found, over all others, fitted for one of the greatest works which Humanity has to accomplish ; namely, the moulding and guiding the African in the conquest of savage nature in the tropical world. The work I am persuaded will present, under his direction, few difficulties. But for this he must act collectively, as making part of a sovereign body politic.

Such were the solemn reflections of Frances Wright when she awoke, between the lassitude and the feverish pulsations of a shattered constitution. to the consciousness of human weakness when considered in the individual. For the first time, she bowed her spirit in humility before the omnipotence of collective Humanity. " MAN SPECIES is alone capable of effecting what I, weak existence of an hour ! have thought myself equal to attempt." After much and repeated solitary reflection, she distinguished that, by an obstinate prosecution of her enterprise, she endangered, with life itself, all chance of rendering any real service to her fellow creatures ; and this at a time when she felt herself to have acquired no ordinary amount of varied experience, and of familiarity with questions upon which hinge the welfare of populations, and the grandeur and duration of empires. She had acquired, also, an intimate acquaintance with American institutions, the American people, and the American territory. She was now aware that, in her practical efforts at reform, she had begun at the wrong end ; although, with a view to the accurate comprehension of the vital interests of the country, and of the world at large, she was satisfied that she had begun at the *right* end. She distinguished, also, that if she had envisaged a practical experiment when she might have been more usefully employed in preparing the popular mind for the exercise, with knowledge, of popular power, *without* that practical experiment, and without the extended and varied observation which preceded it, she could never have acquired the information and the experience at all times requisite to guide the efforts of a really efficient leader of the popular mind.

During the three years and a half which she devoted to the slave question, Frances Wright is conscious that she learned more than during any other period of her life. It was in the cotton field, and while watching the extraordinary fluctuations in the cotton market, and the fearful catastrophes in the mercantile and industrial world consequent thereupon, that she seized the clue of the banking system, which she gradually followed up, through its ramifications of State Banks, and United States Bank and commercial credits, and commercial failures, until it landed her in the Bank of England, and the omnipotent Parliament of Great Britain, as the great source of that financial power, stronger than thrones or republics, which convulsed the world at pleasure, and robbed all the fortunes and the industry of the earth under pretence of aiding them.

Once satisfied as to the course to be adopted, with a view of forwarding the one object of her life—the advancement of human knowledge and happiness—she abandoned, though not without a struggle, the peaceful shades of Nashoba, leaving the property in the charge of an individual, who was to hold the negroes ready for removal to Hayti the year following. In relinquishing her experiment in favor of the race, she held herself equally pledged to the colored families under her charge, to the southern State in which she had been a resident citizen, and to the American community at large, to remove her dependents to a country free to their color. This she executed a year afterward.

On leaving Tennessee, she went to New-Harmony, Indiana, in order to assume the proprietorship of a peri-

odical which had hitherto been there published, under
the patronage of Mr. Owen, and which had been conducted for two years by different editors, with varying
ability and fluctuating objects, but of which the tenor had
been invariably liberal. This publication, constituting,
at the moment, the only one removed from party or sectarian influences, appeared important to sustain, at a time
when the whole social and political horizon throughout the
United States, appeared charged with clouds.

It was in this year, 1828, that the standard of " the
Christian Party in Politics" was openly unfurled. Of
this party, which had been long secretly at work, Frances
Wright had previously detected the manœuvres in all
sections of the country. This was an evident attempt,
through the influence of the clergy over the female mind
—until this hour lamentably neglected in the United
States—to effect a union of Church and State, and with it,
a lasting union of Bank and State ; and thus effectually
to prostrate the independence of the people, and the institutions of the country. Clearly distinguishing the nature of the move, Frances Wright determined to arouse
the whole American people to meet it, at whatever cost
to herself.

It is here necessary to explain that, during her residence in the south, she had visited New Harmony several times. She was there when the German colony left
it, and when Mr. Owen took possession. She subsequently visited the village twice, after one-half of it had become, by purchase, the property of her friend, Mr. William Maclure, whose life and fortune had been devoted
to the cause of education. This benevolent and estimable
man was a native of Scotland ; of large fortune, which
he employed in travelling, and in visiting every institution of interest in every country ; in making extensive
mineralogical and geological collections, and furnishing
with the same the cabinets of public institutions. He
took an active interest in the educational experiments of
Pestalozzi, aided him with funds, and supplied his school
with many scholars, whose expenses he paid. In the
United States, of which he was an adopted citizen, he

favored every liberal opinion and every attempt at reform, and was the founder and president of the Academy of Natural Science in Philadelphia.

In France, previous to his final return to the United States, he had—with the aid of his scientific friend and associate, Phiquepal d'Arusmont—undertaken in his own house in Paris, to prepare for the foundation of a normal school, by the efficient, moral, intellectual, physical and industrial education of a limited number of youths. The novel specimen of comprehensive education and synthetic instruction there presented, fixed the attention of the most remarkable men of the epoch. Among these it will suffice to enumerate—among the dead: Lebrun (Duc de Plaisance;) the philosophic and truly philanthropic member of the opening triumvirate consulate of France— soon driven into retirement by his colleague, the military Cæsar, Napoleon. The Hypocrates of modern France, the enlightened, benignant, modest and chivalrous Pinel; in his youth a besieger of the Bastille, and, in his maturity, the reformer of the treatment of the insane, and, at all times, the generous encourager and mild preceptor of youth. The distinguished and amiable philosopher and naturalist, M. Turpin. And, among the living: the celebrated Magendie, Villermè, Ferus, Rostan, and other distinguished members of science, physic, and the bar. This interesting private institution—although conducted with the greatest prudence, and visited with the utmost caution by the enlightened individuals above quoted— could not escape a formal domiciliary visit from the police of the Bourbon government. This event, and the consequent hasty return of Mr. Maclure with his friend, Mr. Phiquepal d'Arusmont, to the United States, led to their first acquaintance with Miss Wright; to whose counsel and assistance they applied, to facilitate the quiet transfer of their undertaking from Paris to Philadelphia.*

* It is truly difficult in this age to know what to believe. It is not two years since there appeared in the *Gazette des Tribunaux*, (the organ of the French law courts) a civil case, in which M. Phiquepal d'Arusmont was made (himself absent and confined by sickness) to

Upon their arrival in the latter city, and previous to their removal to New-Harmony, they had opened a most interesting institution for youth in the neighborhood of

plead his own cause, in the sense of his adversary, by the mouth of an attorney speaking in his name ; in consequence of which M. Phiquepal d'Arusmont lost his suit. And yet this again, not in consequence of any argument or any evidence, however foreign to the truth in every particular, which appeared in the official account of the trial, but upon the strength of a violent tirade from the Advocate for the Crown, against the public course pursued by his wife in the United States ; which tirade, astounding to those who heard it, was not even alluded to in the published record. The sentence of the Bench—as carried by storm at the close of this (to say the least of it) irrelevant attack upon a person entirely foreign to the case—not content with refusal of justice to M. Phiquepal d'Arusmont, pronounced, in addition, a stigma upon his honor. At a second hearing of the cause, when M. Marie, the head of the French bar, appeared as the duly appointed counsel of M. Phiquepal d'Arusmont, and appeared with credentials in hand from the most distinguished characters of France, substantiating, at one and the same time, the justice of his claim and the disinterested, as well as enlightened, nature of his unremitting exertions in the cause of juvenile education—At this second hearing of a most interesting cause, M. Marie was interrupted, silenced, and seated by the Presiding Judge at the opening of his speech, and before he had concluded the perusal of the following letter, from the Duc de Plaisance to Baron Cuvier :

" Monsieur le Baron,—

J'ai l'honneur de vous adresser un homme que j'aime, que j'honore, que je respecte—M. Phiquepal d'Arusmont, qui s'est voué avec le plus noble désintéressement à la plus noble des fonctions. Entendez-le avec bonté : il vous expliquera lui-même le bien qu'il fait, et de quelle manière il le fait. Je vous demanderai de lui faciliter l'entrée du Jardin des Plantes et du Cabinet d'Histoire naturelle. Je vous prie de seconder ses vues, d'encourager la bonne œuvre qu'il poursuit, avec tout l'interêt que vous donnez à tout ce qui tient au bien public.

" J'ai l'honneur d'être avec le plus sincère attachement et la plus grande considération, Monsieur le Baron, votre très humble et très obéissant serviteur.

" Le Duc de Plaisance.

" Paris, le 22 Janvier, 1822.

Copy of the letter of M. Lebrun, Duc de Plaisance, to Baron Cuvier :

" I have the honor of recommending to Baron Cuvier a man whom I love, honor, and respect, M. Phiquepal d'Arusmont, who has devoted himself with the noblest disinterested-

Philadelphia. Frances Wright had visited it with intense interest ; and received with regret, in Tennessee, the news of Mr. Maclure's removal and that of his friends, at the urgent entreaties of Mr. Owen, to New-Harmony. She regretted the interruption of labors already so successfully opened, and feared the new position and circumstances would prove less favorable to the object. Upon her second visit to New-Harmony, however, and after the opening of Mr. Maclure's Educational Society, distinct from the operations of Mr. Owen, she experienced true delight upon inspecting the school of industry there in full operation, and fully adequate to its own support at the expiration of the first six months. This really wonderful creation was the only successful experiment, and, indeed, the only real experiment of any kind, made in New-Harmony.*

ness, to the noblest of functions. Listen to him with kindness. He will explain himself the good he is doing, and in what manner he does it. He will ask you to facilitate for him the entrance of the garden of plants, and of the cabinet of natural history. I pray you to second his views, and to encourage the good work which he pursues with all that interest which I know you to bestow upon everything tending to advance the public weal.

"I have the honor to be, with the most sincere attachment and the highest consideration, &c.,

"Le Duc de Plaisance.

"Paris, 22 January, 1822."

Let not the public accuse those who shrink from rendering it disinterested service. At the time present, there is no prudence that can ward off vengeance from those who bear the reputation of serving humanity for herself. M. and Madame Phiquepal d'Arusmont, thus brutally outraged in a case which presented in itself no one political feature, were residing in all but absolute seclusion from a world with which, in its present state, they have no sympathy. They have never, either of them, had any direct or indirect relation with the reigning government of France, nor, indeed, with any government in any country.

* Community of property, which—to mean anything, or to mean what is not as decidedly immoral and pernicious as the order of things now existing, with an extra addition of injustice and absurdity to boot—should mean *the consolidation of land and capital in the name and for the benefit of a population, constitutionally organized for the most just and most effective administration of the capital, and*

The institution here adverted to, satisfactorily solved one of the most important problems in human economy— to wit, *whether the correct education of youth*, i. e. *an education judiciously calculated so as to develope simultaneously the moral, intellectual, physical, and industrial faculties of the human being—may not be made to cover all its own expenses, together with those of the preceding state of infancy.* Although the duration of this institution did not

for the most judicious development of the resources of the territory— Community of property, nor indeed any collective tenure of land or capital for this or any other purpose, there never was, nor any attempt toward it, at New-Harmony; and as the population had been assembled together under that pretext, the consequence of a practice in discordance with the profession, necessarily generated dissatisfaction and confusion. The character of the persons who generously answered what they conceived a generous call, to make an experiment of new principles, was of the first order, presenting among them every useful branch of industry; and many persons of high standing and wealth, from various quarters of the American Union, and also from Great Britain. Among the latter, was a very remarkable young Scotchman, an accomplished officer in the British army, Captain Macdonald; who had resigned his commission, to accompany Mr. Owen to America. Ardent, generous, intelligent, and of the mildest disposition, he won universal affection and confidence. When he suddenly and irrevocably withdrew from the village, all hope of any satisfactory result disappeared. After the departure, in disappointment, of this first population, the estate was indeed besieged, and the proprietor entangled, with intriguing lawyers and desperate speculators.

Such is a short and true reading of the much vexed and much distorted history of New-Harmony. In an age like the present, it is little astonishing that a thousand romances should be connected with it which never had existence. Among these Frances Wright herself was once led to give credit, and even circulation through the *Free Enquirer*, to a well-conducted and successful experiment of *labor exchange.* It proved, upon investigation, to have been neither more nor less than the pattern experiment of what was afterward practiced in London, and which closed very little to the satisfaction of any of the honest interests involved. It is time now to distinguish that all individual experiments neither have been, nor can be, of any practical account, beyond the inquiry they may elicit, the ideas they may generate, and perhaps the warning they may teach. Reform, to be effective, must be rightly understood *in its principles* by a collective body politic, and carried forward wisely and consistently, with due regard to the interests of all concerned, by that body politic.

extend over a year, and from the modesty of its creator and conductor, Phiquepal d'Arusmont, its existence has been scarcely heard of, its influences have been powerfully felt in the United States, from that hour to this. Many youths who there received the first elements of industrial knowledge, have since risen to useful stations, exhibiting a fearlessness of inquiry and experiment which has quickened the popular ranks with intelligence and invention. It is thus that the silent labors of the good and the wise, though they may pass unheeded in their generation, sink, in their effects, deep into the bosom of society, and prepare for that great advent of human redemption, when ignorance, error, and, their consequent misrule, shall disappear from the earth.

It is proper under this head to state, that the juvenile schools, and instruction of the whole village of New-Harmony, were founded and conducted in Mr. Maclure's half of the village at his entire expense, and under the direction of his friends—Phiquepal d'Arusmont, before mentioned ; the distinguished naturalist and botanist, (since deceased,) Thomas Say, of Philadelphia ; Doctor Troost, professor of natural philosophy and chemistry, in the University of Nashville, Tennessee ; the distinguished artist and naturalist, M. le Sueur, of the *jardin des plantes*, Paris, and the companion of the famous French voyager, Du Perron, the first explorer of New Zealand ; and Joseph Neef, one of the most distinguished disciples of Pestalozzi.

To return from these digressions to the subject of this memoir. Frances Wright found in New-Harmony no trace of the School of Industry which a year previous was so full of interest and promise. The parents, as resident in Mr. Owen's section of the village, had withdrawn ; the children, as resident in that of Mr. Maclure, were scattered, with their parents, to the four winds of heaven. Of her scientific friends, some had withdrawn to the cities and universities of the different States, and some were following, in the seclusion of the neighboring woods, their favorite pursuits. The talented and energetic conductor of the School of Industry was struggling with the depres-

sion of his disappointment, and applying himself in retirement to the instruction of three youths who had accompanied him from France. Frances Wright, touched with
a disappointment which she knew from experience how
to appreciate, observed that he, like herself, had erred in
counting for too much the power of the individual ; and
for too little, the counteracting influences existing in the
very motive principle of society in which the individual
moves. That both, in this manner, had mistaken the
road most directly leading to their object—the public
good. What we are insufficient to effect, let us engage
the mass to do for themselves. Here the people are sovereign. Here, too, free speech, written and spoken, is
secured by the law of the land. All that is wanting is
to start the American public in the true path of inquiry
and political reform, until it shall finally distinguish that
the care of infancy, the just training of youth, the useful
direction of adult strength, the protection of age, and, in
general, the whòle administration of the collective interests of the population, regard the population itself. Their
views meeting on this ground, Mr. Phiquepal d'Arusmont volunteered in a month s time to acquire and to
communicate, to his three French pupils, a thorough
knowledge of the printing business, asking, only for that
period, free accession to the printing office in which the
Harmony Gazette, now issued on Frances Wright's responsibility, was executed. If it be stated that she knew
the friend who made this offer, to possess, at the time, no
more acquaintance with the printing business than she
possessed herself, the confidence she had in his ability, to
seize at once upon the details of any branch of science
and its appropriate art, may be estimated. So entire was
her confidence, that she made arrangements for the whole
printing establishment to be placed in Mr. Phiquepal
d'Arusmont's hands on that day month. She then appointed
Mr. Robert Dale Owen, Mr. Owen's eldest son, as her
assistant editor, and leaving editorial matter in his
hands and forwarding other regularly by post, she proceeded to Cincinnati, and woke up the city, at the time
depressed and alarmed by the machinations of the clergy

of the different sects, united under the name of "the Christian Party in Politics." At the close of the first meeting in the Court House, she announced the paper for the day agreed on with its new publisher, and which was to present the Prospectus of Principles that was to guide its course. While engaged in delivering in the city and neighborhood stirring addresses to the population, the paper arrived on the day announced, and was universally noticed for its general appearance and correctness of typography. It is proper here to explain, that the reliance of Frances Wright on a promise, which to many appeared impossible of realization, arose from her having watched minutely the operations of her distinguished friend in the wonderful, but only too short-lived institution created by him on the property of Mr. Maclure, in New-Harmony. For she had there seen him master himself—by watching, analyzing, and simplifying the operations of different workmen—and then communicate to his pupils, the process peculiar to almost all the leading trades—such as carpentering, turning, coopering, blacksmithing, tinning, weaving, tailoring, shoemaking, hatmaking, broom and brushmaking. All of these she had seen going on under his direction at one time, and all of these were studied and practiced by the same youths who changed their occupations in rotation.

On leaving Cincinnati, she made a tour as far west as St. Louis; and then, crossing the Alleghany in the opening of the winter, addressed the people of Baltimore. Arriving in that city in December, 1828, she found a committee organized to receive her. Various were the proposals as to the place of meeting. A large and fashionable saloon, with tickets at a dollar, was strongly urged. The money, as she took none, it was suggested might be devoted to a popular library. Her reply was to the effect, that the object was not to raise money, but to give knowledge; and that her opinion would be for a theatre, and to throw it open to the public. It was urged by some that Baltimore was a populous city; a seaport; that the clergy were rabid; that they had fanatics at command; that her life might be endangered. She replied,

that she knew the American people, and to one riotous
fanatic who could be found, there were many hundred
citizens of good sense and right feeling ; and that, if a
theatre could be procured, she would engage to address
the public, and with the aid of the committee, to keep the
peace. It so happened, that a theatre was immediately
placed at her disposal by a public-spirited proprietor.
The only regulation adopted, and the one she invariably
followed, was to have the committee distributed at the door
and through the House, so as to distinguish on the instant
any ill-disposed individual. On her part, at the opening
of the meeting, it was her custom to request the audience,
in the event of any attempt at disturbance, to keep silent
and keep their seats. In this manner the detection of bad
subjects could instantly be distinguished. And so it was,
that in a seaport and populous city, armed only with the
sacred character of her sex, with confidence in the cause
she advocated, and in the people she addressed—a young
woman, raised in the circles of European aristocracy, and
whose habits were those of a student and quiet observer
of men and things—encountered a mixed multitude of
both sexes, of every class and profession, in an open theatre crammed from pit and stage to ceiling, without expe-
riencing, and without apprehending, anything but silent
respect and enthusiastic sympathy. Such. in general,
were the American cities, when inhabited by an American population— that is, by a population raised under free
institutions. As those cities have become gradually, and
of late rapidly, occupied by a mixed populace, raised
under the institutions of all the kingdoms of Europe, their
character has completely changed. The native population of the United States, born to, and raised in, the exercise of sovereignty, is now altogether engaged in agriculture, and occupies the soil as independent proprietors ;
while the manufacturing and commercial cities are generally occupied by the European population ; of which
an immense number are not citizens, many altogether
without instruction, and others ignorant of the very language of the country. It matters not certainly where
men are born, but it matters everything where and how

they are raised. The late disgraceful scenes in Philadelphia, others of a similar character on various points of the American Union, and the generally disordered state of the cities sufficiently show, that the rule of *laisser faire* and *laisser passer*,* excellent in its day, requires at the present some modification.

From Baltimore she proceeded to Philadelphia, and addressed a vast multitude, pressed in and around the old State House. From thence to New-York, the head seat at once of popular energy, sectarian, and clerical, wealth and power, and financial and political corruption.

On the clear and fiercely cold night, the last in the year, when a north-western gale detained her in the steamboat, on the contrary side of the bay from the city, she passed an hour or two on the deck, gazing on that which was to be the chief seat of her exertions, and as sne foresaw, of painful and complicated sacrifices and persecution. In that city were some heart affections, which dated from her first landing in the country. These, the course prescribed to her by duty, was perhaps about to sever. Friends in official situations or political standing, whom considerations of propriety would oblige her in appearance to forget. Houses in which she had been as a daughter, and which she must now pass with the regardless eye of a stranger. Some she knew would understand her course and in silence appreciate her motives. Others might feel embarrassed. Among the latter her heart recalled the amiable, kind, polished and cultivated Charles Wilkes, late president of the New-York Bank, a native of England, and the nephew of the John Wilkes of opposition and parliamentary celebrity, the same friend to whom she had dedicated her first volume on America. Imbued, as by inheritance from a fond and aristocratic mother, with other political views from herself, this difference of opinion and even feeling had never been allowed to check their intimacy, nor to chill their friendship. Her first care, upon arrival in the city, was to address to him a few lines, leaving it to

---

* *Leave alone* and *let pass.*

himself to regulate their future relations. That whatever might be his decision, she should never do injustice to what she knew would be always his secret sentiments of respect for a devotion whose object he would probably regret, and for exertions, the nature of which he would condemn. On her side, the remembrance of past years would ever live in her heart, together with those sentiments of affection for himself and family, which she had cherished for years, and which would remain unaltered through life. In a few lines, couched in the same strain, he accepted, as she thought wisely, her suggestion of dissolved or suspended intimacy. He resigned, moreover, the charge of her worldly interests, and (what she much regretted,) those of her sister; which last had been more especially and entirely in his hands from the time of their first arrival in the United States. This circumstance afterward involved serious and painful losses.

Again, she would observe that the public has no right to sit in judgment upon those who shrink from rendering it service ; or even who fail to that service when undertaken. The injury and inconvenience of every kind and every hour to which, in these days, a really consistent reformer stands exposed, none can conceive but he who may experience them. Such becomes, as it were, excommunicated, after the fashion of the old Catholic mother church ; removed even from the protection of law, such as it is, and from the sympathy of society, for whose sake they consent to be crucified.

The course of events which followed her arrival in New York, would probably present more interest to the reader than any which have been here recounted. But pressed with business at the moment of departure from the country, and having to hasten to Liverpool, to take the steamer of the coming 17th for New-York, the author and subject of this memoir, is' obliged here to interrupt her narrative.

DUNDEE, 13th August, 1844.

NOTE FROM THE PUBLISHER.

Before the departure of Madame d'Arusmont from Dundee, she revised hastily, with her own hand, the proof-sheets of the biography here presented. In the belief that the circumstances which called for this production from her pen will possess some interest for the public, I subjoin the following letters, which appeared two months since in the *Northern Star* :

MISS FRANCES WRIGHT.

I believe it may be safely asserted that less is known with respect to the personal history, origin, and family connections of Miss Frances Wright, or Madame d'Arusmont, than of any other character of existing notoriety. This has, doubtless, been caused by the fact, that when not impelled by the hope of achieving some great public good, she has lived in retirement, bordering on absolute seclusion. Many and various surmises have consequently run current relative to the life and character of that distinguished and eloquent lady ; and, singular to relate, few, if any, of these surmises have had any foundation in fact.

As the reader may be curious to know by what means I arrived at that knowledge which her numerous admirers in this country seem altogether destitute of, I may briefly state that Madame d'Arusmont lately visited Dundee, for the settlement of important business connected with property she has inherited from a cousin of her father— the last of the name. The news of her arrival soon spread through the town. Feeling anxious to see a woman whose eloquence has gone so far to effect a revolution in the mind of America, I embraced the earliest opportunity of soliciting an interview ; I was received with the greatest kindness.

Madame d'Arusmont is among the tallest of women ; being about five feet ten inches high ; she walks erect, and is remarkably handsome. Her brow is broad and magnificent; her eyes are large ; her face is masculine, but well formed.

In the course of conversation, I mentioned to her that certainly little was known of her life, as I had seen it stated in an Edinburgh Magazine that she belonged to Glasgow.

She replied, that was not surprising ; she had seen biographical notices of herself which did not contain a single fact. Adding, "The reason is obvious. I have always avoided speaking about myself; and, of course, no one knows from whence I originally came, nor anything about me."

After a desultory conversation, and a promise from her to call at my abode, we separated.

After waiting a few days, and finding that Madame d'Arusmont did not call, I wrote to her, stating that my views in calling upon her were to obtain from her such facts of her life as she might think proper to favor me with, to be published in some liberal newspaper or magazine, for the information and gratification of her numerous admirers in this country.

On the same day this was posted, Madame d'Arusmont called at my residence, with the following note, remarking that she intended to leave it if she had not found me at home :

" DEAR SIR,—Should I not find you at home, let this line, which I shall leave in that case, in token of ready sympathy with your wishes, satisfy you that I did not, that I could not, misinterpret your only too flattering enthusiasm. So far as this may have been in-spired by those principles of truth and liberty which it has ever been the effort of my mind to interpret correctly, and the object of my life to advance—that enthusiasm can only meet with an echo in my own breast. So far again as in the ardor of youthful feeling, you may have apotheosized the advocate of those principles, instead of purely and entirely those principles themselves, my censure cannot, and will not, be too severe, since I can recal the time when I was prone to err in the same manner and in equal excess.

" I beg that you will dismiss all fears of intrusion, and call on me as frequently and freely as inclination may dictate. I look for my husband and daughter by the next London steam-packet.

" Yours, dear Sir, with much respect,

" F. W. D'ARUSMONT."

The reader will now perceive, that my opportunities of ascertain-ing the information so much wished for were of the best description. In my next article, I will endeavor to give a lucid and succinct bio-graphy of a woman, who is unquestionably the most intellectual fe-male defender of liberty in the present age.

J. MYLES.

Dundee, May, 1844.

The *Northern Star* of the week following, presented a biographical notice of Madame d'Arusmont, drawn, from my best recollections, of the information with which she had favored me. The following criticism of the same then appeared from her pen ; and, subsequently, the po-litical Letters now in the Press, and which will appear in the same form as the Biography :

MADAME D'ARUSMONT.

TO THE EDITOR OF THE NORTHERN STAR.

SIR : In your columns of the 18th ult. and the 1st inst., I have seen some biographical notes respecting myself, from a gentleman of this, my native city. With every intention on his part to render them correct, I find them somewhat erroneous in several particulars, not otherwise important, it is true, than that fidelity even in trifles is important, if trifles occupy us at all.

Having swerved from the rule, strictly followed to this time, of withholding all information regarding myself, not only as of no real importance to the public, but as calculated to divert its attention from the principles I have endeavored to advocate, and the truths it has been my effort to expound—having swerved from this rule, it seems befitting that, if I meet the curiosity of the public at all, I should meet it to the best of my ability. And in truth, at this point of time, and in this my native country and city, to decline doing so, might expose me, not unreasonably, to the suspicion of moroseness or affectation.

When my townsman, Mr. Myles, called on me in the manner he has related, and solicited the information which I readily promised, my answers to his inquiries were short, and strictly to the points inquired after. To string these afterward into a narrative, would doubtless be difficult; and as he again applies to me for corrected and fuller information, in the view of supplying a biographical notice, as a preface or appendix to such of my works as are current in this country, it appears to me the better way to take the pen in hand myself. I do therefore furnish him with a sketch of my parentage, family connections, and early years, fully sufficient, I imagine, to satisfy any curiosity with which the public may honor me. In do-ing this, it seems but fair that I should secure to a young bookseller of my native city, and one too (if report speaks true, somewhat per-secuted for opinion's sake) any little advantage that may arise from its publication. The publishers of my works in London will doubt-less appreciate my motives, and obtain from him permission of af-fixing the same to any future editions they may issue.

But, sir, after the appearance in your columns of the somewhat imaginative and too eulogistic notice already alluded to, not merely of myself as a consistent and untiring advocate of truth and liberty, but also of such of my works as are known in this country, I feel called upon to express my dissent from the unqualified approbation passed upon the latter.

It is seldom that an honest inquirer after truth—and such I feel myself to have ever been—has not to correct and to modify his views more than once, before he can hope to present such as are unmixed with error. But whenever he discovers himself to have been mis-taken, imperative is the duty for him to correct his reading of the book of nature, or of the human mind. Such has ever been my

BIOGRAPHY,

NOTES,

AND

POLITICAL LETTERS

OF

ERANCES WRIGHT D'ARUSMONT.

FROM THE FIRST BRITISH EDITION.

No. 2.

Containing the Political Letters.

NEW YORK:
PUBLISHED BY JOHN WINDT
99 READE STREET.
1844.

POLITICAL LETTERS

FRANCES WRIGHT D'ARUSMONT.

LETTER I.

Prefatory Letter addressed to the *Northern Star*, (Leeds, England,) explanatory of the circumstances which led to the correspondence now published under the title POLITICAL LETTERS, and of the more immediate object held in view by their author.

Sir : I have already adverted to the biographical notice of myself which appeared in your columns of the 18th ult. and the 1st instant, and requested permission to make a few observations suggested by the perusal.

I feel this a duty on my part, Sir, necessitated by the tone of eulogy in which those letters were couched. Had the eulogy been merely personal ; I mean, had it been confined to rendering tribute to the rectitude of my intentions, to the consistency of my public career, and to the devotional ardor of a life consecrated, as I honestly believe, without intermission, to the search after truth, and to the propagation of the same truth, with a view to its final triumph in human practice ; had the eulogy been confined to this, I should have let it pass without comment. But, however willing to let pass a tribute of enthusiasm to my public course in general, I must be permitted to dissent from the unqualified approbation bestowed on my published works.

With respect to these, Sir, they were well enough

under the circumstances, and with the young experience which inspired them. And, even now, take them in the whole, I think it probable they may contain more truth and less error, than has been often put forward by any leader of the public mind. I take this, in all probability, to be the case, for three reasons:

1. That I have written and spoken in a country which, by the acknowledged principle of its institutions, guarantees the freedom of human thought, speech, and action; and even renders the exercise of that freedom, on proper occasions, incumbent on its citizens.

2. That I have never looked to any moneyed or other reward; never courted or accepted any party support, and never ambitioned popularity, either among the many or the few.

3. That I have never, at any moment of my public life, made a suggestion, or uttered a word, that I did not conscientiously believe true, either in the absolute or the relative; and useful, either to the public safety at the time, or to the course of human progress in the future.

Thus much of sincere conscientiousness, most of my hearers and readers may have attributed to me. But what they cannot have suspected, is what I am about to explain.

Not only have I never, as a public teacher, expressed a sentiment which I did not regard as both true and useful, with reference, either to the exigencies of the present, or to the requisitions of absolute justice in the future; but, whenever I have distinguished the slightest admixture of error, or of danger, in any view or any counsel presented to the public, I have withdrawn it on the instant.

An admixture of the two elements, error and danger, I distinguished in my discourse on religion, after I had published the second American edition of the volume of lectures now current, in a cheap and popular form, in this country. No sooner did I clearly distinguish the error and danger, to which I advert, and which it is my intention to elucidate, than I endeavored to prevent any further general circulation of the work containing it. Unfortunately, however, the stereotyped plates of my lectures were removed, during a period of time, from my control; nor was it until many editions had been thrown off, that I could conveniently recover the plates and bury them, as I have done for eight years past, in the darkness of a cellar.

I must observe, however, that with respect to the circulation of the volume of lectures known in this country, I have always regarded the evil as comparatively small, conceiving the error it comprised to be so little developed, and so much counteracted by the whole tenor of the context, as might authorize me to hope the good effected by the volume would more than counterbalance the evil. Not so, however, with respect to "Epicurus," or, as it was christened to soften the alarm of its first London publisher, "A Few Days in Athens."

That little work, hastily entered on at the age of eighteen, to enliven a few winter evenings of some friends in the country, and then as hastily thrown aside, was first published in London, (down to the close of the twelfth chapter,) at the request of a Greek scholar. One edition of the same, from a London copy, appeared in the United States.

It is true, that I had even then penned the substance of tne three chapters preceding, and preparing for, the speech of Epicurus on religion. But, at that time, these I carefully withheld, not only from publication, but from every eye, feeling that I could not as yet have matured my views, and being harassed with some doubts as to the utility or safety of cutting through the root of superstition, while that of the tree of knowledge was scarcely planted in the soil of the human mind. How far this might have been done by other writers, I knew but imperfectly. The philosophical works of Voltaire and other French authors I had not then opened; and the few English works in the sceptical, argumentative, or metaphysical style, which had fallen in my way, appeared to me obscure, and insufferably dull and tedious. My own views of nature were simple conclusions of the mind, drawn from the study of chemistry and physics. This

will explain my continual reference to natural phenomena, in support of every view I may at any time have
advanced ; and will further explain the censure I have
ever passed on disputatious argumentation, and mere
bandying of words with ignorance and error—an operation which, as alike conducted by our sects, Christian
and anti-Christian, has ever appeared to me to originate,
equally in both parties, in a total misconception of the
nature of opinions, and equally of the *nature of all truth,*
whether physical, moral, or intellectual.

An observation here occurs to me, which may not be
altogether without instruction. I had not read, nor did I
know of the existence of Holbach's " System of Nature"
for good two years after the speech of Epicurus on Religion was written and published. When the works of that
philosopher were put into my hands by a French friend,
I was already suspicious of the accuracy of my own
views, and was astonished to find the whole ground,
whether correct or defective, covered by my Epicurus, to
have been embraced fifty years before by a French
moralist. The only difference indeed to be found between
the French author and myself is, that what in his hands
occupies two or three volumes, in mine, from a peculiar
habit of mind, is condensed in as many pages. The apparent singularity of this coincidence led me to distinguish
the fact : that there is for the human mind, no less than
for human events, an order of progress as certain and necessitated as is the concatenation of physical phenomena
in the material world. This order of inquiry, and, consequently, of intellectual conclusions, has to be followed
by all the pioneers of truth, until the higher summit of
synthetical perception is attained, and from thence a vista
of the general horizon of things is embraced. The short-
est road between two points may then easily be drawn,
and the less reflecting mass of existing society, and, more
surely, that of future generations, may be led safely by it
to the great *look-out* or *Belvidere* of intelligence. From
that time forward, circuitous windings and break-neck
pitfalls may be shunned by all, and Ignorance may be led
forward to Knowledge without having to grope his way

through all the mazes and the doublings of error. Oh! Knowledge indeed is Power! Knowledge is Salvation! And there is no other Power that will stand the test of time; no other Salvation against all the wrongs, the miseries, and the crimes, which mislead, deform, and brutalize our race!

But to resume my confession. It was in the year 1828, and while engaged in the State of Tennessee, in my experiment on the slave question, that I was led, by the general fermentation of the public mind on religious matters, to revert to the little philosophical treatise for some years forgotten.

This fermentation, excited by the cabals and restless ambition of the Clergy of multitudinous Christian sects, was met, either by confused and contradictory lucubrations of liberal writers, or by the disputatious dogmatism of anti-Christian writers. Both appeared to me equally unworthy of the occasion.

I was at the time struggling for life between the relapses of fever; and, expecting to succumb, made an effort to render, what I conceived would be my last services to the cause of truth and human improvement. Unable to sit up or to bear the light, I dictated from my bed, and in darkness, first the deed of trust of my Tennessee property, consecrating it, and the laborers upon it, to the object for which I had made the investment, and, afterward, with many interruptions from disease, the speech of Epicurus on Religion.

I am somewhat minute in the detail of circumstances, because it is my wish to convey to the public a sense of the deep conscientiousness which inspired that production, and which equally inspired its first circulation by myself in a flying sheet, and then through the columns of a liberal publication, the *New-Harmony Gazette*, to which I forwarded it for insertion. It is thus, perhaps, that I may best win credit for equal conscientiousness in my subsequent endeavors to withhold from circulation all the parts of a work, which I soon distinguished as generally defective, and even in some of the tendencies of its last chapter, decidedly mischievous.

My intention had always been, to defer any regular
publication of the work in a volume until its completion
and satisfactory revision ; desiring to present in it, a
beau ideal sketch of society in an advanced stage of
civilization, and as we may rather expect it to be in the
future, than conceive it to have been in the past. And
my intention also was to bequeath in it, to posterity, a
Treatise of Practical Philosophy, as devoid of error and
as replete with truth, as my most conscientious reflection could supply to my fellow creatures. This had been
a favorite idea with me ; and I had already prepared
some chapters with more care, and, therefore, probably
with more skill than any of the preceding, when I received, in Paris, a request that I would consent, as a good
moneyed speculation, to the publication in New-York of
the work, as then existing only in the obscure pages of a
forgotten journal. I, of course, refused consent, and
distinctly motived my refusal ; when, to my amazement,
the volume was issued with my name on the title page,
not only as author, but as associated publisher. This
sudden appearance of my Epicurus, with all his imperfections on his head, occasioned me so much mortification
as completely to disgust me with my offspring, and has
prevented me from ever putting my hand to him again.

To have exposed this singular violation of property and
propriety, though it might have gratified the hostility of
Christian sects and political parties, could not have reme-
died the evil. I contented myself, therefore, with seizing
the first occasion of presenting new and corrected views of
the subject erroneously treated in my earlier efforts. This
I did in a Course of six Lectures on *the Nature and History
of Human Civilization, considered in the Past, the Present,
and the Future.* This Course, delivered in various cities
of the American Federation, between the years 1836
and 1840, has not been published, nor am I in any hurry
to publish it. I have been, and am desirous of matu-
ring and enlarging my own views, by repeated revision ;
well knowing, by experience, that it is easier to give cur-
rency to imperfection and error, than to amend either
when circulated. The spoken errors of a public teacher

can be amended by successive lessons; but his printed
and published errors ever glare upon his sight, like the
fabled writing on the wall. Nay! they stick, as they
ought to stick, to his conscience, like the poisoned shirt
to the back of the demigod; for, worse than all! they fix
a plague-spot on that very human mind which it is his
sacred mission to sanify and enlighten.

Few, I trust, are the serious offences of this nature,
which lie at my door: that there should be one, is to me
a source of pain. In my adopted country I am, perhaps,
authorized to hope that my more recent labors, and the
removal of my works from the hands of the public, until
circumstances shall permit to me their careful revision,
have tended to weaken any former erroneous impressions.
In this my visit to my native country of Britain, I find, at
once with regret and satisfaction, with mortification and
pleasure, that the works which I have temporarily stifled
on the other side of the Atlantic, are generally current
here. The chief error which they comprise, it is my
intention to explain. When I shall have done so, I trust
that the publishers of my works in London, will see the
propriety of prefixing to any future editions, the stric-
tures upon them furnished by their author.

I am, Sir,

With the highest respect, yours,

F. W. D'ARUSMONT.

Dundee, June 20th, 1844.

LETTER II.

Nature of the error common to public teachers, and its danger to society. Unremitted effort of the author to avoid that error. Criticism
of her own more popular works. Important distinction in two words
and two things. Theology: its meaning in the word; its origin in
the thing.

IF error unmixed with truth were presented to the
human mind, the human mind, when not in the most barbarous state of savage ignorance, would instinctively re-

ject it. And so, also, if truth unmixed with error were
presented to the human mind, the human mind, when not
either in the most barbarous state of savage ignorance,
or in the most brutalized state of vicious degradation, or
when not blinded or perverted by temporary interests at
variance with the self-evident conclusions emanating
from the same—the human mind would as instinctively
receive it. 'And, again, when error is received by the
human mind, it is received because presented in company
with truth ; and so also, if truth is refused by the human
mind, it is because it appears in company with error.

Leaders of public opinion are always individuals who
advocate some truth not generally familiar ; but with that
truth, they generally advocate some, and very frequently,
much error. Weak judgments, relying on the judgment
of the leader, swallow the error with the truth. Stronger
judgments, disgusted with the error, not unfrequently refuse the truth.

The leaders themselves—either unconscious of the admixture of poison which they have administered with the
sound food, or, it may be, smitten with the vanity common
to persons raised by circumstances or by their own ambition, to positions more conspicuous than their absolute
knowledge fits them to occupy—defend all which they
have once advanced with the ardor of proselytism or the
obstinacy of self-conceit. Thus is it, that contention so
generally interrupts the even course of inquiry ; that
party and sect ever arise to turn aside Reform ; and that
those who open their career as the scourgers of abuses
and the friends of human progress, close it, but too often,
with attempts to extinguish the light which they at first
assisted to kindle.

I distinguished at too early an age, and have ever too
deeply deplored, the erroneous course so generally followed by public teachers, not to have held myself on
guard against following the same. Let me, therefore,
suggest to that portion of the public in my native country
who honor me with confidence, that there exists in my
works, and in the very parts of those works which I understand to be the most popularly approved, a very fun-

damental and a very dangerous, because a most demoral·
izing, and a socially and politically disorganizing, error.
In various parts of the volume of my popular lectures,
known in Great Britain, Theology and Religion are con·
founded; and, most true it is, that (with single and sin·
gular exceptions) they have ever been, and still are, con·
founded both in the theory and the practice of empires.
The words, however, like the things they represent, are
essentially different. To precise and establish this differ·
ence, is a matter of no small importance; since their
association, nay! their absolute blending together and
confounding in the language, thoughts, and feelings of
men, have been the source of most fatal mental and moral
aberrations, and ruinous political convulsions.

Theology, from the Greek *theos, logos*, renders distinctly
the meaning of the subject it attemps to treat. *Theos*,
God, or Gods, unseen beings and unknown causes. *Logos*, word, talk, or—if we like to employ yet more familiar
and expressive terms—prattle or chatter. *Talk, or prattle,
about unseen beings or unknown causes.* The idleness of
the subject, and inutility—nay! absolute insanity of the
occupation, sufficiently appear in the strict etymological
meaning of the words employed to typify them. The
danger, the mischief, the cruelly immoral, and, if I may
be permitted to coin a word for the occasion, the *unhu-
manizing* tendencies both of the subject and the occupation
—when and where these are (as they have for the most
part ever been throughout the civilized world) absolutely
protected by law and upheld by government—sufficiently
appear also from the whole page of human history.

Religion, from the Latin *religo, religio*, renders with
equal distinctness the thing signified. *Religo*, to tie over
again, to bind fast; *religio*, a binding together, a bond of
union. The importance of the great reality, here so ac·
curately shadowed out, appears sufficiently in the etymo·
logical signification of the word. Its utility will be evi·
dent, if we read, with intelligence, the nature, the past
history, the actual condition, and the future destiny of
man.

But now, taking these two things in the most strict

etymological sense of the words which express them, it
will readily be distinguished that the first is a necessary
creation of the *human intellect* in a certain stage of inquiry; the second, a necessary creation of the *human soul*
(by which I understand both our intellectual and moral
faculties, taken conjointly,) in any and every stage of
human civilization.

Theology argues, in its origin, the first awakening of
human attention to the phenomena of nature, and the first
crude efforts of human ingenuity to expound them.

While man sees the sun and stars without observing
either their diurnal or their annual revolutions; while
he receives upon his frame the rain, and the wind, and
the varying elements, without observing either their effects
upon himself or upon the field of nature around him, he
is as the brute which suffers and enjoys, without inquiring
why it experiences light or darkness, pain or pleasure.
When first he puts, in awkward language, to himself or
to his fellow, the question, *why does such an effect follow
such a cause?* he begins his existence, if not as a reasonable being, (a stage at which he has not yet arrived,) at
least *as a being capable of reason.* The answer to this
first inquiry of awakening intelligence is, of course, such
as his own circumscribed observation supplies. It is, in
fine, in accordance with the explanation of the old nurse
to the child, who, asking, when startled by a rolling peal
of thunder, "What makes that noise?" was fully satisfied
with the answer: "My darling, it is God Almighty over-
head, moving his furniture." Man, awakening to thought,
but still unfamiliar with the concatenation of natural
phenomena, inevitably conceives of some huge being, or
beings, bestriding the clouds and the whirlwind, or wheel-
ing the sun and the moon like chariots through the blue
vault. And so again, fancy, most naturally, peoples the
gloom of the night with demons, the woods and the water
with naiads and dryads, elves and fairies, the church-
yard with ghosts, and the dark cave and the solitary cot
with wizards, imps, and old witches.

Such, then, is Theology in its origin; and, in all its
stages, we find it varying in grossness according to the

degree of ignorance of the human mind, and refining into
verbal subtleties and misty metaphysics in proportion as
that mind exchanges, in its progress from darkness to
light, the gloom of ignorance for the mazes of error.
My next letter will contain the hasty developments at
present within the scope of my leisure to offer, touching
the nature and uses of Religion.

LETTER III.

Danger of confounding Theology with Religion. Uses of Religion.
Its essential union with civilization. The character of the one decides that of the other. The four Religions and four Civilizations of
the World. Exposition of the first. Its union with Theology in Hindostan; and its existence distinct from Theology in China. Consequent ruin of the one empire, and lengthened duration of the other.

In my last, I defined the meaning of Theology and
Religion, both in the words and in the things signified;
elicited, satisfactorily as I trust, the difference between
them; exposed the futility and absurdity of making the
former a subject of human study, and suggested the danger to individual rectitude of associating it with the law
of right and wrong in the human mind, and the utter ruin
to all the dearest interests of the human race—nay! even
to the great scheme of human improvement itself, involved in the blending together of its dreams and fictions,
its delusive hopes and terrors, its demoralizing threats
and promises, to take effect in a remote, unearthly, and
inconceivable future, with the solemn obligations contracted in society between man and man, with the pure
devotion owed by each individual to the species, and with
all the other glorious inspirations of civilizing and human-
izing Religion.

Religo, I tie. And Religion alone *has* tied—according
to the state of progress of human thought and human
practice, on various spots of the globe, and at various
epochs of time—Religion alone *has* tied the slave to his
master, the subject to his king, the citizen to his brother
citizen, the patriot to liberty; and—even under the most

2

erroneous systems of government and defective forms of civilization—all classes of society and sects of opinion to the ark of public safety, and the altar of a common country and a common cause !

Religo, I tie. And Religion—she, and she alone, *has* tied man to woman, woman to man, men to each other, youth to age, age to youth, the human mind to Truth, the human soul to honor and to virtue, the civilized world together, with the bonds of common interest, human brotherhood, and the instinctive belief in an ever improving future, as now preparing, and as yet to be prepared, upon this earth by ever improving generations of our race.

Religo, I tie. And woe be to the hand which rashly seeks to sever those bands, loose as they are and rotten, which still hold a diseased society together, without supplying stronger and better ties—nay ! chains of adamant, wherein to receive and hold cemented the falling fabric of, defective indeed, but still sacred and improvable, civilization !

Taking Religion in the most strict etymological sense of the word, it will readily be distinguished that no tribe, race, or nation, could subsist in a state of association, or in any state or stage of civilization, without a *Religion* or *common bond of union.* Even a band of robbers—and the very word *band* implies the idea, *banded or bound together* —even a band of robbers must have some such tie, some pledge of honor or common and sacred rule of conduct, or their association would be annihilated.

The first associations of men, and of many nations and potent empires at this hour, have indeed been made, or do now exist, as much for the purpose of despoiling their neighbors as for protecting themselves. Still, although the overthrow and destruction of such nations might be a desirable object to those who are preyed upon, it is certainly not one to be desired by themselves; nor would any reasonable—not to say benevolent—member of such nations propose their destruction as the best means of forwarding the purposes of general philanthropy. He would rather propose their reformation—which, at the existing point of generally awakening intelligence and of generally

altering circumstances in the affairs of the civilized globe—
is certainly a consummation as distinctly attainable as it
is desirable. With this in view, however, he would
most scrupulously refrain from weakening the religious feeling of the community, while he would direct his
most strenuous efforts to change its object and correct its
aberrations.

At all times the character of the religious bond decides
that of the civilization. In other words, the religion of a
country presents, at once, the principle and the theory of
its political association.

There have been among men precisely as many religions as there have been civilizations, i. e., there have
been, up to this period, four.

The first, that of Asia, (Egypt inclusive) may be denominated the religion of the priest.

Taking its rise with agriculture in the fertile regions
of Southern Asia, this civilization was probably mild and
paternal in its youth ; and, when at the full apogee of its
power and splendor, must have exhibited a wonderful
scheme of administrational science and imperial magnificence. But, resting as it did, on the knowledge of the few
and the ignorance of the many, it degenerated, of necessity, into the most cruel despotism on the one part, and abject slavery on the other.

Of this civilization the object was *statu quo ;* the binding principle *undoubting adherence to, and devoted venera-
tion for, all that had been established in the past by the will
of Heaven, as expounded by the priest.* Its political organization, however varied in the mode, as here held and
guided by the Priest King, there by the King Priest, and
again in other empires (and in such the state of things was
decidedly the worst) by temporal and spiritual heavenly
vicegerents, acting conjointly—Its political organization
was that of *the feudal system, in its most perfect state.*
Well defined and hereditary castes or classes, (it matters
not as to the name, the thing, with slight modifications in
the mode or the degree, is in nature and effect the same ;)
a landed aristocracy at the head, and servile laborers
forming the base.

The first master measure employed for the more certain enslavement of the species was the subjugation of
woman in her body and her soul. She—the intellect, the
soul, the providence of society—being made the tool of that
sex who represent the selfish instinct of animal life—that
which looks to individual conservation and selfish gratification—the nobler instinct inshrined in her—that which
looks to the conservation and happiness of the species—
was necessarily thus made subservient to the baser. The
consequence has been what we witness at this hour : brute
force quelling the inspirations of mind ; noise drowning
reason; disputation knowledge ; fraud subtracting from
weakness what violence may have failed to rob ; law
usurping the place of justice ; selfish interest that of generous friendship ; prostitution, contraband or legal, that of
love ; theology of religion, and rapacious government
that of benign administration.

Under the first civilization of the world, it is worthy of
remark, that religion—and certainly, however the reverse
of truth in its principle, and however consequently defective in the theory and practice which that principle
generated, the religion of the Asiatic civilization has
proved more binding and durable than any which has
ever swayed the fate of empires—It is worthy of remark,
that religion has existed in one Empire, and probably
was, in the outset, established in all, distinct and apart
from theology.

In China, Religion is evidently at this hour as it has
ever been, a social and political bond alone ; holding men
bound to each other, and all fast to the throne of the King
Priest, whose mandate is held from Heaven.   In the absence of all doctrine of a future state, or hopes and fears
of rewards and punishments out of this world, human duties, however interpreted, are all *here*.   Reverence for
the past has to inspire the present, and the approval of
posterity for religious adherence to ancestral rules is all
that is thought of the future. The Reformer (*not Founder*,
as is the vulgar belief in Europe,) of the Chinese religion,
Confucius, was a just, vigorous, and patriotic statesman, an
a ble administrator, and as enlightened a philosopher and

consistently virtuous a man as ever adorned the records of humanity or the annals of a nation.

Wherever there is ignorance, there is superstition ; and so China has hers. It is compounded of trifles as numerous and ridiculous as the ceremonials of Chinese politeness, and in character, is pretty similar to those current among the more ignorant European peasantry, and silly persons in all countries. The bonzes and monks, who make a traffic of these popular whims and mummeries, have never commanded respect either for their persons, or their trade ; but are regarded much in the same light as our fortune-tellers, jugglers, and mesmerizers. On the other hand, China has felt, in the duration of her empire, the advantage of the absence of any great scheme of humbug, such as in Europe is protected by law, remunerated by the state, and confounded in the popular mind with religion. If the vice inherent in the religious principle has kept her stationary under the yoke of despotism, the separation of that principle from the scarecrow of a national faith in shadows and incomprehensible dogmas, and a national worship of unknown causes and unseen existences, has aided to preserve her civilization during untold generations, until—to the disgrace of a Christian empire—it yields, in our day, to the sap and the mine of commercial fraud, and to engines of destruction, forged under a civilization, more powerful it is true, but also more cruel and less stable as being less religious, than her own.

In Hindostan, from circumstances not difficult to interpret, did time permit, the course of circumstances was different. There, at an early period, Theology absolutely stifled Religion. The same has been long growing to be the case in Christian Europe. And in Christian Europe, the consequence will be the same as in Hindostan. Her empires will fall to pieces, or rot away in corruption, unless some principle more potent than that which has expired, and more in unison with the wants and the intellect of the epoch, shall gather together within its bond the scattering and warring elements of society, and inspire them to take a new start in the race of civilization.

In my next, I shall pass in hasty review the second civilization of the world ; and define its binding principle and its political theory and practice.

LETTER IV.

Exposition of the second civilization of the world; its religion; its theory, and its practice. Causes of the abortion of the second civilization. Rise of the third civilization. This, a compound of the two preceding. Explanation of its rise. Its religion of slavery, a temporary good. Its contradictions, a consequent of its parentage, and its vices, a compound of the conflicting vices of the two civilizations to which it succeeded. Disorganization of the third civilization when commenced. How this disorganization gave rise to the fourth civilization

THE second civilization of the world was that of the classic empires of Greece and Rome. Of this the binding principle, or Religion, was *love of country ;* the political theory was *government by the greatest number of influential citizens ;* and the political practice was *struggle and confusion.* This abortion of the classic empires may be attributed to the following leading causes :

1. To an imperfection in the religious or binding principle, which looked to the false greatness of the ill-defined existence called country, instead of to the happiness of the population.

2. To the absence of constitutionally specified, and administrationally regulating, principles.

3. And a consequent of the second : To the absence of administrational science, and the presence of governmental power.

4. And a consequent of the third : To a vicious, all-absorbing, all-devouring centralization, in lieu of a common-sense re-partition of affairs among the population of the different localities.

5. And a consequent of the fourth : To the lawless passion for war and robbery as national occupations ; and the consequent homage awarded to martial prowess as the first qualification of the citizen.

6. And a consequent of the fifth : The slender respect and reward afforded to useful industry.

7. The sale of land, and its re-partition ; together with the re-partition of capital among individual monopolists.

8. And a consequent of the seventh : The competition of capital as divided among individual and warring monopolists, in lieu of the single but full and unbounded competition of laborers ; that only source of industrial, artistal, mental, or indeed of any, excellence.

It will be seen that the second civilization was, in general, the extreme opposite of the first. In the absence of sufficient experience, the human mind, swayed by impulse rather than reason, usually swings like the pendulum, as far in one direction as it has previously done in the other.

In that first dawn of the earth's new era, when—in gifted Greece—the hopeless lifeless *statu quo* of antiquity first gave way before the voice of a sovereign people, enthusiasm was high, energy potent, experience wanting. An old and wily enemy too was in the field. The Priest of Egypt held the science of the world, and smiled to see the blunders of the first sons of liberty. In the outset of the revolution, (it has been so in all revolutions,) he found no room for his ministry, save by the new altar of country, and no ear for his dim fables until these were dressed in poetical imagery, adorned by the sculptor's genius, and blended with the deeds of patriotic heroes, and the strongest passions of humanity. In democratic Greece and republican Rome, the classic religious principle, love of country, ruled the souls of men, apart from the dogmas of theology or the fables of mythology, until the imperfections inherent in the political system brought corruption on the people and ruin on the state. It was then—when liberty and religion had been finally crushed under the throne of the Cæsars ; when all the ties which bound citizens to their country, men to each other, and even soldiers to their chief, had been severed ;—when society was falling to pieces, and civilization menaced with destruction ;—it was then that the priest of Egypt, recurring to his old Asiatic model, and fastening it to one of the thousand wild stories and wild sects current at the period (in the style of our Joanna Southcotes and Mormons,) and by aid of some tricks of jugglery stolen from India, and no small familiarity with astronomical science, the medical art, and with chemical and physical phenomena, and—adorning the whole mass of contradictions and confusion with some ill-rendered moral axioms of Confucius and philosophical dreamings of Plato—offered a new binding principle of servitude to the tottering throne of Constantine, a new political theory of self-abasement, helplessness, and natural depravity to a population who might well receive the doctrines for true, and proposed to bury for ever in the political practice of the *statu quo* feudal system, the stirring remembrances of Grecian liberty and of Roman virtue.

It is here curious to remark, that though the Christian Gospels were not penned before the age of Constantine, and, though the new religion of servitude was only then systematized and incorporated with the state, the expiatory sacrifice of the Man-God was dated from the reign of Augustus; thus marking the final death of the Republic, and its religion of love of country, and the birth of the Monarchy, and its religion of servitude.

It is curious to remark also, that though the principle of Christianity is self-abasement and innate human depravity, and the direct object and tendency of its theory is to hold men bound as helpless slaves to the " powers that be," yet that the curious mass of disjointed inconsistencies which compose the sacred books of the Christian system, are besprinkled with sentences and axioms leaning to democracy. If the page of history be present to the mind, and if the position and object of the priest of Egypt, and equally those of the Roman Cæsar, to whose aid the priest of Egypt came, be held in view, the necessity of shaping the new system so as best to make it appear all things to all men, and to make it look toward classic freedom while it moved toward Asiatic despotism, will become evident.

And, let us observe, that—in the horrible epoch in which the Christian delusion was fastened upon human kind—it

was at once a necessity and a blessing. The civilized
world was in moral ruin, preparatory to being shaken
into physical ruin by the Goth, the Hun, and the Vandal.
Society had lost its bond of union; religion was dead in
the human soul; citizens had no more a country. The
sons of the Scipios, of Cornelia, and of the Gracchii were
sensual reprobates and soulless slaves. A Religion of
servitude alone could band the degraded race together.
Submission and fear, in this world and another, was a
theory fitted to their degradation. But the whole became
otherwise useful when the savage hordes of the north bore
down upon the fields of agriculture, and levelled the
works of science, the creations of genius, and the arts of
industry, with the cities of pride. The barbarian had
then to be tamed to servitude before he would exchange
the battle-axe for the ploughshare, or learn to amass and
invent over again the knowledge and the arts which he
had destroyed.

It was then that the priest of Egypt became again a
civilizer; and that, in establishing the religion of modern
servitude, Christianity, and the theory and practice of the
feudal system, he gathered together new elements of society—rude indeed, and for ages cruel and still miserable, but which the patriot, warned by old errors and on
guard equally against new ones, may see to cement and
improve into a stronger and better order of civilization
than any known in the past or at the present.

The third order of civilization then has been that of
modern Europe. Of this, the religion has been that of
serfs, bound together by a common belief in their own
helplessness and innate depravity, and bound also to their
feudal lords and to the throne of kings, under protection
of the priest, by a common belief in their divine right to
rule over them. Christianity has been, and is, that religion, which, considering it in its origin, purpose and history, may be denominated *the religion of kings*.

This civilization, following upon the two preceding,
has presented a compound of the vices of both. It has
indeed been purely and evidently, transitory. Two
forces — that representing the first civilization, and

that representing the second—have been continually opposed.

The classes placed, by the power of conquest, or by hereditary descent, or by the power of money, or by the arts of legislation, or by the quibbles of law, or by the tricks of commerce, in possession of the land and the capital of the human family, have represented, and represent at this hour, *the first civilization*; and have ever been, and yet more forcibly are, pulling backward to the consolidation of the feudal. with a view of arriving at the old Asiatic system; with its anti-human and inhuman principle of *statu quo ;* its dull, asinine, mill-horse theory of castes or immovable classes, hereditary occupations, community of class-property—securing hereditary tenure of capital and of administrative power to the higher summities, and hereditary labor to the masses. No competition; no excellence; no talent; no genius; no ambition ; no independence ; no liberty ; no praise ; no blame ; no reward of ease, and wealth, and honor, according to merit, and no merit according to works ! Ha ! let humanity be decoyed thus into communities raised after the model of Catholic monasteries, (and such are called, and have ever been called Communities on the continent of Europe,) or after the model of Protestant Poor-houses (and such I have heard, with my own ears, called Communities in England;) or after the model of American-Shaker, German-Moravian, and other establishments, in which labor and rigid rules are common to the mass, and tenure and administration of property, fingering of funds. and secret laxity of asceticism are common to the few : let, I say, humanity be decoyed thus into an impass, and she may find her chains harder to break than they are at this hour !*

---

* It will be borne in mind that these letters were written *in* Europe and *for* Europe. The danger in America of a people, virtually sovereign, being lured into a system of which the design is here exposed, is evidently null. In Europe, however, the danger has been real. A population in the lowest stage of misery and degradation, may well be expected to lay hold of any project, however visionary or deceptive, which may appear to offer any relief from absolute starvation and nudity. In America danger assumes another form.

The classes, on the other hand, who are born portion-less, and whose labor goes only (their own bare subsist-ence subtracted,) to swell the fortunes of those born to rule, pull in the sense of *the second civilization*, threaten-ing confusion and consequently ruin, to the whole of so-ciety, themselves inclusive.

We have now to observe, that the disorganization of the third civilization—a system never indeed fully estab-lished, nor capable of being established, as present-ing, (in consequence of its mongrel origin,) radical im-perfections in its principle, inconsistencies in its theory, and contradictions in the frame-work of its practice:—The disorganization of the third civilization distinctly com-menced with the *Reformation*—more properly the *Dis-pute ;* and such, historically and philosophically, I am wont to denominate it. Reformation in fact there was none, but only an immense deal of arguing, quarrelling, fighting, hanging, drowning, and burning : and this, on all hands and all sides, whichever got the uppermost. But there was also, and this made the gist of *the dispute*, an immense deal of scrambling after the lands, and tithes, and dues, and goods of the Catholic church ; by German Princes, British Monarchs, Swiss, Swedish, Dutch, Dane, Scotch, and other high-seated, long-armed, and long-gowned, greedy rulers, and fire-and-faggot fanatics ; while the poor, ignorant, and by ignorance besotted, pop-ulations executed, as a holiday exploit, the Vandal work of heaping in ruins time-worn abbeys and cathedrals, abusing Popes and Cardinals, church music, and holiday amusements, and shouting for Protestant ascendency, but dreamed not of relieving their own shoulders of burdens, which, with many additions, they carried thereafter in honor of Protestant Monarchs holding direct from Heaven, instead of from Heaven by favor of the Pope. Oh ! glo-rious work of theological, metaphysical, and governmen-tal disputation, which cost in Germany, (that huge and heavy cradle of every modern mystification,) a first Pro-testant war of *thirty years duration*, which turned fertile states into barren deserts, buried cities, whole populations millions of treasure and stores of wealth, such as migh have colonized and outfitted the New World, with Australia, Oceania, and Siberian Russia to boot!

The binding principle of the third civilization—that is, *the Christian Catholic religion*, having thus given way to disputatious Protestant theology, its theory and its practice had to give way also. Vigorous were the assaults made upon these in republican Holland and revolutionary England. By *revolutionary England*, I mean England of the Commonwealth; and not England (so called) of the Abdication, and the Transaction with a foreign Prince, and that foreign Prince he who had overthrown the liberties of Holland.

This assault upon the principle, and shaking of the theory and practice of the European civilization, commenced in the stronger souls and bodies of Europe's population a fermentation which developed the first seeds of a fourth civilization.

The hasty consideration of this will form the subject of my next letter.

LETTER V.

Fourth civilization of the world. Its birth in the wilderness of America. Its Religion, as first set forth at the Revolution, 1776. Its political theory, and its practice. These three defined. Of these, as now existing, two supplied by relative truth, and one by absolute truth. The two first efficient during the past, but inefficient at the present. The nature of the change now demanded. Social compact, as yet non-existent. Necessity of such in every civilized country. Counsel of the author to the British people. Destined influence of the Fourth civilization, over the whole of humanity. First effort now demanded of the Reformers of Europe. Sovereignty of the people. What constitutes a people.

THE fourth civilization sought its refuge from the persecution of the third, in the howling wilderness, with savage beasts and savage men. Its foundations were laid on the shores of the New World, by choice spirits of the Old.

Britain sent her patriots and her sages: her iron men of the Commonwealth; her polished statesmen of the

Tory court; her Scotch schismatics and invincible mountaineers; her Welsh peasant, armed with the spirit of his ancestry; her high-souled martyrs of liberty, and her obdurate of every defeated party or sect. France, sent her conscientious Huguenots, her valiant soldiers, her learned Jesuits, and her modest philosophers; Holland, her exiled Republicans, her sagacious and upright merchants, whose word was their bond, and whose creed was the equal right of nations to the seas; Spain, her fearless adventurers; Ireland, her unsubdued patriots: from every shore and climate, the brave, the persecuted, and the free. Such laid, with the arm of strength, and the soul fired with the *religion of liberty*, and nerved by the same with resistance unto death, the foundations of America's opening civilization.

Of this civilization, the religion was thrown into words on the 4th of July, 1776 : " All men are born, and of right ought to be, free and equal." And to this tie of human brotherhood and doctrine of national faith, were pledged, by a young people in arms, " life, fortune and honor." The political theory and political practice, were subsequently consigned in the constitutional law of the States and the United States.

These three, *necessarily component parts of every organized political system*—ITS RELIGION, ITS THEORY, and ITS CONSTITUTED CODE OF PRACTICE, may, as presented in America's opening civilization, be thus rendered :

Binding political principle, or Religion : *Love of liberty.*

Political theory : *The right, inherent in every political association, and the propriety, inherent in things, of changing at all times the forms of the political system, so as to keep pace with the progress of the public mind.*

Political practice : *Government by a male majority.*

Now, it is important to distinguish that, of these three necessary parts of the whole, *one only* is sought in *truth absolute ;* and that the two others, as supplied by *truth relative*—that is, *by truth shaped and tempered so as to fit with the exigencies of temporary circumstance ;* these two are consigned to future correction and amendment by the second.

Wonderfully powerful, and all appropriate to effect the first objects of the nascent popular association and States' Confederation—namely, the conquest of independence from metropolitan power ; and, equally, the conquest of the soil from savage nature and savage men ;—perfectly calculated to effect these objects, were the American religion and practice, as presented above. They were fitted, and admirably fitted, to achieve revolution, and establish national strength. And, equally fitted were they, also, to effect the overthrow of that demoralizing false credit and fraudulent financial system, which—after having served the first indispensable purposes intended—was good for nought, but to aid in the general corruption and enslavement of Humanity. But, all these objects achieved, the American religion and practice, as presented in the opening scheme of the fourth civilization, is found inefficient and defective.

To meet the new wants of the epoch, recourse must be had to the beautiful principle involved in the theory— *progressive improvement.* In keeping with her motto, " Ever onward," America has now to give a new reading to her religion, and a new form to her practice. *Love of liberty and aim after equality,* have to mould themselves into *love of the species and aim after justice,* in lieu of the vague and very disputable assertion : " *All men are born, and of right ought to be, free and equal,*" she has to proclaim the self-evident moral truth : *All are born with, and in justice ought to possess, equal right to equal chance.* And her mode of practice, in accordance with the amended declaration of faith, should be such as to present the practical illustration of the equally self-evident axiom : *To every man, woman, and child, according to his and to her works.*

With a view to effect the gradual realization of this golden rule, her citizens have to pass *a social compact,* presenting at one and the same time a new code of principles, as regulative of the future, and a compromise of interests at the present, in the view of preparing for the gradual, prudent, and peaceful passage of society into that future.

In all reforms, in every country, the habits and the feeling, no less than the existing interests, of society have to be taken into view. All those exigencies, existing in the present, as entailed on it by the past, have to be provided for; and the apprenticeship of a population must evidently be lengthened or shortened, according to the greater or less amount of virtue, intelligence and political experience, spread through the mass of its population; to the greater or less approach toward homogeneity in mind, manners, habits, and condition existing in the same; to the greater or less embarrassment, debt and complication entailed on the present, by the malversation of the past; to the greater or less amount of resources existing in the soil, climate, and industry of the country; and—more than all, perhaps—to the greater or the less number of useful, compared to useless, members found in the community.

We have heard and read of social compacts—all of us: for of what have we not heard and read? But *seen* a social compact we never have. None such have ever been passed on the face of the earth. There never has been anything else than a sacrifice of the interests of the many to a greater or a less number; nor anything better ever seriously proposed than a sacrifice of the interests of the few to the will of the many.

This last mode of scramble and injustice has been, as yet, the best theory of the United States; for *out of this* Democracy moves not. A majority! Of what? The experienced? The intelligent? The virtuous? The industrious? No: a majority as of brute force counted by numbers, and of the male sex. A worse rule, at the present point of time, could scarcely be devised or followed; unless indeed it should be that which submits, as in Europe, the control of all things and all interests to *a minority* of landed and moneyed monopolists upheld by the brute force of armies, coercive law, and all the machinery and corrupting influences of Government.

Any further developments touching the future course of the fourth Civilization are, of course, now and here, uncalled for. I may add, however, for the encourage-

ment of the friends of human improvement in Europe,
that I entertain few, if any, doubts, that it will be such
as the wise and good throughout the civilized world will
approve.

It remains for me to offer to British Reformers a few
observations touching the prospects of Reform in this my
native island : and the general course, which would appear
to me, best recommended by prudence and wisdom under
existing circumstances. I feel this incumbent on me from
the honorable testimonies of popular regard addressed to
me from various quarters, coupled with requests, by me
declined, to address the public in some of the principal
cities of the kingdom. Even had compliance with those
flattering wishes been possible to me, I should still have
considered the mode I have selected—of addressing the
more intelligent portion of the mind of my native country
through the columns of an extensively circulated popular
journal—the more consistent, at the time present, with propriety as with utility.

If I am correct in the view I take of the actual position
of things throughout the civilized world, no nation standing within the pale of the third civilization nor even within that of the first, can long be removed from the influences of the fourth.

This civilization indeed had its rise, as we have seen,
in the bosom of the third. From Europe it carried the
seeds both of its excellencies and its vices. From European loins the first wise and mighty fathers of a real
sovereign people drew existence. And, again ; in that
struggle for national existence which shook the thrones
of Europe to their foundations, how many of Europe's noblest and bravest sons—of her Montgomery and Lafayette,
her Jones, her Steuben, de Kalb, Pulaski and Kosciusko—
laid their lives, their fortunes, and their unstained honor
upon the young altar of Freedom ; nor asked, nor dreamed
of worldly reward for service beyond price. Of latter days,
indeed, the idle speculator or the idle indigent, the vain
or the ambitious, may have swelled the tide of European
emigration, adding rather elements of disorder, commo-
tion, corruption, and party discord to the American fam-

ily, than those of unpretending good sense, modest worth, and wholesome industry. Still, if the helpless pauper, the fomenter of disturbance, the angry partisan, the caballer for office, or unblushing electioneering canvasser— a character little respectable or respected even when found among native citizens, but which becomes far otherwise offensive when those born and raised under other institutions thrust themselves forward to solicit confidence to which they have no claim, and the rewards and distinctions of office, which to be honorable must be at all times unsought: still, if such be found among the ranks of adopted citizens, how many are there of laborious habits, steady occupation, unsullied integrity, retiring manners, and delicacy of sentiment, who are proud to aid the national strength and the national wealth, or to lend their unbought influence to the side of peace, union, and reform, and who would shrink even from the acceptance of office, how much more from its demand. Every State and City in the Union boasts foreign citizens of this stamp; men who do honor alike to the nations they have left and the nation they have sought, and whose foreign birth is forgotten by all but themselves. And, in Europe, where is the family renowned by its virtue, influential by its fortune or descent, honorable by its integrity, its steady habits of hardy labor or honest occupation, which owns not, and is not proud to own, ties of consanguinity, of friendship, or of interest—sons, brothers, friends, alliances, ancestral remembrances, or business associations—with the young Republic of the New World?

Nor are these connections and associations, however multitudinous, altogether of a private nature. Every child of liberty—every lover of humanity—every honest patriot in Europe, recognizes in America, and recognizes with pride and with hope, THE COUNTRY OF A SOVEREIGN PEOPLE.

And here appears to me should be the first great and undivided effort of all Europe's intelligent populations— to effect, in each country, *the acknowledged and practical sovereignty of the people.*

But now comes the question— *What constitutes a people ?*

All those who possess, in their property or their labor, a real stake in the country. This stake may be very disproportioned, the one to the other : this is a disadvantage, but does not alter the case. Whatever the proportion, all such may be classed as *of the people* ; for all such are interested in the country's salvation, and in the country's reformation, by orderly and peaceable means. In short, all these are directly interested *in the passing of a social compact*—*i. e.*, a compact in which the worldly interests of each and of all should be as fairly adjusted and compromised as may be within the compass of the public fortune, all public exigencies being met and public duties fulfilled. It would be now premature to enter into any developments touching the nature of those exigencies and duties, or touching the nature of the public fortune, or into any of the details of a compact which one great event must evidently precede—*the acknowledgment and practical establishment of the popular sovereignty.*

It would be ill making a compact where the few are in arms and the many in chains—where the Few hold the seats of power, and command all the avenues of authority, and the Many have to move and to speak at the risk of liberty at least, if not of life. But worse would be that compact to make, where a vicious system, pushed to its utmost limits, should have created such a mass of *slaves* under the form of a *pauper population*, or of a population *in any manner directly dependent upon the few* as should make *the many among the people* stand in a *numerical minority.* Is it impossible that the same governing and all mystifying power which has produced this state of things in the Island of Jamaica, under the name of negro emancipation, may not attempt to produce it at home under some other name ? These are not days, nor is this a country, in which mischief can be effected without a fair mask to cover its deformity. Philanthropy ! Reform ! may be the rallying cries employed where perhaps fraud may suggest the means, and enslavement be the object intended. In the strength *of the people,* (as distinct from a dependent and degraded populace,) in the union *of the people*, in the elevation *of the people* in their own eyes and in the estimation of the governing power, are (as appears to me) the only safe, and the only certain means for securing a happy result. Knowledge! knowledge!—a true understanding of how things are, and of how they ought to be; and this knowledge spread far and wide among the more honest of the working classes, and of the middle classes, is what the hour demands, and what every patriot, capable of aiding the work, should volunteer to accomplish.

Having pointed to a social compact as to the *terminus* at which this and all other countries have, sooner or later, to arrive, it occurs to me to call the popular attention to one feature in the present complicated system of Government, which if properly turned to account, may greatly hasten the opening of reform. But this must supply the subject of another letter.

LETTER VI.

Two Powers in all existing Governments. History of both in England. Essential character of Government. Advantage gained in England by the Transaction. Future good purchased by temporary evil. Monarchy when, and how changed into Aristocracy. Principle and Theory of European civilization, how and when attainted, and destroyed in England. Immediate effects of British Policy. Future consequences of the same. Objects held in view by the Tory land power of Great Britain. Exhibition of its policy and position. Its actual design exposed. Its estates, how forfeit to the nation.

THERE are now, in all our half-civilized countries, two powers in the Government—the Tory landholding power, and the Whig financial power.

The first of these dates in Britain, as in every other country, from the first rise of agriculture. It was founded under the Roman government, and grew to greater force under the Saxon. The Norman invasion brought to it a new accession of religious, as well as warlike power and feudal organization; changing the land-owners from those of a weakened, to those of a stronger race, but only temporarilv disturbing the mass of the population. At the same time it advanced England to the rank of a powerful and ever rising nation, which it cannot be said to have ever occupied before. Under the Anglo-Saxons, themselves invaders, it was unable to protect itself from the stronger invasion of Danish, or other sea and continental, robbers.*

The second, or financial power, dates, distinctly and governmentally, from the Transaction of 1688, and marks the accession of a foreign prince to the British throne, by aid, and under cover of an *omnipotent Parliament.*

This transaction consisted of a compromise made between the old landed interest and the new industrial, commercial, and professional interests, which had been struggling, during a course of centuries, into life, and by their continuous efforts, and one violent explosion (in 1640 Charles and the Commonwealth,) had burst asunder the bonds of the Christian Catholic feudal system. This had become too narrow, oppressive and ignorant, to contain a society ever expanding with new and powerful interests,

* It is to be wished that we might hear no more in America of the *Anglo-Saxon race;* an epithet of which our reviewers and newspaper editors seem to think they can never give us enough. The pride of America is that her *Sovereign People* are descended from the boldest and bravest of all the more civilized nations of Europe. As to the Anglo-Saxons, there would be little in their especial ancestry to boast of. A population which submitted to be plundered, taxed, ridden and driven by every band of freebooters who chose to set foot on their island, could only gain by a plentiful cross with their Norman conquerors. This cross took place largely in the outset, by intermarriages with Saxon heiresses, who did nobly in selecting the fathers of their children from a troop of valiant soldiers rather than from a herd of craven slaves. Since the Transaction of 1688, the crossing of the two races has gone steadily forward, and with it the blending of the money-power with the land-power. Besides, if men did but think when they talk and write, they would make fewer flourishes about the blood of races and honorable houses. While—with the usual inconsistency of a system founded upon male supremacy—name and descent are handed down on the doubtful side of the house, a looker-on upon the curious game of silly and fraudulent society, is strongly tempted to quote the old adage : *He is a wise man who knows his own father.*—[NOTE TO THE AMERICAN EDITION.

as created with and by the development of the thoughts, wants, and arts of rising civilization.

The same causes which impelled to the colonization of North America, and to the birth therein of a first really sovereign people, could not but force a modification of the order of things in Europe. True it is, that this modification benefitted but little the mass of the population, but rather submitted them to the burden of a new and all but unlimited class of riders, who were now admitted to take their places at the government table ; which means, *at all times, in all places, and in all cases,* a table more or less well covered with the loaves and fishes—the same being subtracted, by force or fraud, from the labor of society. This subtraction, by one of these two modes—force or fraud—constitutes, indeed, the essential nature of government ; and can only give way, under a better order of things, when *government* shall be exchanged for *administration,* and when every sane, sound, and useful member of society shall have an understanding of, and a voice in, the affairs which regard him.

The Transaction, as being passed without any comprehension of the matter by the laboring classes, could not but involve a sacrifice of their interests. Knowledge is power, and in the present warring and wicked state of society, a nation, a people, or a class without knowledge is always trampled on. Let the British people acquire it now, and they may see to effect another and a better compromise ; one which shall not only embrace all existing interests, but in whose beneficent results not one creature wearing the human form shall be forgotten.

But to resume. The public debt, funded or unfunded, of Great Britain,—as now governmentally made and acknowledged by act of Parliament, and which would at this day absorb, for the full payment of its interest alone, all the labor of the civilized world, the barest subsistence of the producing laborers subtracted,—dates, together with its manager and agent, the Bank of England, from the accession of William of Nassau to the British throne. That prince was not selected without deep reflection by the Tories of England, perplexed at once by the unmanageable race of Stuart, (who adhered religiously to the doctrine of holding their crown, and all their powers, from gift of Almighty God;) by the accumulation of royal debt, which they knew not how to cover without coming on their own fortunes, drained as these were by the civil wars and other causes; and by the deep and general dissatisfaction of the industrial, commercial, and moneyed classes. In this dilemma they turned their eyes to the triumphant Captain of Continental Protestantism, and successful assassin of the Republic and Republicans of Holland, who had already opened the compound system of war, debt, credit, and inflated commerce, of which it was now proposed to transport the head seat from Amsterdam to London.

This transfer of the prince, and of the great scheme associated with him, was purchased by a round sum of money paid to Holland. This sum, together with the crown debts of the exiled Stuarts, being scored on the opening leaves of the great book of the nation's liabilities as the first items of that debt which was (by the hocus-pocus of an omnipotent Parliament, and a Government Bank,) to represent, henceforward, the moneyed capital of the British nation, and to command, as based thereupon, the credit of the world.

But now there was an important change in the government principle involved in all this, which it would be useful for the people to distinguish. This change had two sides, a bad and a good one. The bad side is that which has been forcibly felt by the masses to this hour. The good is that which they may turn to account for the future.

Under the old Tory Kings, England was a monarchy; that is, a government holding of the *monos*, one; an uneasy monarchy it is true, but still a monarchy in principle, and in fact. The sovereign was responsible to Heaven theoretically, and (Heaven being a great way off, and not very definitely situated in the most chimerical chart ever drawn of the universe,) to the people practically This Charles I. experienced, when he answered for malversation with his head. The consequence of all this was despotism, with continual resort to anarchy. The people had a good chance of getting the upper-hand. But then to keep it, by turning it to fair and wise, that is, just account!—Ah! they wanted the knowledge, the union, the practical experience, the deep reflection upon, and understanding of, the nature and importance of principles!

Under the new Whig race of monarchs—foreign in origin, alliances, and affections ; politically null and void, (since they who can do no wrong, can do no right ;) placed nominally at the head of the nation, but in reality, at the head of the aristocracy—Under this new race the sovereign now held his crown, and his means of subsistence from the Parliament ; Heaven appearing no more in the matter than as a flourish of rhetoric, *Dei gratia*, and so forth. As he who feeds us, rules us ; the sovereign has become a puppet, of which the wires are pulled by the Lords and Commons. The advantage here gained to the fundamental principle is immense ; so that whatever may be the increase of vice, in existing practice, the final defeat of error, and triumph of justice and truth, has been insured by every leading political event, and every move made by every power in the government. Whatever the existing force of England's territorial aristocracy, the government vested in its hands is unsound in the root of its principle. And, whenever and wherever, a flaw is effected in the principle, *which makes always the title* of a government, if such government be not forced to concessions, or expelled from its throne, it must be infinitely more powerful than the current of events ; and infinitely more wise and united than the people which it rules.

The principle of European government received a first mortal blow in Great Britain, when the Christian Catholic feudal theory was overturned by Henry VIII. ; greedy to absorb the power and wealth of the altar with those of the throne. It received a second, when its political framework was shaken by Elizabeth, who smote the pride and the power of the nobles, the surest stay of a throne. It received yet a third, when the English people—insurgent equally against theory and practice—laid the anointed

head of Charles upon the block. It received yet a fourth
—and that the most deadly of all—when, in 1668, the
embarrassed, and greedy territorial aristocracy, united
with the threatened and the ambitious moneyed classes in
a compact, of which the object was—on the part of the
land-owners—to associate the power of capital and credit
with that of landed monopoly ; and, on the part of the
holders of that capital and credit, to secure a voice in the
government, and to break through those barriers of name
and descent, which—whatever might be their pretensions,
their wealth, or their merit—held them back as inferior
castes in society.

But if, in Great Britain, the principle of the third civilization was severed at the root, and if its theory was
scattered to the winds, at the epochs, and by the events
here pointed at, its practice—as galvanized by the Transaction of 1688—has exhibited, through a period of time,
centupled energy. And truly if skill, daring, and deep
design could impart to measures the sustaining force of
principles, it is the British government that would have
worked the miracle.

The long, intricate, astute, daring, and persevering
policy opened by the Tory land power, as aided by the
money power, at the period of the Whig accession, and
from thence carried steadily forward, it is not now indispensable to unravel. Under this head let these general
observations suffice.

If its immediate effects at home have been as deplorable
as those abroad ; if here, it have annihilated an independent yeomanry, and crushed down whole masses of the
British people into a foul and degraded populace ; if
abroad, it have undermined the thrones of ancient kingdoms. and the cradles of popular government ; if it have
stifled all *religion* in the souls of populations, crazed their
intellects with theological chimeras, perverted their
moral sentiments by commercial fraud, and bowed down
their bodies to the earth beneath the yoke of oppression ; if
it have raised vanity, and meanness, and mediocrity in
all but cunning and crime, to wealth and honor, and
driven pride, and greatness, and wisdom to the shade ; if

it have demoralized the whole of the species, savage as
well as civilized, and steeped the earth with human gore
and human tears: if such have been its ostensible and
immediate effects, still its ultimate tendencies, as now
checked and influenced by other causes, must hereafter
be such as to induce the birth and the spread of a new
and higher order of civilization over the whole face of the
earth.

But it is necessary to say a word in elucidation of the
precise objects held in view by the Tory power in Britain.
These were:

1. To monopolize the whole commerce of the globe, and
thus to render the whole industry of the globe subservient
to the ruling power in England.

2. To employ, and so to pacify, the activity and ambition of those classes which threatened the repose of the
ruling land-holding interest.

3. To concentrate all the capital and credit of the
country in the hands of the government; the government
consisting of the same land-holding interest, and that interest being vested in a small and ever-diminishing number of families.

The third clause in this scheme seemed for a time the
most difficult part of it, until a sudden discomfiture of the
first has finally endangered the whole. With respect to
the third, a thousand accidents abroad, and, as encouraged
by these, a thousand accidents at home, have forced concessions from the ruling power, and made occasionally the
balance tremble as if the secondary power was about to
fling into air its creator.

To avert the catastrophe of a revolution, such as in
France prostrated the old feudal fortunes, and threw all
Europe into confusion, the policy has ever existed so to
entwine and identify the interests and vanities of all the
heads of the moneyed, industrial, and commercial classes
with those of the ruling power, as shall lead them, at all
moments of crisis, to identify with it individual salvation,
and induce them to immolate to that individual salvation,
the interests of the classes which they represent. But the
Tory power has yet a further and more direct hold over

the Whig power. The fact is, that these are in much conjoined. The landholding interest is also, to an immense extent, the fundholding interest ; the surplus funds, arising from enormous estates, rich offices and sinecures, being scored on the book of the nation's account current. These, however, from being often passed into the hands of daughters, younger sons, and collaterals, constitute (where not thrown back by marriage alliances, as is more generally the case, into the same Tory interest) another set of claimants. But, again : individuals of all classes, the industrial, the commercial, and the professional, and, among these, a most interesting, as in the present monstrous order of things, a most helpless class in society— orphans, single women, and the aged of both sexes—stand as creditors on the immense book of the nation's liabilities.

In order to render the general position of things evident to the popular comprehension, it yet remains to be observed that, on the old and long successful scheme of governmental and national rapacity—as upheld by a false capital ever swelled by Act of Parliament, and a false credit based upon that false capital ; by extensive colonies and dependencies spread through the richest soils and climates of the globe ; by a commerce upheld by fleets and armies ; by strongholds and fortresses scattered around the globe ; by ever extended conquests ; by treaties and alliances formed under the cannon's mouth ; and, more than all, by that scheme of debt, and of loans and of credit based upon that debt, which has made it the interest of foreign governments to uphold that of Britain at the expense of their own honor and of the ease and welfare of their people ;—and, yet farther, by a tariff or duties upon all imported articles of general use, and which, even now, as reduced by recent acts of Parliament, amount to *four hundred per cent.* upon every pound of coffee, from *two to three hundred* upon every pound of tea, the same upon sugar, without noticing those, yet higher, upon tobacco, peppers, spices, and all those tropical productions which have been ever employed in Europe as the surest and most disguised mode of making the mass of the poor and of the middle classes support the expenses of a government of which every lucrative office, with all military, naval, clerical, judicial, and other preferment, is absorbed by the families of the same class which holds the land and wields the power in the House of Lords and its dependent Commons ;—It yet remains to be observed, that—by this old and long successful scheme of foreign robbery, human butchery, colonial oppression, financial and commercial swindling, and home extortion, the means of supporting the same have been drawn from all the soils and industries of the earth, no less than from the productive classes of Great Britain and Ireland. But, at the time present, one part of this scheme—that which regards foreign countries—is giving way. Powerful nations have withdrawn and are yet withdrawing from the commercial grasp and diplomatic and financial control of the British Parliament. The consequence is, that a large part of those supplies, until lately extorted or subtracted from abroad, has now to be found at home, or—*to be dispensed with.* This is the sum of the matter.

But now, if found at home, these supplies, off what and off whom are they to come ? Off the landed estates, and off the incomes of those who hold them ? But, if the Tory land-owners are called to pay the interest of the debt they have created, they will clearly, in so far as they own that debt, have to take out of one pocket what they put into the other. And again : in so far as they do *not* own it, they will have to take the interest out of both their pockets to put it into the pockets of other people. In short and in fine, they will have to take on their own shoulders those burdens which as yet they have not touched with one of their fingers.

The matter being so, what is the course followed by the Tory land-power ? *Why it is spunging the debt of its own creation,* and this in a sly and indirect manner, so as to distress, and finally to ruin, all moderate and narrow incomes ; and so also as to threaten annihilation to the fortunes of those heads of the industrial, commercial, and professional classes which, after all, do really represent the interests of the laboring mass no less than the intellect and the liberties of society.

Now that every Lord spiritual and Lord temporal, whose name, or the name of any of his immediate family, may stand on the list of public creditors, should spunge the same from the records, would seem fair and honor. able. But that, instead of this, he should vote a three per cent. income-tax to take effect on widows and orphans, and families in moderate circumstances, and small land. owners, of whom there are so few, and *no* land-owners of whom there are so many; and which last have ofttimes sold their properties, in city or country, in ships, or manufactures, or trade, or any of the thousand forms of value or of industry, and transferred the same to the pub- lic funds in full confidence of their Government's faith : that one, or any, or all of the ruling land-power should do this, must seem *to* cast a strange and foul stain of fraud on the honor of baronial escutcheons, and on the purity of episcopal lawn! The frequent and arbitrary reduction of the rate of interest, and now, even upon those reduced dividends, a direct tax of three per cent. constitute a commencement, and a bold and a broad one, on the part of the governing power, of an intention finally *to spunge a debt* (the phrase is already in fashion) from which it now foresees, to the fortunes of its constituent members, loss and not gain!

Let this process be carried forward, and to what will it amount ? *To a silent and surreptitious destruction of the mortgages held by the nation on the estates of the ruling Lords spiritual and temporal.* Will it be said that such deeds of mortgage are not individually made out, signed, witnessed, sealed, and legally registered ? There is more than this. The estates of the omnipotent land-power are governmentally pledged, given and surrendered in the wholesale, in legislative acts, signed by the three powers of the Monarch, the Lords spiritual and temporal, and the Commons ; and the same are witnessed and attested by the whole civilized world! The parties who contract a debt are clearly bound for the debt in all their posses- sions ; but, when the contracting parties constitute a na- tional government, and the party contracted with is the nation itself, the contracting parties are clearly bound, in honor and duty, to redeem the pledge, or to vacate the seat of power, to surrender the administration of the public fortune, and to place their own possessions at the discretion of the nation whose confidence they have abused.

It remains for me—in the view of more distinctly developing the course of policy pursued by the Tory land-power toward the whole mass of the British people — to present a true reading of its conduct toward the resident population of the island of Jamaica, and of other British possessions in the West Indies. This will form the subject of my next and closing letter.

LETTER VII.

Exposition of British Policy in the British West Indies. Direct purposes aimed at, and objects effected by the act of Abolition. Identity of the process followed in Jamaica, and that followed in Great Britain. Woman, her noble impulses how misdirected and imposed upon by fraudulent government and vicious civilization.

In connection with, and in fuller elucidation of, the subject embraced in my last letter, it occurs to me as useful to present to the more intelligent mass of the British people, a few simple facts explanatory of the conduct of the Tory land-power toward the West India colonies. These will, I think, convince every impartial individual, that in nothing have I misrepresented or exaggerated the actual policy pursued, and intended to be pursued, toward the middle and laboring classes of society in the financial crisis now preparing. They will, I think, also convince the same classes, that what they have more especially to hold themselves in guard against is mystification, humbug, and quackery. If the British public have been decoyed into the direct robbery and ruin of the smaller proprietors together with the resident trading and professional classes of Jamaica—and this under the most taking pretexts of reform and philanthropy—let them beware of similar lures here. Let the people stand with eyes and ears open and intelligence awake. Let them be-

ware of all schemes and proposals tending, under the plea
of bettering their condition, to place them in direct dependence upon the land-power as now constituted. Let
them look to the helpless and enslaved populace now cared
for under the best arrangements of Tory mercy, in poor-
houses, alms-houses, bridewells, and jails ; and let them
ask themselves in what these differ, in principle and direct tendency, from communities, placed at high rents on
long leases or short leases, on the estates of landed monopolists, supreme in the British Parliament, so to order
things as to render it impossible for the body of collective
tenants ever to liberate themselves, and who in the mean-
time raise buildings, and effect other improvements, which
will remain when they are tired out or ejected ?   I ask if
these things have not already happened ?

It remains for me to explain the act of fraud committed under plea of abolition of negro slavery, against all
the interests of the people of the West Indies and of the
people of Great Britain, by the consolidated Tory Land
power of the British empire.   I shall present a general
view of the case under as few heads as possible.

1. The governing power which decreed the act subversive of all the existing relations political and social in
the West Indies, was not West Indian but British.

2. The same power was in standing hostility against
the local Assembly of Jamaica ; the leading, and from
the superior size of that Island, the only constitutional organ of British West Indian interests.

3. The British Parliament held in its bosom a powerful body of absentee West India proprietors, the same forming part also of the governing land-power of England.

4. The estates of these absentee proprietors were sugar estates ; the largest, the richest, and the most heavily
covered with negroes in the islands.

5. These sugar estates—in consequence of the necessary malversation of all colonial interests, as controlled
and despoiled by a distant government, and by a distant
metropolitan bank, of which the action was to drain the
islands of specie and to prevent all local credit institutions—
these sugar estates were mortgaged to London commer-

cial and financial houses to the amount of one-third of their value.

6. In consequence of ever increasing malversation, the estates became inefficient for payment of the interest of the debts with which they were burdened ; and were liable to be sold for payment of capital and interest.

7. In the event of such sale the natural purchasers of the estates, divided into small lots, were the mountain and city proprietors and other residents, white and colored, of the islands.

8. Such subdivision of the great sugar estates among resident proprietors, would have annihilated at one blow the metroplitan power as existing in the great absentee proprietors, and have so strengthened the colonial power in the Jamaica Assembly, as to have effectually prepared for the independence and welfare of the islands, or have forced their open subjugation by armed force ; an alternative that must have kindled a war in which all the powers of Europe, and those of America must, in course of its progress, have taken part.

` 9. To obviate all this, to pay their debts, and to clear their estates, the absentee land-power of the West Indies, in understanding with, and forming part of the land-power of Great Britain, decreed an act of abolition and indemnity.

10. By this act the value of the negroes was estimated at one-third the value of the estates.

11. The people of Great Britain, already bowed down under the weight of taxation, were burdened with twenty millions of additional debt to meet the provisions of the same act. This, with the exception of such small amount as was counted to the resident West India proprietors, holders chiefly of coffee plantations in the mountains, was paid into the great mercantile houses in London which held the claims on the sugar estates, and the mortgages were burned.

12. In despite of the most stirring remonstrances on the part of the Jamaica Assembly (comprising in its body several members of color,) the negro population, of which the great mass was found on the sugar estates, was warn-

ed by the Royal Governor, that being henceforth free, it was no longer to consider itself entitled to remain on the estates of their former masters, nor to consider the houses and gardens which they had hitherto occupied, as their property. In like manner they must, in future, support their own families and relatives, the young and the aged; and to do all this, must make the best terms they could with their old masters or with new masters, overseers alone in both cases, without any of those habits of mutual dependence and kindness of feeling existing between master and servant, born and raised on the same estate in the mountain plantations. But the system to which the negroes *now called free* were to be subjected, will better appear in the Proclamation itself, as published throughout Jamaica and the other islands:

Jamaica, ss.

PROCLAMATION.

By his Excellency Sir Lionel Smith, Knight, Commander of the Most Honorable Military Order of the Bath, Knight Grand Cross of the Royal Hanoverian Order, a Lieutenant General in her Majesty's Land forces, and Colonel of the fortieth Regiment of Foot, Captain-General, Governor-in-chief and Commander of the Forces in and over her Majesty's Island of Jamaica, and the other territories thereon depending in America, Vice-Chancellor and Admiral of the same.

PRAEDIAL APPRENTICES !*

In a few days more you will all become FREE LABORERS—the Legislature of the island having relinquished the remaning two years of your apprenticeship.

The first of August next is the happy day when you will become free—under the same laws as other freemen, whether white, black, or colored.

I, your Governor, give you joy of this great blessing.

Remember, that in freedom you will have to depend on your own exertions for your livelihood, and to maintain and to bring up your families. You will work for such wages as you can agree upon with your employers.

It is their interest to treat you fairly.

It is your interest to be civil, respectful, and industrious.

* So called under the apprentice law, first form of the abolition. And a form so utterly unmanageable that all were willing to change it; but not to change it for the still worse state of things, that is to say for all but the absentee proprietors, established by the Proclamation.

OF FRANCES WRIGHT.
45
Where you can agree and continue happy with your old masters, I strongly recommend you to remain on those properties on which you have been born, and where your parents are buried.

But you must not mistake, in supposing that your present houses, gardens, or provision grounds are your own property.

They belong to the proprietors of the estates, and you will have to pay rent for them in money or labor, according as you and your employers may agree together.

Idle people who will not take employment, but go wandering about the country, will be taken up as vagrants and punished in the same manner as they are in England.

The ministers of religion have been kind friends to you—listen to them—they will keep you out of troubles and difficulties.

Recollect what is expected of you by the people of England, who have paid such a large price for your liberty.

They not only expect that you will behave yourselves as the queen's good subjects, by obeying the laws, as I am happy to say you always have done as apprentices; but that the prosperity of the Island will be increased by your willing labor, greatly beyond what it was in slavery. Be honest toward all men—be kind to your wives and children, spare your wives from heavy field work as much as you can—make them attend to their duties at home, in bringing up your children and in taking care of your stock—above all, make your children attend divine service and school.

If you follow this advice you will, under God's blessing, be happy and prosperous.

Given under my hand and seal at arms, at St. Jago de la Vega, this ninth day of July, in the first year of her Majesty's reign Annoque Domini 1838.

LIONEL SMITH.

13. The negroes, who, under the above proclamation, might be taken up as "vagrants" whether "idle" or infirm, as it might be, were thus, under the English Poor Law system, to be supported at the expense of the small proprietors and other resident population of the islands.

14. The number of "vagrants" was certain to accumulate with all the refuse and all the helpless of the sugar estates. Their managers, selecting only the more able-bodied and laborious, and throwing off "the dead weight," as age, infancy, and infirmity, are denominated by modern British economists—upon the charity of a ruined public. The policy is the same as that followed by the land power in Britain, which has thrown off the mass of the agricultural population into the cities, thereby crushing

it down into a populace to be supported at the expense of the middle and commercial classes, or to die by the slow process of misery, insufficient food, and the diseases generated by the same.

15. A crowd of ignorant fanatics and preachers (more especially of the Baptist persuasion) were openly encouraged by the executive influence to excite the negroes against the white resident population. "The sword of the Lord and of Gideon" was the text and rallying cry of those misguided and misguiding wretches, who not only disturbed with impunity the peace of the islands, but exposed to assassination the best families—men, women, and children.

16. Ruined in their fortunes, menaced in their lives, the resident planters of Jamaica had either to fly, or to sell their estates for a few shillings in the pound to the agents of the great absentee holders of the sugar estates.

17. Considered in all its effects, of which but a small portion can be exhibited here, the Act which cost the producing and middle classes of Great Britain twenty millions sterling, was most justly denominated "An Act of Abolition." The only misnomer is to be found in the words appended to it " of Negro Slavery in the British West Indies." It should evidently read, *an Act for the abolition of the debts, and of the moral and political duties and obligations of the great absentee Tory proprietors in the British West Indies.*

One observation appears to me important to subjoin.

This most nefarious Act of fraud and spoliation ever enacted by a Government against its own people, was mainly brought to bear through the moral influence of woman. It is a homage paid to her nature, that men cannot be led to effect even a semblance of good but through her agency. O! what would it be if her virtuous instincts were enlightened by knowledge : if her all-quickening as all-enduring energies, were at once strengthened and steadied, rightly aimed and justly balanced by wisdom and experience ! And O! if she could understand that wisdom and experience are only to be acquired by observation and reflection ; a familiarity with things, with the active business of life, with matter of fact realities, with positive practical truth!

Some equally extraordinary and astounding developments with those which appear above, might be presented in explanation of the efforts of the governing land-power of the British Empire to effect, not *the abolition but the control* of the African slave-trade as still prosecuted by several British allies. If, in accordance with Lord Palmerston's assertion, the Tagus only flows by permission of British power! if Spain and Brazil are under direction of her diplomacy; if her dominion of the seas be not a vain boast—how is it, that instead of enforcing a cessation of the slave-trade by those powers, she only enforces THE RIGHT OF SEARCH? Thus, in effect, permitting the slave-trade under exercise of piracy by her vessels of war upon their slave ships: slaves so captured being forthwith carried to Jamaica, and worked under the name of apprentices, held bound for fourteen years. The advantages of this course of proceeding are numerous. The possession of negroes without either the original cost of purchase from African traders, or the cost of raising them on the plantations. Also the absence of all " dead weight" either at the present, or in the future: such captured slaves being all males in the force of youth, and destined to be thrown off as free, at the expiration of their strength, and of their apprenticeship. Also the absence of inconveniences from strikes and insurrections, such negroes being ignorant of civilized language, and objects of hatred to the colonial negroes of the plantations, whose ejection is the consequence of their arrival. Much more might be said under this head, but my time expires. Let me subjoin the warmest wish of my soul, for the effective union of the whole British people against the desperate system of which the history, the nature, and the tendency have been most faithfully, although imperfectly, portrayed in these letters.

FRANCES WRIGHT D'ARUSMONT.

American Women: Images and Realities
An Arno Press Collection

[Adams, Charles F., editor]. **Correspondence between John Adams and Mercy Warren Relating to Her "History of the American Revolution," July-August, 1807.** With a new appendix of specimen pages from the "History." 1878.

[Arling], Emanie Sachs. **"The Terrible Siren": Victoria Woodhull, (1838-1927).** 1928.

Beard, Mary Ritter. **Woman's Work in Municipalities.** 1915.

Blanc, Madame [Marie Therese de Solms]. **The Condition of Woman in the United States.** 1895.

Bradford, Gamaliel. **Wives.** 1925.

Branagan, Thomas. **The Excellency of the Female Character Vindicated.** 1808.

Breckinridge, Sophonisba P. **Women in the Twentieth Century.** 1933.

Campbell, Helen. **Women Wage-Earners.** 1893.

Coolidge, Mary Roberts. **Why Women Are So.** 1912.

Dall, Caroline H. **The College, the Market, and the Court.** 1867.

[D'Arusmont], Frances Wright. **Life, Letters and Lectures: 1834, 1844.** 1972.

Davis, Almond H. **The Female Preacher, or Memoir of Salome Lincoln.** 1843.

Ellington, George. **The Women of New York.** 1869.

Farnham, Eliza W[oodson]. **Life in Prairie Land.** 1846.

Gage, Matilda Joslyn. **Woman, Church and State.** [1900].

Gilman, Charlotte Perkins. **The Living of Charlotte Perkins Gilman.** 1935.

Groves, Ernest R. **The American Woman.** 1944.

Hale, [Sarah J.] **Manners; or, Happy Homes and Good Society All the Year Round.** 1868.

Higginson, Thomas Wentworth. **Women and the Alphabet.** 1900.

Howe, Julia Ward, editor. **Sex and Education.** 1874.

La Follette, Suzanne. **Concerning Women.** 1926.

Leslie, Eliza . **Miss Leslie's Behaviour Book: A Guide and Manual for Ladies.** 1859.

Livermore, Mary A. **My Story of the War.** 1889.

Logan, Mrs. John A. (Mary S.) **The Part Taken By Women in American History.** 1912.

McGuire, Judith W. (A Lady of Virginia). **Diary of a Southern Refugee, During the War.** 1867.

Mann, Herman . **The Female Review: Life of Deborah Sampson.** 1866.

Meyer, Annie Nathan, editor.**Woman's Work in America.** 1891.

Myerson, Abraham. **The Nervous Housewife.** 1927.

Parsons, Elsie Clews. **The Old-Fashioned Woman.** 1913.

Porter, Sarah Harvey. **The Life and Times of Anne Royall.** 1909.

Pruette, Lorine. **Women and Leisure: A Study of Social Waste.** 1924.

Salmon, Lucy Maynard. **Domestic Service.** 1897.

Sanger, William W. **The History of Prostitution.** 1859.

Smith, Julia E. **Abby Smith and Her Cows.** 1877.

Spencer, Anna Garlin. **Woman's Share in Social Culture.** 1913.

Sprague, William Forrest. **Women and the West.** 1940.

Stanton, Elizabeth Cady. **The Woman's Bible** Parts I and II. 1895/1898.

Stewart, Mrs. Eliza Daniel . **Memories of the Crusade.** 1889.

Todd, John. **Woman's Rights.** 1867. [Dodge, Mary A.] (Gail Hamilton, pseud.) **Woman's Wrongs.** 1868.

Van Rensselaer, Mrs. John King. **The Goede Vrouw of Mana-ha-ta.** 1898.

Velazquez, Loreta Janeta. **The Woman in Battle.** 1876.

Vietor, Agnes C., editor. **A Woman's Quest: The Life of Marie E. Zakrzewska, M.D.** 1924.

Woodbury , Helen L. Sum n er. **Equal Suffrage.** 1909.

Young, Ann Eliza. **Wife No. 19.** 1875.